FEVER SEASON

FEVER
SEASON

THE STORY OF A TERRIFYING EPIDEMIC
AND THE PEOPLE WHO SAVED A CITY

JEANETTE KEITH

BLOOMSBURY PRESS
NEW YORK   LONDON   NEW DELHI   SYDNEY

Published by Bloomsbury Press, New York

All papers used by Bloomsbury Press are natural, recyclable products made from wood grown in well-managed forests. The manufacturing processes conform to the environmental regulations of the country of origin.

LIBRARY OF CONGRESS CATALOGING-IN-PUBLICATION DATA

Keith, Jeanette.
Fever season : The story of a terrifying epidemic and the people who saved a city / Jeanette Keith. —1st U.S. ed.
p. cm.
Includes bibliographical references and index.
ISBN 978-1-60819-222-9 (alk. paper)
1. Yellow fever—Tennessee—Memphis—History—19th century.
2. Epidemics—Social aspects—Tennessee—Memphis—History—19th century.
3. Medical personnel—Tennessee—Memphis—Biography. 4. Journalists—Tennessee—Memphis—Biography. 5. Memphis (Tenn.)—Biography.
6. Memphis (Tenn.)—History—19th century. 7. Memphis (Tenn.)—Social conditions—19th century. I. Title.
RC211.T3K45 2012
614.5'410976819—dc23
2012010176

First U.S. Edition 2012

1 3 5 7 9 10 8 6 4 2

Typeset by Westchester Book Group
Printed in the U.S.A. by Quad/Graphics, Fairfield, Pennsylvania

Contents

Introduction

September 1878

WHEN THOSE WHO LIVED THROUGH the epidemic tried to describe it, they talked about the sudden, eerie quiet. Built on high bluffs over the Mississippi, Memphis, Tennessee, was the only major urban center between St. Louis and New Orleans and the de facto commercial capital of a rural hinterland encompassing parts of Tennessee, Arkansas, and Mississippi. Although small compared with the nation's largest city, with a population of roughly fifty thousand to New York's one million, Memphis was about twice the size of Nashville, the state capital, four times the size of Little Rock, Arkansas, and ten times the size of Jackson, capital city of Mississippi. Half the population had fled upon the outbreak of yellow fever, but an estimated twenty thousand remained. You would think that many people would produce noise sufficient to demonstrate their presence, but the voices we have from Memphis in the summer of 1878—mostly doctors, nurses, and journalists—agree that the city felt abandoned.

A young journalist described the empty streets on a Sunday, the silence broken at long intervals by the slow passage of a mule pulling a vacant streetcar. A nurse from Texas named Kezia DePelchin wrote of the waterfront district, "The large stores and warehouses on Front St. were closed. A woman with a few apples to sell on one block and two children sunning themselves on the steps of a large building on another block were all the signs of life." From the high bluff over the water, "no curling smoke heralded the approach of a steamer, it was calm, unruffled by an oar, as when DeSoto first gazed in wonder and admiration on

1

its broad expanse of water." Dr. William Armstrong, one of the cadre of physicians pledged to stay in the stricken city, described a "lonesome-ness" that was "in itself, lonely, making a gloom that cannot be conceived of nor described on paper." Newspaper editor John McLeod Keating said that the city by day was as desolate as the desert, at night as silent as the grave. Fifty years later an aged physician described how Memphis nights had sounded to him that summer: "the rattle of the death wagons and the eerie sound of a moaning city, praying, dying."[1]

That was how Memphis seemed to the people who stayed behind during the great yellow fever epidemic of 1878. On the other hand, the few individuals who came into the city, who defied warnings and common sense on errands of mercy or profit, talked about the stench. They said that you could smell Memphis from several miles away.

FROM AUGUST TO OCTOBER 1878, the people of Memphis suffered through an experience unique in American history. Yellow fever is a viral hemorrhagic fever passed from human to human by mosquitoes. Although mild cases produce flu-like symptoms, at its worst yellow fever is comparable to Ebola. The virus strain that caused the 1878 epidemic was extremely virulent. The fever spread up the Mississippi Valley from New Orleans to Illinois and killed an estimated eighteen thousand people. But it was Memphis's plight that riveted national attention. At least two thirds of the people in Memphis contracted the fever, and about one quarter died, more than five thousand in all. The mortality rate for African Americans was around 10 percent, but the disease was even more dangerous for the white population, where the mortality rate was as high as 70 percent. People ran fevers with temperatures over 105 degrees. In their delirium they stripped, ran naked into the streets, or crawled off to hide in back rooms. Victims in the late stages of the disease vomited up a black, viscous liquid containing coagulated blood; their skin turned bronze. So many people died so quickly that the bodies had to be buried in trench graves.[2]

Histories of epidemics tend to follow a couple of patterns. One is the "victory of science" theme. In this formula, a disease kills a large number of people but is eventually brought under control by scientists who discover its etiology and use that knowledge to either cure it or stop it from spreading. The other formula asks what impact the disease had on something human beings were doing: making war, building cities, colonizing countries, organizing public health services. Here the emphasis is on disease as catalyst for human action. The way that we construct epidemic narratives, whether fictional or factual, is suspiciously comforting—for us, not for people who live through such disasters. See, we say, things got better! We learned from this! Thus we whistle past the graveyard.

Although scientific research eventually led to the eradication of yellow fever in the United States, this book is not about that victory. Major Walter Reed's team of U.S. Army doctors did not discover that mosquitoes spread the fever until 1901. Once the method of transmission was understood, it was relatively easy to stop the fever. However, to telescope the 1878 epidemic and Reed's 1901 triumph, thus providing a happy ending, is to falsify the lived experience of the epidemic. The orphaned children of Memphis were adult men and women by 1901. The mass graves along the banks of the Mississippi had long since grown green. Those aging adults who had survived the epidemic must surely have been happy—and astonished—to finally understand how the disease was transmitted and hopeful about eliminating it. It is hard to believe, however, that the new knowledge eased the old grief. What had happened to the city in 1878 could not be undone by any team of army doctors.

What follows is no scientific romance. Instead, this story of what happened in Memphis during the fever season of 1878 is informed by the most basic of questions: What was it like to live through that? Our focus here is on personalities and what the people of 1878 would have called, simply, character.

In extreme peril, surrounded by death and squalor, living on the bacon and coffee supplied by the nation's charity, people in Memphis remained fascinated by character. They were most disconcerted to find that neither heroism nor villainy could be predicted by public standing, gender, or race. Upstanding citizens abandoned their families, and prostitutes and sporting men stepped up to care for the sick. White elected officials deserted their posts, but black militiamen stood fast as guardians of the city. Nurses risked their lives in houses full of pestilence—or robbed those houses and took off with bags full of loot. Some religious leaders left their flocks to die without spiritual comfort; others martyred themselves nursing the sick. The epidemic turned all common categories of trust and honor upside down and reduced good and evil to the most basic questions: Do you leave your people to die, or do you help?

To UNDERSTAND WHAT HAPPENED in Memphis, a little natural history is in order.

Yellow fever is caused by an arbovirus of the genus *Flavivirus*; arbovirus indicates that the virus is spread by an arthropod (insect) vector. In the case of yellow fever, the virus's natural habitat is high in the canopies of West African rain forests, where *Aedes* mosquitoes such as *Ae. africanus and Ae. simpsoni* breed. After mating, female mosquitoes must consume blood in order to lay eggs. In the rain forest, the mosquito gets that blood by feeding on monkeys. Fortified by her blood meal, the female then deposits between one hundred and two hundred eggs on the sides of a hole in a tree filled with rainwater, typically going from pool to pool and tree to tree to spread the egg batch around. She does not mate again, but can keep on laying eggs, one batch per feeding, up to five times. In a life span of two to four weeks, therefore, a female *Aedes* mosquito can produce as many as a thousand eggs. The eggs are quite durable. They can withstand desiccation for months and will still hatch with the return of water, as when fresh rain fills their tree hole. In the tropics, the mosquitoes develop from eggs to larvae to pupae to mosquitoes in about a week, although the mosquitoes may stay in the larval stage for months at lower temperatures. The *Aedes* mosquito is very much a tropical insect, most active at temperatures between 70 and 90 degrees Fahrenheit. The mosquito becomes dormant at temperatures below 50 degrees, and it cannot survive freezing. The eggs also do not survive prolonged freezing. Female *Aedes sp.* mosquitoes not only carry the yellow fever virus but can also pass it on to their offspring.

When an infected mosquito takes a blood meal from a monkey, it acts as a vector to transmit the virus to the monkey. Although the monkey does not get sick, it carries the virus. Should an uninfected mosquito feed from the infected monkey, it will pick up the fever. Thus the cycle of the yellow fever virus: from mosquito to monkey and back again for generations. When people go out in the rain forest to hunt monkeys or fell trees, they come into contact with *Aedes sp.* females, who feed on them and pass on the yellow fever virus. The infected people may then carry the virus back to their human habitat, whether village or city.

Ae. aegypti mosquitoes thrive in human habitats and continue the yellow fever cycle in urban populations. Unlike the *Anopheles sp.* mosquito—the malaria carrier that lives in stagnant water and infests rural areas—the yellow-fever-transmitting mosquito prefers to live in towns. It prefers to lay eggs in still water that is relatively clean. People need a lot of water, and unless it is provided by municipal water systems where it is piped in, they tend to store it close to their houses in jugs, barrels, or cisterns. These storage vessels approximate *Aedes*'s rain forest tree hole nicely. Today the mosquito lays its eggs in cemetery urns, birdbaths, flower vases, old tires, discarded cans and jars, toilet tanks—any container that can hold clear water, whether provided by nature or by people. If infected humans bring the virus back with them from an endemic area into town and are then bitten by an urban-dwelling mosquito, the yellow fever cycle can easily be transferred from the tree canopy to the street. The mosquito will carry the virus for the rest of its short life. The mosquito incubates the virus for eight to eighteen days, depending on environmental conditions. After that the mosquito can spread the virus each time it feeds on a human being.

The unfortunate person who is infected by the mosquito gets sick three to six days later. At this point, with the virus present in the individual's bloodstream, uninfected *Ae. aegypti* mosquitoes take up the virus with a meal from the sick host, but the window of opportunity is short: humans can pass the virus to mosquitoes only in the first three days of the illness. This first stage of the disease can be so mild as to go unnoticed by the infected person. However, the disease can also present with severe headache, nausea, and fever up to 104 degrees. Most people pass through this stage and begin to recover. They have acquired immunity for life. This is not the case for about 15 percent of the cases. They appear to recover, but they relapse and enter what doctors call "intoxication." In this final, deadly phase, the patient's fever begins to rise again, the headache comes back, and the patient becomes restless. As the patient's heart, liver, and kidneys begin to fail, delirium sets in. The victim's skin turns a dark yellow, giving the disease its New Orleans nickname, "Bronze John." This signals the beginning of the end, either of the disease or the victim. Hemorrhaging internally and deathly ill, the patient may vomit coagulated blood, the infallible sign distinguishing yellow fever from other tropical fevers like malaria. Black vomit, or *vomito negro*, looks like coffee grounds. Once the black vomit commences, few victims survive. Those who do struggle with the illness for weeks. Convalescence is very slow.[3]

The National Institutes of Health, the Centers for Disease Control, and the World Health Organization today agree: "There is no specific treatment for yellow fever . . ." Physicians today can do no more than provide palliative care and treat the symptoms, using IV fluids for dehydration, transfusions for blood loss, and dialysis for kidney failure.[4] Lacking these options, healers in the past tried different "cures," none of which worked. Nursing was of more value than potions. By keeping delirious patients quiet and supplying nourishment and liquids to those able to take them, caregivers gave the sick their best chance to recover.

Yellow fever's ancestral virus has apparently existed in Africa for at least fifteen hundred years. Over the centuries, the transfer of the virus from rain forest to West African villages probably took place repeatedly. Some strains of the virus may produce a relatively mild illness that is comparable to the flu. Moreover, like several other diseases, yellow fever seems to be less dangerous to children than to adults. In communities where the fever was endemic, a child could easily contract the disease, resulting in a mild case of the fever, perhaps so mild that it was unnoticed, resulting in a lifetime immunity. On the other hand, centuries of observation suggest that some African populations may have developed hereditary resistance to the disease. "The whole human family is equally susceptible to infection by the yellow fever virus," according to the historian Khaled J. Bloom, "but the severity of the disease varies considerably according to race; blacks, at least those of West African extraction, suffer much less than Caucasians." Dr. Michael B. A. Oldstone notes that "black African peoples, although easily infected, nevertheless withstood the effects in that fewer died from the infection than did Caucasians."[5]

Yellow fever came out of Africa to the Americas on slave ships. One fever-carrying female *Aedes* mosquito flitting around on the deck of a slaver bound from West Africa to Barbados could have spread the disease to the New World. As the mosquito fed off the crew, infecting them with fever, she deposited her eggs under the rims of water barrels. When the original female mosquito's offspring reached maturity and mated, they fed from the infected people, picked up the virus, and spread it to more of the slave cargo and crew. Six weeks later, when the ship docked in Jamaica, Haiti, or Barbados, the mosquitoes came ashore with the passengers and crew, and the cycle of urban yellow fever had been transplanted to the New World. Barbados suffered the first reported American yellow fever epidemic in 1647. Soon the mosquitoes, and the virus, had colonized the Caribbean and tropical areas in Central and South America. Since the bright yellow flag traditionally flown to signify quarantine was called a Yellow Jack, the name came to apply to the disease as well.[6]

In the eighteenth century, yellow fever epidemics were confined to tropical cities and the temperate-zone seaports that communicated with them via oceangoing ships. Northern winters were too cold for *Ae. aegypti* to survive, but summer outbreaks hit Portugal and Spain and, in the United States, New York and Boston. In 1793 ships carrying refugees from the Haitian revolution brought the fever to Philadelphia, then the capital of the new United States. Five thousand died. Outbreaks that far north remained uncommon, dependent as they were on unusually long, hot, wet summers coinciding with the arrival of yellow fever cases from the Caribbean.[7] Given the long-standing trade route linking New Orleans, Savannah, and Charleston to the Caribbean, it is not surprising that nineteenth-century Americans came to associate the fever with the Gulf Coast in general, but especially with New Orleans. The Crescent City had eight major epidemics before the end of the century; in 1853 almost eight thousand people died.[8]

Living in a region where yellow fever could break out any summer, longtime Gulf Coast residents spoke of being "acclimated" to yellow fever. The term was dangerously ambiguous. Yellow fever victims, being immune, were acclimated. However, people claimed acclimation for reasons other than acquired immunity. If you had passed through several epidemics untouched, you might consider yourself acclimated. Natives to the region claimed to have "Creole immunity," or what might be called hereditary acclimation. In French and Spanish colonial usage, "Creole" denoted the American-born children of colonists. Along the U.S. Gulf Coast, Creole could mean someone of French, Spanish, or African ancestry, or any combination of the three. In nineteenth-century Gulf Coast outbreaks, a smaller proportion of the Creole population died than of the non-Creoles. It seems likely that the children of old French families and of their former slaves contracted mild cases of the disease, cases so mild that they were not even noticed, and thereby acquired lifetime immunity. However, it has to be noted that Creoles of color along the coast and African Americans up the Mississippi River simply assumed that African ancestry gave them immunity. During the 1878 epidemic, people who had thought themselves acclimated by ancestry or long residence in the South would learn to their sorrow that only acclimation by survival conferred immunity from the disease.[9]

If yellow fever ceased to be quite as frightening to long-established families in the region, it devastated newcomers. In New Orleans they called it the Strangers' Disease. In the multiple New Orleans epidemics, Irish immigrant laborers died by the thousands, but the families of wealthy northern merchants who had relocated to the Crescent City were also susceptible. This meant that unlike other diseases common in the nineteenth century, yellow fever could not easily be stigmatized by Anglo-Americans as the fault of immigrants or the depraved lower classes. In nineteenth-century New Orleans, piped-in water fit to drink was rare. Most families depended on rainwater collected in barrels or aboveground cisterns. *Ae. aegypti* was just as likely to lay its eggs in the cisterns of Garden District mansions as in the rain barrels of the poor. Yellow fever struck waterfront prostitutes and Presbyterian matrons who had nothing in common except being newcomers to New Orleans, undercutting arguments that the fever was a punishment for depravity. The transmission pattern peculiar to yellow fever made it difficult to single out any group, whether defined ethnically, racially, religiously, or behaviorally, and scapegoat that group for "causing" the fever.

Two centuries after yellow fever arrived in the Caribbean, no one had yet figured out how the disease was spread. Doctors knew well the symptoms of a bad case of yellow fever (it is hard to miss black vomit and pumpkin-colored skin) and could predict with some accuracy a patient's chances for survival. They understood that the fever was worse in some years, milder in others. They had many nostrums for it, although none were sure cures. But they could not predict which summers would be blighted by epidemics, nor could they foretell which areas might be hit.

The yellow fever virus moved up the Mississippi River from New Orleans, its passage facilitated by technological innovations. Steamship travel on the Mississippi extended the summer range of the fever, and the railroads carried it farther. Memphis had cases of yellow fever in 1828, 1855, and 1867, and a serious outbreak in 1873. Increasingly rapid transportation by rail could carry a person bitten by a virus-carrying mosquito in New Orleans to his whistle-stop hometown in Mississippi in time for him to get sick and spread the disease to the local mosquito population.

Plus, like sailing ships, locomotives carried water barrels in which *Ae. aegypti* could deposit its eggs. In 1878, railroads helped spread the fever from the Mississippi River east into the interiors of Mississippi, Alabama, and Tennessee, and north to Kentucky and southern Illinois.[10]

If you know that the disease-causing virus is transmitted by mosquitoes, it is easy to see how it spread from Africa to the Caribbean and eventually up the Mississippi River. But we need to remember that in 1878 no one knew how the disease was transmitted. Therefore, according to historian Margaret Humphreys, "Yellow fever was a central disease in disputes about contagion, the germ theory, and public health action in nineteenth-century America." Doctors debated the disease's etiology for decades without coming to firm conclusions.[11]

A combination of knowledge and ignorance, confidence and fear distinguished the 1878 yellow fever epidemic from other historic outbreaks and makes it peculiarly relevant to twenty-first-century America. In the 1340s, when the bubonic plague hit Eurasia, it was a new thing. As they grasped for understanding, Europeans devised explanations that ranged from the exalted (maleficent astronomical alignments or that perennial favorite, the will of God) to the vicious (in parts of Germany, Jews were murdered by the hundreds because people suspected them of spreading poison). In the first half of the nineteenth century, cholera was new to people outside the disease's endemic home in South Asia. When cholera hit New York in the 1830s, wealthy native-born Americans blamed immigrants, particularly the Irish, whom they stigmatized as drunken, dirty, and depraved.

Yellow fever was no new thing to southerners in 1878. Memphians did not scapegoat any particular race or ethnic group for the outbreak. Like contemporary Americans, some of them thought about disease in religious terms, some in scientific terms, and many—perhaps most—combined religious and scientific worldviews without any apparent worry that those perspectives might be inherently contradictory. Thus Memphians spoke of the disease as a scourge and prayed for mercy, but they also searched for answers in science and used the technology available to them (railroads and telegraph) to organize relief efforts to care for the sick. In short, their response was modern. Yet science failed them, and their best organizational efforts could not keep the stench of death from pervading their city.

The epidemic did not further scientific research into the disease in any way that helped end the scourge. When Major Reed and his team went to Havana in 1901 to investigate the connections between mosquitoes and yellow fever, they were testing a hypothesis floated by Cuban physician Carlos Finlay in 1881 but also influenced by British scientist Ronald Ross's recent demonstration that mosquitoes transmitted malaria.[12] Although various people in Memphis pointed out that there were an awful lot of mosquitoes in the summer of 1878, and at least one suggested that maybe mosquitoes had something to do with the disease, no one took it seriously enough to embark on an investigation. Readers will look in vain for the optimistic "victory of science" happy ending here. This is a much darker narrative, serving as a reminder that centuries of heroism, courage, hard work, research, and education may not suffice to build us a shelter against the indifferent assaults of the natural world.

The 1878 fever is the closest example we have of what a killer epidemic might be like today. The 1918 influenza virus infected one third of the world population and killed at least fifty million people. In seasonal flu outbreaks, less than 1 percent of those infected die. In the 1918 outbreak, the mortality rate was more than 2 percent. That does not sound like much, but in the United States a 2 percent mortality rate translated into over half a million deaths. In Philadelphia, one of the hardest-hit cities, volunteers in trucks and horse-drawn wagons picked up shrouded corpses and carried them to mass burials in trench graves excavated by steam shovels. If the H5N1 bird flu virus mutates enough to be communicable not just from bird to human, but between humans, as the Centers for Disease Control and the World Health Organization have feared for years, we could be facing a disease we have seen before, but in a much more deadly form. The human mortality rate from H5N1 is about 60 percent. Like the people of Memphis in 1878, we will know enough to understand what is happening, and even to treat the sick with some modicum of success, but we will not be able to "cure" the flu any more than nineteenth-century Americans could cure yellow fever, and we will bury our dead in mass graves. Looking at Memphis's catastrophe may give us insight into what it might be like to live through our own modern-day worst-case scenario.[13]

Some human reactions to epidemic disease are so common as to be all but universal. For example, when people see the sick falling down dead all around them, the normal tendency is to run away (and possibly spread the disease by fleeing from it). Among those who don't make it out of town before the city gates are closed, the highways blocked, the trains canceled—in short, among the trapped—some will react by isolating themselves, avoiding human contact, and others will take the epidemic as an occasion for wild, end-of-the-world bacchanals. Despite these commonalities, however, epidemics call forth responses that illuminate the diverse social strengths and weaknesses of the locale in which they occur. Natural history is not enough to explain what happened in Memphis. Human history is needed too.

Memphis's response to the yellow fever epidemic spotlights the racial, social, and political conflicts dividing the city in the wake of the Civil War. Although African Americans in Memphis experienced the war as a time of liberation and new hope, the 1860s left deep and permanent emotional scars on the town's white population. The Union army captured the city early in the war and maintained occupation forces there for the duration. In occupied Memphis, Confederate sympathizers felt themselves humiliated, politically oppressed, and denied what they considered to be their proper place at the top of the urban social and racial pyramid. The most startling reversal of all involved the fate of the enslaved. The Emancipation Proclamation did not free slaves in Memphis—the document specifically exempted slaves in loyal southern states and many Union-occupied areas of the Confederacy, including Tennessee—but the slaves in the nearby plantation districts liberated themselves and came to Memphis seeking the protection of the Union army. They settled in camps clustering around the federal installation, Fort Pickering, just south of town. As the war continued, the federal government enrolled former slaves as soldiers and, in Memphis, employed them as occupation forces.[14]

Nothing galled defeated Confederates more than the ascendency of victorious black soldiers. In addition, Memphis's Irish working class saw freedmen and women as unwelcome competitors for jobs. On May 1, 1866, an "affray" between discharged black soldiers and Irish policemen set off one of the worst race riots in American history. Whites swept through Memphis, burning black houses and schools, raping women, and murdering men. Although the police force appears to have been at the center of the riot, the mob included native white southerners, prominent businessmen, and city officials.

The Memphis riot had a major impact on the nation's history. Radical Republicans used the riot to help convince Congress to pass the Reconstruction Acts, ushering in a decade of tumultuous political and social change. Congress placed the former Confederate states under military rule. The Fourteenth Amendment established citizenship for African Americans, and the Fifteenth gave black men the right to vote. Republican governments were elected throughout the South, but backed by determined, violent white resistance, southern white Democrats took back control of much of the region. By 1876 federal troops had been withdrawn from all the former Confederate states except Louisiana, South Carolina, and Florida. The outcome of that year's presidential election depended on disputed returns from those three states. After months of controversy, southern Democrats in Congress acquiesced to a Republican victory in the presidential election. In what appears to have been a quid pro quo, in 1877 President Rutherford B. Hayes removed troops from the South, bringing Reconstruction to an end.

This history was fresh in the minds of politically active blacks and whites in Memphis in 1878, although the city itself, being part of the state of Tennessee, had been readmitted to the Union before Reconstruction proper ever got under way. The anomaly of Tennessee's "reconstruction" derived from the state's peculiar politics. Although the majority of Tennesseans supported secession, most people in the eastern part of the state remained stubbornly loyal to the United States through all the travails of the war. In the early months of 1865 these Unionists formed a government and elected a governor, William "Parson" Brownlow. With Brownlow's Radicals in control of the state government, the legislature ratified the Fourteenth Amendment in June 1866, and Tennessee reentered the Union before the passage of the Reconstruction Acts. Brownlow's methods enraged former Rebels, but they also alienated conservative Unionists. As his support melted away, the governor pushed through legislation enfranchising former slaves, who therefore obtained the ballot years before the passage of the Fifteenth Amendment. With their backing, Brownlow ran the state until he left to serve in the U.S. Senate in 1869. Following his departure, conservative whites wrested control of the state from the East Tennessee Radicals. They repealed Brownlow-era legislation—including the acts creating a state school system and banning racial segregation on public transportation—and gave the vote back to former Confederates. But they did not disfranchise black men, and in

1878 black voters were still a political power to be reckoned with in Memphis. The war and the postwar period left many Memphians bitter and suspicious of one anothers' motives. The city's internal conflicts would play a major role in shaping its response to the epidemic.[15]

IN SOME WAYS the America of the 1870s was very similar to that of today. For example, consider transportation and communication. Americans could get from city to city by train almost as fast as we can today by automobile. A train trip across the country, from the East Coast to California, took about a week. Telegraph wires linked west to east and stretched under the Atlantic to England. The Associated Press, a cooperative that existed in large part to enable newspapers to capitalize on telegraphic communications, had a reporter stationed in Memphis. His stories went out on the wire, spreading news of the city's plight and within days transmitting its pleas for help around the world.

In other ways, however, the Memphis of 1878 may seem foreign. Many of the people you read about here would today be condemned as virulent racists, incorrigible sexists, immoral womanizers, insufficiently subservient to family values, politically incorrect in every possible way—in short, ordinary people by the standards of their time. Just the same, many of them were heroes. In the dirty streets of Memphis, when death was random and survival uncertain, people behaved badly in the predictable ways. Irresponsibility, debauchery, craven selfishness, and dereliction from duty abounded. Against that background, some people put themselves at risk to help strangers.

This is a story about character, a history of a time when natural forces pushed people to moral extremes. And here are some of the characters through whom the story is told:

John McLeod Keating, editor of the *Memphis Daily Appeal*, who reported daily on what he saw during the fever season. An Irish immigrant who loved books, music, and the Democratic Party, Keating was convinced that Memphis's poor sanitation had caused the epidemic. He helped organize the relief effort and stayed at his job when all his coworkers fled, sickened, or died. Through his paper, Keating became the voice of Memphis in extremis. A partisan southern Democrat with a long history of opposing racial equality, he came to praise the black citizens of Memphis, without whose help the city would not have survived.

Kezia Payne DePelchin was a teacher and nurse from Texas. The daughter of a British wine merchant who migrated to the Republic of Texas, Kezia lost most of her family to a yellow fever epidemic when she was a child. Raised by her stepmother to be self-supporting, she taught school, gave music lessons, and, having acquired immunity to yellow fever, nursed patients through Houston's frequent epidemics. In 1878, at the age of fifty, she volunteered to nurse in Memphis. Kezia Payne DePelchin was well educated, highly literate, and profoundly religious, and her letters to her surviving sister provide an intensely personal chronicle of the fever season. Originally chatty, descriptive, and amusing, her letters became darker and sadder as she confronted her own helplessness in the face of the epidemic.

Dr. William Armstrong's adored wife, Lula, had just given birth to their eighth child when the epidemic broke out. Armstrong sent the family to safety but stayed in Memphis to help the sick. In his letters to his wife, he presents his decision to stay as being motivated in part by the need for money, but despite his assumed practicality, his compassion for his patients is evident. The most domestic of men, the doctor missed the routines of family life and was afraid to sleep in his house alone for fear of falling ill.

Nathan Menken was a wealthy merchant, co-owner of Menken Brothers dry goods store in downtown Memphis. When the epidemic began, he volunteered for the Hebrew Hospital Association and helped evacuate the Jewish community to safety in the North. Although he sent his family out of town and planned to follow them, Menken saw so many people who needed help, and so few left to help them, that he decided to stay, and he went to work for the citywide medical relief organization. A proud veteran of the Union cavalry, Menken risked his life to help people he had fought against only a few years previously.

The Reverend Sylvanus Landrum, pastor at Central Baptist Church, had the distinction of being the only white Baptist minister who stayed in the city during the epidemic. Landrum did not condemn other Protestant ministers for fleeing to safety, but he felt that the duty of a pastor, as a shepherd, required him to stay with his flock in times of trouble. His decision to stay cost him more than he could have anticipated. At the end of the epidemic, when his fellow survivors asked him to open his church and hold services, he spoke to a bereaved congregation on loss and faith.

Robert Reed Church's presence in the city during the summer of 1878 went almost unmarked. Yet there was no man in Memphis who benefited more from the changes brought by the epidemic. Church was a former slave, the almost-white son of a steamboat captain and an enslaved woman. He had already made a reputation as a man prepared to defend his rights in court and on the streets. When the epidemic transformed Memphis's demography, Church capitalized on the changes to found a fortune.

And finally, Memphis itself. Not to anthropomorphize the city: Memphis had no character other than that given to it by the people there. Yet the epidemic deeply affected the place, forming its future and making it into one of those few American cities known throughout the world. As strange as it may seem, the Memphis that gave birth to the blues, the city that was the cradle of rock 'n' roll, was born in the hot summer of 1878, during the fever season.

ONE

Bluff City Panorama

THE *MEMPHIS DAILY APPEAL* BUILDING normally resounds with men's voices talking politics and business, gossip and news. Today the quiet lies as thick as the dust on the desks in the front offices. All you might hear—if there were anyone to hear—is the soft tap of lead type slotting into a composing stick. John McLeod Keating, managing editor, is setting into type the news from Memphis: the corpses lying unburied for forty-eight hours or more, the baby trying to nurse at the breast of its dead mother, the man found dying, alone, naked, and covered with flies. Line by line, he spells out the names of the dead; eventually there will be thousands of them. Here is the name of a woman, gentle and refined. This man was brave, and Keating admires nothing more than courage. For weeks he has been preaching fortitude to the people of Memphis and embodying it himself, but every man has his breaking point. He sets into type his despair: "Hope, we have none."[1]

Outside, the sun beats down on empty streets. The waterfront is deserted, the saloons and brothels silent, downtown businesses closed, locked, and shuttered. People hide in their houses, fearing prolonged illness and a painful, degrading death. It is the summer of 1878, and in Memphis, Tennessee, thousands lie sick, dying, or dead of yellow fever.

WE DON'T KNOW what Memphis looked like in 1878. Most of the surviving nineteenth-century photos of street scenes were made twenty years later, in the 1890s. The best depiction of the city is actually a map, a panorama done in 1870 by Albert Ruger, at that time the nation's most successful panorama artist.[2] The "bird's-eye view" map he produced there shows a city laid out on a high bluff over a river bustling with traffic. Ruger drew packets, old-fashioned flatboats, rafts, and steamboats, the latter rendered in such detail that you can read their names on the paddle wheels: the *Natchez*, the *Republic*, and the famous *Robert E. Lee*. At the riverbank wharves, cargos are being unloaded and carried up the hill by tiny but deftly sketched horse-drawn wagons. At the top of the hill, cotton brokerages line Front Street. One block east of Front the city's business district begins. Main Street runs parallel to the river, crossed by avenues that begin at the bluff and continue east into distant green fields. Tall buildings—up to four stories, some of them—stand next to columned churches, schools, and the occasional small peaked-roof building (maybe a house or a grocery store). Downriver, the tall buildings get fewer and farther between and the houses and small stores more numerous after Main crosses Gayoso Avenue and Beale. Bayou Gayoso, which in other cities would be called a creek, winds through the city. Horse-drawn trolleys roll along tracks linking downtown to the residential areas north and east. Court Square, a green park in the midst of downtown, provides an easy orientation point. Ruger drew people on horseback, in wagons, and in buggies, designated by the smallest drops and curlicues of ink.

Detailed as it is, Ruger's map is a work of the imagination. Like all maps, it imposes rationality from above, and of necessity it omits the sensory cues of sound, color, and scent that people use for orientation. It also flatters the buying public, in this case the people of Memphis. In the map key Ruger designated by number important public buildings (courthouse and post office, railroad depots) and civic amenities such as parks, schools, and many, many churches. The panorama shows a neat, clean, orderly, and quiet city. But if we could bring up the color, the sounds, and the smells of Memphis on a July day in 1878, the map's pleasing order would disappear into a cacophony of noise, an assault of aroma, a blaze of color: steamboat whistles, the shouts of roustabouts, the clopping sound of mules pulling a trolley car, the stink from sewage-choked Bayou Gayoso, coffee brewing in the kitchen of the Peabody Hotel, stacks of watermelons and cantaloupes piled high at the Beale Street farmers' market, the sour smell of beer, the somber black clothing of grandmothers coming home from Mass at St. Patrick's Church, sunlight glittering on water, the swish of a young woman's long skirt sweeping along the sidewalk, the chatter of conversation, quarrels over politics, and news of the town and the river.

This was J. M. Keating's world, and by borrowing the panorama maker's license, we can picture Keating in it: forty-eight years old, dark hair shot through with silver, broad brow over dark eyes, bushy graying chin whiskers, walking past Court Square to the *Appeal*'s offices on the Fourth of July. Here is a man of business, a town booster, with a good word for the merchants along Main Street and an ear open for the town's chatter. With his partner, Matt Galloway, he runs the town's most successful newspaper. They make no pretense of political neutrality; they are Democrats, and the *Appeal* stands for the interests of that party. In their open political biases Keating and Galloway are typical of their time. Yet as managing editor, the person who makes the nightly decision on what to publish, Keating does offer a forum for civic controversy, publishing letters on all matter of local issues. Personally, he is a steady, sober, responsible man, although his life has been marked by sudden radical transformations. He has been an Irish rebel, a traveling printer, a Confederate general's aide. He has used his skills to defend the liberties of Irish Catholics and to disparage the liberty of newly freed slaves. He once wanted to be a priest. Now his interests are more scientific.[3]

He is obsessed with urban sanitation. He worries a lot about disease and writes about prevention so much that people in the town complain about the paper's fearmongering. Just now he and his friend Dr. Robert Mitchell are engaged in a protracted struggle to get the city government to authorize a quarantine against a potential outbreak of yellow fever. They are losing.

In February a virulent form of yellow fever struck Rio de Janeiro, and in March cases began to appear in Havana. Years of observation taught doctors and laymen alike that the fever killing Cubans in early spring usually hit New Orleans in early summer and upriver communities in late summer. Since 1855 the region's bastion against disease had been the Mississippi River Quarantine Station, seventy miles south of New Orleans, where resident physicians inspected incoming vessels for signs of illness. If they found any, they required the ship to spend ten days in quarantine.[4]

As news of the Caribbean outbreak spread, health officials upriver became nervous about the efficacy of quarantine at New Orleans. On

John McLeod Keating, from William S. Speer's Sketches
of Prominent Tennesseans, *1888.*

May 21 Dr. Maury of the Tennessee State Board of Health wrote a letter
expressing his concerns to the head of the Louisiana Board of Health, Dr.
Samuel P. Choppin. According to Keating, Choppin's reply was "curt"
and uninformative: the Louisiana physician said that he would send
Dr. Maury official information on a regular basis. He did note that at
that moment a British ship was already quarantined at the station. The
Borussia had passed through Havana on its way from Liverpool and arrived at the mouth of the Mississippi with six cases of fever on board.[5]

Dr. Robert Mitchell was chair of the chronically underfunded Memphis Board of Health. A man his contemporaries considered quiet, kind,
honest, and fair, Mitchell was better trained than many of the physicians in Memphis. In the 1850s medical training was not standardized,
and doctors throughout the nation often apprenticed themselves to experienced physicians to learn the trade. Mitchell had done that, but he
had also obtained a medical degree at the University of Louisiana, the

Dr. Robert Wood Mitchell, from John McLeod Keating and
O. P. Vedder's History of the City of Memphis and Shelby County,
Tennessee, Vol. II (Syracuse, N.Y.: D. Mason & Co., 1889).

ancestor of present-day Tulane, in New Orleans. Given that the University of Louisiana was one of the nation's best medical schools, you can get an idea of what medical education was like by looking at the school's prospectus for 1852. A term (a "course of lectures") lasted from mid-November to March. To obtain an M.D., a student had to finish two terms, write a thesis, present it to the dean, and pass examination by the faculty.

Mitchell studied chemistry, anatomy, physiology, surgery, and obstetrics, as well as "materia medica," now called pharmacology. He graduated in 1856, and in 1858 he opened a practice in Memphis. When the Civil War began, he volunteered to serve as surgeon to the Thirteenth Tennessee Regiment of Confederate Volunteers. He was captured at Shiloh but released, and he continued with his regiment through battles at Stones River, Missionary Ridge, Atlanta, and Franklin. As that (dismal) trajectory suggests, Mitchell had extensive surgical experience.

He also knew as much as anyone about yellow fever. As a medical student, he had taken charge of the Vicksburg city hospital during a yellow fever epidemic. He had cared for patients through the Memphis epidemics of 1867 and 1873. In addition to experience, Mitchell had other attributes that were to prove invaluable in the days ahead: he could organize men and get them to work together. Dr. Mitchell knew that in 1873 the Louisiana cordon sanitaire had failed, allowing yellow fever to slip through to Memphis, where it killed almost two thousand people. He feared another epidemic, and a bad one.[6]

On May 22 the steamer *Emily B. Souder*, in from Havana via Key West, arrived at the Quarantine Station. The captain explained to the doctor on duty that one of his crew had a fever. The doctor diagnosed malaria and sent the man to the station infirmary. The man was obviously not well, but the doctor accepted his self-diagnosis of facial neuralgia. He examined the rest of the passengers and crew, ordered the ship to be disinfected and fumigated, and sent them on up the river to the New Orleans docks. The ship's purser got sick that night. The next morning, a New Orleans doctor took him to the home of a nurse, where he died two days later, on May 25. Although the attending physician recorded that he had died of "intermittent bilious fever," a board of health officer interviewed the people who had been in the house with the purser and concluded that he had died of yellow fever. The *Emily Souder*'s engineer died in a New Orleans hospital on May 29. The attending physician attributed the death to intermittent fever. When two board of health medical officers autopsied the body, they came to the conclusion that the engineer had died of yellow fever.[7]

On June 3 Dr. Mitchell ignited a public controversy by telling the Memphis Board of Health that they should make preparations for quarantine against yellow fever. Mitchell was not advocating shutting Memphis up and refusing to let anyone out. By quarantine, he meant closing avenues of transportation and trade from fever-stricken regions. If Memphis quarantined against New Orleans, people and goods from New Orleans would not be allowed to enter the city without some form of intervention. In its strictest form, quarantining against New Orleans would mean that nothing from the Crescent City—neither trains nor boats nor the people and goods they carried—would be allowed into Memphis. Less stringent forms of quarantine might include posting health officers to inspect passengers before allowing them to enter the city or requiring that shipments of goods be stopped, inspected, disinfected, and held outside the city for some set period of time. Mitchell was not suggesting that the city quarantine immediately against New Orleans, only that they get ready to do so.

What followed was the reverse of what might have been expected. Mayor John R. Flippin supported Mitchell, but Dr. John W. Erskine and his colleagues on the board disagreed. Erskine acknowledged that yellow fever was transportable, but he believed that the disease required malignant environmental conditions in order to spread.[8] While Mitchell prepared to ask the city council for funds to implement quarantine if needed, the other physicians on the board organized the city's doctors against it.[9]

The physicians' dispute may have been fueled by local political or personal issues—the record is not clear on this point—but it certainly reflected legitimate scientific conflict over the nature of contagion. In 1878 biological science was on the brink of rapid advancement. By the end of the century new discoveries and methodologies would lay the foundations of bacteriology and transform the practice of medicine. As yet, however, there was no single paradigm explaining the origins of infectious disease. Physicians cobbled together remnants of the ancient miasma theory, modern medical discoveries, and socially acceptable prejudices to formulate theories about the etiology of yellow fever. Although these could vary wildly from person to person, two centuries of observation had produced some consensus. Most physicians no longer accepted the theory that the fever spontaneously generated in miasma, or bad air. Few, if any, disputed the disease's origins in Africa and its preference for tropical climates. For generations, doctors had observed that people could breathe the atmosphere of the sickroom and swab up black vomit without catching the disease. Anti-contagionists insisted that yellow fever was therefore not catching in the manner of smallpox or measles.[10]

Yet the fever moved from place to place. The pattern seemed clear: fever broke out in the Caribbean, ships came from the islands to New Orleans, fever broke out in New Orleans. On the Mississippi, yellow fever seemed to travel by steamboat from New Orleans to cities upriver. Before the Civil War, Mississippi Valley yellow fever outbreaks rarely extended far from the river. An infected person can pass the virus to a mosquito only in the first three days of his illness, so the slowness of antebellum transportation, by horse or by foot, worked against the spread of the fever. After the Civil War, a railroad building boom reduced the distances to matters of days or even hours: from New Orleans to Memphis by train was a journey of about fifteen hours, from Memphis to Little Rock, about twelve. Although physicians and other interested observers did not know how the disease was transmitted, when yellow fever broke out in whistle-stop towns along the railroad lines, they understood the implications. Clearly, Yellow Jack had learned to take the train.[11]

So the fever was not contagious, but it was transportable. How, exactly? Groping for a reasonable answer, mid-century physicians advanced the theory that there was a yellow fever "germ," the nature of which had yet to be discovered. It might be an "animalcule," or a type of fungus. This germ attached itself to objects, such as articles of clothing or bedding that had been in contact with a fever patient or in his vicinity. Such objects (or "fomites") could transport the yellow fever germ. In the 1870s, doctors hypothesized that the yellow fever germ was transported in this way. Yet the presence of fomites did not suffice to explain why fever broke out in some cities and not in others.[12]

Anti-contagionists argued that the answer could be found in the environmental conditions prevailing in infected cities. They believed that yellow fever required filth to propagate. Although the component parts of filth were neither clearly defined nor quantified, mid-century doctors and laymen knew it when they smelled it. Kitchen slops, rotting vegetation, sewage, manure, and carrion decomposed under the sun on southern city streets, melting into a layer of sludge that emitted offensive odors. Anti-contagionists believed that these effusions contaminated the atmosphere and made it hospitable to the yellow fever germ.

Today science has proved that yellow fever has nothing to do with filth. Dirty streets do not cause the fever, nor do open sewers, piles of food scraps, unwashed people, or polluted water. Mosquitoes are vectors for the yellow fever virus. But in 1878 people did not know that. Updating the miasma theory, physicians argued that while the bad atmosphere did not cause yellow fever, its presence made it possible for the fever to develop. Therefore, yellow fever epidemics could be avoided in two ways: by interdicting or sanitizing fomites and by making sure that the environment would not be hospitable to the germ.

Not all physicians accepted these theories as accurate or even logical, and physicians who accepted the general validity of the anti-contagionist

position did not always agree with one another on the details. One New
Jersey physican asked how the noninfectious bodies of patients could
shed infectious materials on fomites. Others pointed out that outbreaks
occurred in some filthy tropical cities but not in others. Dr. Samuel Choppin of New Orleans, arguably the country's leading expert on the disease,
professed to only modest knowledge about it: "I believe that yellow fever
is an exotic; that its germ is a living organism and reproduces itself. It
multiplies itself, first on surfaces and then in the atmosphere, until it
becomes epidemic. Yellow fever is a self-limited disease, like all specific
diseases. *It must run its course, and nothing that we know of can stop its
progress.*"[13]

Dr. John Erskine was an anti-contagionist. In a *Public Health Papers
and Reports* article he argued that the fever, while not contagious, was
certainly transportable to places with conditions suitable to its growth.
His proof came from the 1873 Memphis epidemic. Erskine described the
waterfront district Happy Hollow, home to "a low class of Irish," as a text-
book example of the perfect environment for yellow fever: "It is under the
Chickasaw Bluffs, so sunken that in high water it is largely submerged,
and after the tide has fallen is left partially covered with stagnant pools
and slimy ooze, whose exhalations are noisome and offensive." He added
that garbage was continuously thrown onto the alluvial soil. "It is the
natural drain for the sewers of the overhanging bluff, through which the
sewage steadily trickles." During the summer months the decomposing
"filth" emitted "mephitic gases . . . potent enough to induce infection,
needing only the germ of yellow fever to be sown to yield all the fearful
fruits of this great epidemic." Once seeded, Erskine said, the fever "obeyed
the law of gradual extension," taking a month to spread a quarter mile.
After that, cases began to appear in "different centres at variable distances." Twenty thousand people had left Memphis during the 1873
epidemic, but thirty thousand stayed. Erskine estimated that the fifteen
hundred people who died represented about 15 percent of the ten thousand actually infected with the disease.[14]

As Erskine and other anti-contagionists saw it, yellow fever's spread
could be stopped by cleaning out the filth that clogged Memphis streets.
By the end of June, thirty-two Memphis doctors had joined the health
board dissenters. Their petition stated that quarantine was not needed,
too expensive, and impractical. "There is no yellow fever in New Orleans,"
the petition read; establishing quarantine at this point "would be most

detrimental to the business interests of Memphis." Instead, the doctors argued that the city funding used for quarantine could be best expended "to abate nuisances in the city." Memphis needed a "well-regulated sanitary department" and would need it more as the "hot weather advances." Finally, they said that making quarantine work would require guarding the city's railroad depots, "which can only be done at an additional cost, and then very ineffectively."[15]

While the doctors opposed quarantine, many of the city's business interests supported it. To counter Erskine's petition, Mitchell submitted one signed by twenty leading merchants—the very people who would, presumably, lose business if quarantine were enacted. Mitchell also received support from Keating. On June 30 the *Appeal* respectfully disagreed with the anti-quarantine doctors, finding their reasoning "insufficient to overcome the strong desire the people have for any and all protection against epidemic disease they can get, be it little or much." The editors considered preparing for quarantine an inexpensive "precautionary measure" that should enhance Memphis's reputation throughout the region and actually encourage trade. The paper agreed that the city needed to be cleaned up, adding that doing so would provide more security against disease. The editorial concluded with a quote from the American Public Health Association's journal, *The Sanitarian*: preventing yellow fever "is possible only by thorough quarantine and civic cleanliness."[16]

The *Appeal*'s Independence Day edition, however, focused on the city's major and constant preoccupation, the state of "trade" and the prospects for the cotton season that would start in September.

The world's largest inland cotton market centered on the Front Street offices of Memphis's cotton factors. According to a Memphis historian, a cotton factor "financed the operator's crop from planting through harvest with seed, provisions, and equipment. He then sold this crop and received a commission plus payment for all of the provisions furnished from the plantation operator. He was the planter's banker."[17] A cotton factor's entire year's work culminated in the autumn cotton season. Each September, bales of ginned cotton arrived at Front Street by rail, steamboat, and wagon and were graded and sold, thousands of acres worth, to buyers in the United States and overseas. Four railroad lines connected to the city, making it a crossroads of land and river transportation. When prices rose or fell on the international cotton exchange in Liverpool, England, the information crossed the Atlantic on the new undersea cables and was transmitted via telegraph to Memphis to appear in local newspapers. The black roustabouts unloading bales on the riverbank, the farmers buying boots on Main Street, the cotton factors dining at Gaston's Hotel, the sons of planters and of slaves—all derived their living from the process by which cotton became silver, gold, and lines of credit in British banks.[18]

Native-born southern whites dominated the city's cotton trade, but the businesses on downtown streets were run by people with names like Flaherty, Schmidt, Lowenstein, and Youn Wo. Memphis had four Catholic parishes, German Evangelical Lutheran and Protestant churches, two synagogues, and more black Baptist congregations than white. Fraternal organizations abounded, from the Odd Fellows, Masons, and Knights of (respectively) Pythias, Honor, and Innisfail to the Società di Unione e Fratelanza Italiana.[19]

Memphis was densely populated, with about fifty thousand people crammed into a waterfront space two and a half miles long north to south, a little over one mile wide east to west. Workers walked past middle-class homes, shops, churches, and schools en route to their jobs, and middle-class men walked past livery stables and factories to get to theirs. Merchants lived over their stores; domestic servants lived down the alley. Bars operated throughout the city, and brothels sold sex from Front Street into the exclusive suburbs. A British visitor to Memphis thought Memphis girls the prettiest in the nation, although she noted that they were dressed badly in "modes which, however pretty they may be, a French milliner would not allow a *lady* to buy, simply because they were *porteés par la demi-monde.*" Perhaps the girls observed were not ladies.

The British tourist Thérèse Yelverton Longworth, Viscountess Avonmore, praised the supper she had at Gaston's, where the food really was French. She praised the availability of good music in private homes and public concerts, attributing it to the influence of Germans. What struck her most strongly was the mud. Outside of the paved main streets, she wrote, "for miles and miles in every direction the roads and waste lands are impassable, from oceans of liquid mud. In most of the streets it concentrates into porridge again." On the other hand, the riverfront was impressively busy, with the finest landing she had seen on the Mississippi.[20]

The viscountess's comments highlight Memphis's contradictions. It was a dangerous, dirty place with finely dressed, cultured people who carried guns and enjoyed opera. There were pigs in the streets, but also luxurious accommodations and first-rate public spaces. Take, for example, the Peabody Hotel. Now a Memphis icon, the hotel then was in a different location, but it was already a venue for socially significant events. With Moorish arches, tiled floors, carpets, and Persian rugs, the Peabody Hotel's public rooms could compete with any hotel of its size in the country, but its rooms were outstanding: each had its own private bath. As the viscountess pointed out, however, Memphis verged on lawlessness. "The Memphis newspapers of January 1st, 1869, published a list of local events during the past year. The list included thirty-three homicides, for none of which had a man been hanged." The local papers published crime stories featuring brawls, stabbings, shootings, and other affrays. Men of all classes and races habitually carried pistols, thus heightening the danger against which they were armed.[21]

As a center for the cotton trade, Memphis was spectacularly successful. As a city, it was a failure. Even by the standards of the day Memphis had embarrassingly few urban amenities. Those that existed tended to be privately funded and to serve only a few well-to-do families or neighborhoods. There was a privately owned water company, but few families chose to pay fees for water drawn from the polluted Wolf River, a small stream that entered the Mississippi just above the town. Instead, Memphians drew their water from more than four thousand cisterns and wells and thereby on any summer day risked bites from the common cistern mosquito—*Ae. aegypti*. Privately owned sewers served about two hundred buildings. The rest of Memphis used approximately six thousand privies, simple pit toilets. Most American cities had dirty streets, which is not surprising considering that horses and mules contributed twenty pounds of manure per animal per day. Keeping the streets clean required a committed effort and a considerable expenditure of money, neither of which Memphis could muster. Regular garbage collection remained an elusive dream. Memphis streets were quagmires in wet weather, strewn with filth and trash in all seasons. Convinced that the city's filth caused disease, J. M. Keating repeatedly crusaded in the *Appeal* for better sanitation, but in vain. The municipal government of Memphis had other priorities.[22]

By January 1878, after more than twenty years of bad decisions, corruption, and political cowardice, the municipality was bankrupt. Before the war, Memphis had issued a series of bonds to help finance rail connections. Those bonds were never paid off. In recent years the city had gone into debt again to put "Nicholson pavement" on the downtown streets. Patented in 1866, the Nicholson process laid down a foundation of wooden boards, topped them with creosote-soaked wooden blocks about six inches thick placed end-grain up, and then filled in gaps with tar and gravel. The blocks "absorbed horse urine and excrement and sweated putrid fluid in hot weather." It is hard to imagine a pavement method less suited to a southern city. The Nicholson pavement was a disaster, and the bonds floated to pay for it added even more to the city's debt. In the 1870s the municipal government continually reneged on interest payments, issued more bonds, paid its employees in scrip, and in general behaved as if the rules of capitalism had been suspended in Shelby County. Indignant creditors besieged the city with lawsuits.[23]

The municipality's incompetence led some members of the white upper class to demand reform. They suggested that Memphis would be better off if the state legislature rescinded the city charter and replaced the elected city government with an appointed commission. Not incidentally, this measure would allow the city to repudiate its debts. Although the Memphis Cotton Exchange and the chamber of commerce supported the plan, it lacked popularity among the city's elected officials and the voting public. Meanwhile, wealthy Memphians benefited financially from the city's bad government. Tax collection was so inefficient that most never paid their assessments. Or, as Keating put it, "taxes were levied, but were not collected." He wrote, "Every interest was carefully guarded and provided for, save that of the health and the life of the people."[24]

So, Memphis: dirty, badly administered, in July 1878 on the edge of a catastrophe that would have strained the resources of the most perfectly functioning municipality in the world.

JULY 4, 1878, was a hot, breezeless day, the latest in a long series. The winter had been mild, and spring had come early. The last killing frost had fallen in February, and by March, daily highs were in the eighties. Trees blossomed, flowers bloomed, and mosquitoes proliferated on the sides of rain barrels and under the covers of cisterns. The *Appeal* noted that the mosquitoes "are increasing in numbers, and are becoming more vindictive and ferocious, if it were possible to do so." People who got bitten scratched the resultant itchy bumps but were not otherwise harmed.

Until they had yellow fever carriers to feed on, *Ae. aegypti* mosquitoes were nothing more than a normal summer nuisance. Like heat and humidity, they were part of the backdrop for the annual celebration of Independence Day.

Thousands of people took special excursion trains to Memphis for the day. This year there would be fireworks, thanks to the organizational skills of local impresario Peter Tracy. Until then there were other things to see. If you stood on the bluff at Front Street, you could see the steamboats at the wharf, flags drooping in the heavy air. You could walk across to Main Street, where merchants had decorated the building facades in red, white, and blue bunting, and down to Court Square. The fountain there was a sight for country eyes. Installed only two years earlier, it featured a statue of Hebe, cupbearer to the gods, a partially clothed pretty woman surrounded by plumes of sparkling water. The municipal fire company also provided free entertainment. Assuming that many of the visitors might never have seen modern firefighting equipment, they rolled out their engines, "steamed up to Court Square, where they attached hoses, and in a short while had their streams playing high into the air."

In midmorning the city's temperance organizations paraded down Main Street to the music of a brass band. In a city that had 125 saloons listed in its directory, plus who knew how many blind tigers, buckets of blood, taverns, house bars, brothels, and grocery stores that would sell a shot out back, temperance was not a popular cause. The crowds on Main raised a cheer for the reformed boozers anyway.

Men nostalgic about their wartime military service or just appreciative of well-executed close-order drill could go to Estival Park, where the city's two white militia units put on an exhibition to raise funds for St. Peter's Catholic Orphanage. The Bluff City Grays and the Chickasaw Guards had spiffy uniforms (gray with black and gold trim for the Grays, blue with scarlet and gold for the Chickasaws). Militia companies, nominally under the command of state government, had not yet evolved into the National Guard. Throughout the nation in the 1870s they were used primarily against labor during strikes and to put down riots. The militia companies also functioned socially as young men's clubs.

At Olympic Park, racing fans watched trotters and waited for news from a much bigger race in Louisville. Molly McCarty, the reputed best filly in California, had come all the way across country by train to race

Ten Broeck, said to be the best stallion in the east. Although no one in 1878 could know it, for more than a century afterward, fiddle-playing bands would sing about how Ten Broeck beat Molly. The ballad transported the race from Kentucky to Memphis and described Ten Broeck running all around the city and beating the Memphis train. Ominously, Molly complains that running in the hot sun has given her a fever in her head. The song makes the race sound more exciting than it actually was. Much to the disgust of the punters, Ten Broeck left Molly thoroughly in the dust. Those who had traveled to Louisville for the event said later that they wished they had stayed home.[25]

Yet despite the parades and drills and general hoopla, there was a subdued quality to Independence Day in Memphis. Although J. M. Keating and his partner Matt Galloway promoted the celebration (and had printed up five thousand extra copies of a special edition of the *Appeal* for the benefit of the country people), not everyone in town cared to commemorate the birth of the United States of America. For some Confederate veterans, the Stars and Stripes was and always would be the flag of their enemy. Even in the *Appeal*, one reporter's account of the festivities struck an ambiguous note. It was too bad, the writer said, that "we are now taught the heresy that this land of Liberty is a union and not a league of free states." Nonetheless, "there is something in the Fourth of July, even in this southern land. It brings up memories long buried but not forgotten."[26]

THE CIVIL WAR cut across the lives of J. M. Keating's contemporaries. In Memphis, white men of a certain age went by such military titles as general, major, colonel, or captain, although they might have fought in different armies. Some carried scars, physical and emotional, from the war; some nursed rancor dating from that complex, incomplete revolution we call Reconstruction. Union man or Confederate, they had been shaped by the war. In Keating's case, the war and Reconstruction transformed an ambitious Irish immigrant into a Confederate supporter and a personal friend of Jefferson Davis. In 1878 Memphis knew him as "Colonel Keating," a loyal southerner with an impeccable record of support for states' rights, white supremacy, and the Lost Cause. However, the southern colonel was but the latest persona in the life of a man who moved through many identities.

Keating was born in Kings County, Ireland, in 1830, the son of an Irish Protestant farmer. Keating's mother was from Scotland, and Keating himself spent years there as a child. With this background he could have defined himself as ethnically Scottish, religiously Protestant, and a loyal subject of Queen Victoria. Instead, he chose to be an Irish patriot. At the age of thirteen he apprenticed as a printer in a Dublin newspaper shop. By age eighteen he was pressroom foreman at the Dublin *World* and secretary to the editor. He joined Young Ireland, an Irish nationalist movement that welcomed both Protestants and Catholics. In 1848 the crushing effects of the potato famine and the examples of revolutionary uprisings across Europe prompted Young Ireland's leaders to organize a rebellion among rural tenant farmers. When it failed, the movement's leaders were convicted of treason and transported. Keating immigrated to America.[27]

For six years he worked as a printer on newspapers in New York. Then in 1854 he moved to New Orleans, ostensibly for reasons of health. Given that the city was one of the most disease-ridden in the nation, beset by regular yellow fever epidemics, and filthy beyond description, Keating's move makes no sense. If a warm climate were wanted, the South offered many more salubrious locales. However, when a man says that he moved because of ill health, he may not necessarily be referring only to his need for sunnier skies.

The wave of Irish immigration prompted by the potato famine sparked anti-Irish, anti-Catholic, anti-immigrant resentment among the Protestant native-born, particularly in East Coast cities like Philadelphia, Boston, and New York. Like all Irish immigrants, Keating faced a world of prejudice. As a Protestant, unlike the majority of Irish immigrants, he could not find community and security in the Catholic Church. The only other major institution that welcomed the Irish was the Democratic Party. Keating attributed his affiliation with the Democrats to his admiration for Jeffersonian ideals. In the 1850s that meant that he stood with the party of the common man, the immigrant, the worker—and with slaveholders, attached to the Democrats by promises of small government and "personal liberty," which they took to mean the liberty to own slaves. In choosing the Democrats, Keating followed the pattern of most Irish immigrants. The other major party, the Whigs, often supported state and local laws closing businesses on Sunday, prohibiting the sale of alcohol, and denying tax funding for Catholic schools. Then in the early

1850s a new party began to build support with a platform that made the Whigs look friendly. The Know-Nothings were nativist, anti-Catholic, and anti-Irish. When Know-Nothings or other nativist groups organized parades in northeastern cities—particularly when those parades deliberately targeted Irish neighborhoods—street brawls ensued.[28] Keating disdained the nativists so much that long after the party disappeared, he still referred to Know-Nothings when he needed an example of political prejudice and oppression. The political climate in New York may not have had anything to do with his decision to leave, but it seems worth noting that in 1854 the New York area had two major riots involving the Irish and the Know-Nothings.[29]

For his health, Keating left New York, and from 1854 until 1858 he drifted from job to job across the South. At some point during his peregrinations Keating began to transform himself from working-class rebel to (in the words of a friend) a "cultivated Irishman." He embarked on projects of self-improvement, assigning himself topics for serious daily study. Moving south gave him new opportunities to move up. The antebellum South had relatively few workers in advanced technological trades such as printing. Keating had been working as a foreman in New York. In Nashville he helped set up the Methodist Book Concern, the first publishing house in the South, then for two years worked as superintendent of state printing in Louisiana. He also worked as a newspaper editor in Nashville. This rapid advancement suggests that he was able to exploit political and social connections, perhaps forged through the Democratic Party or through his membership in the Masons.

In 1856 he married a Nashville belle. Josephine Esselman Smith was tall, blond, and statuesque—what Victorians called a handsome woman. An accomplished pianist, harpist, and singer, she read and translated French and wrote erudite essays on cultural topics. Keating was not overawed. He believed in equality for women—an attitude so uncommon in the antebellum South as to qualify as eccentricity. The Keatings had a son, Neil McLeod Keating, in 1858, and in 1860 a daughter, Caroline, always called Carrie. In 1858 Keating wiped the ink from his fingers, moved out of the pressroom, and became commercial and city editor for the *Memphis Bulletin*. A normal progression for a diligent, self-educated, upwardly mobile working-class man.[30]

Yet Keating was not satisfied. In the late 1850s and through the Civil War he tried repeatedly to leave newspapering. He first studied for the

Episcopal priesthood under Bishop James Otey but decided that he could not subscribe to all the tenets of the faith. The advent of the war gave him different job opportunities.

Memphians were not anxious to leave the Union in 1860, not even after Lincoln was elected president. As a resident remembered, "when news of South Carolina's secession reached Memphis everybody was stunned." In February 1861, when Tennesseans voted against holding a secession convention, Union sentiment was still strong in the Bluff City. Keating counted Tennessee senator Andrew Johnson, a loyalist who opposed secession, as a personal friend. He disliked slavery, although, like many other Americans, he was able to separate morality from questions of legality and political expedience. But he also thought that secession was constitutional.[31]

Lincoln's 1861 call for troops to put down the rebellion placed Keating, and most Tennesseans, in a difficult position. Since the U.S. government would not let the southern states leave the Union, Tennessee's state government had to choose. They could send troops to the Union or join the other slave states in the Confederacy. In early June 1861 the state of Tennessee held a second referendum on secession. This time the secessionists won. In Shelby County the vote was overwhelming, seven thousand to five in favor of leaving the Union. Keating became a loyal citizen of the Confederacy. By summer, he was clerking for General Leonidas Polk, the Episcopal bishop of Louisiana, who was recruiting for the Confederacy in Memphis.[32]

All through the summer of 1861 white men marched off to join the Confederate army. They enlisted in companies with romantic names like the Garibaldi Guards, the Emerald Guards, the Crockett Rangers, the Bluff City Grays, and the Memphis Light Dragoons.[33] Often they left with flags sewn by "the ladies" and presented, with appropriate speeches, to the company commander. Ultimately, hundreds of men from Memphis fought for the Confederacy. Slave trader Nathan Bedford Forrest, a Memphis resident, raised a cavalry troop, promised his men plenty of opportunities to kill Yankees, and became one of the Confederacy's most famous (and infamous) generals. People who did not want to kill Yankees—or in fact supported the Union—found it advisable to keep quiet or leave.

Keating worked for Polk until October, when he was felled by a typhoid attack so severe that it left him bedridden for four months. A physician judged him "incapacitated for military duty of any kind." After the typhoid, Keating developed a debilitating ailment that required major surgery in 1864 and 1866. Although the records do not indicate what the problem was, severe typhoid can cause anal fistulas and kidney disease. To help support the family, Josephine Keating wrote literary and critical pieces for pay. When Keating could work, he took a job clerking for the Southern Express Company, then served as city editor for the *Memphis Argus*. He thus witnessed the Civil War's impact on the city on a daily basis.[34]

In June 1862 the Union river navy defeated Confederate river forces in a brief battle in the Mississippi just above the city, and the federal army captured Memphis. Union forces occupied the city until 1866. Ironically, the city's economy benefited from the occupation. While the Union army turned a tacit blind eye, upper-class Memphians and enterprising northern newcomers made money smuggling cotton out of the Confederacy. In this Casablanca on the Mississippi, the presence of large numbers of soldiers also had a predictably positive impact on saloons and brothels. The latter trade was regulated by the Union army, which licensed prostitutes who submitted to regular medical inspections. At the end of the war, Memphis's real estate values had actually increased, at a time when many southern towns lay in burned-out ruins. However, defeated Confederate soldiers came back to a Memphis that had been profoundly changed. The business class now included northern Unionists, and the streets were patrolled by black soldiers.[35]

In the postwar period Keating dabbled in insurance. He started a newspaper. In 1867–68 he went to Washington, where he served as an adviser to President Andrew Johnson. The president put Keating forward to be postmaster of Memphis, but the Senate rejected his nomination, and while he was away in Washington, his newspaper failed. Despite this run of failure and rejection, Keating was not without resources. He knew people who had money. The Overton Hotel, one of the finest buildings in Memphis, had been used as a hospital during the Civil War and in the spring of 1866 was sold at a Chancery Court. Standing as proxy for New York investors, Keating bought the hotel for $181,000, of which $75,000 had to be paid in cash. Eight years later Shelby County bought the building for $150,000 and turned it into the county courthouse. (Because prices for other goods and services had declined drastically in the interim years, $181,000 in 1866 was equivalent to just less than $140,000 by 1874.) By that time, Keating had become the influential editor of the city's largest newspaper, the *Memphis Daily Appeal*.[36]

The *Appeal* was already a legend among American newspapers. When Memphis fell to the Union army, *Appeal* editor John McClanahan packed up the type cases, dismantled his solid iron steam-driven press, loaded up the pieces (which took eight wagons to carry), and fled south.[37] For years the *"Moving Appeal"* was the effective voice of the Army of the Tennessee, publishing from Jackson, Mississippi; Atlanta, Georgia; and Montgomery, Alabama, generally leaving each town just ahead of advancing Union troops. The *Appeal* returned to Memphis after the war, but the editors died, the heirs quarreled, and the paper was so deep in debt that it went into receivership and was sold at auction. When one of the new owners lost interest in running the paper, he sold a half interest to J. M. Keating. The outstanding debts still had not been paid, and the paper was threatened with sale again. Eventually Keating managed to raise the money needed to redeem the *Appeal* by incorporating and selling stock to thirty investors. Matt Galloway joined him in 1870. Galloway and Keating ran the *Appeal* for twenty years.[38]

The two men were very different. Only ten years older than Keating, Galloway was nonetheless of an older generation and an earlier time. It is indicative that in the 1840s and 1850s, when Keating was learning the printing trade, Galloway developed a reputation as an expert on the etiquette of dueling. He served as a second in two affairs of honor and was frequently called to mediate disputes before they reached the shooting stage. Founder of the fiery *Memphis Daily Avalanche*, Galloway supported secession earlier than most Memphians. The Confederate government appointed him postmaster of Memphis, a position he held until the Union occupation began. He fled to the Confederate army and served as aide to General Forrest. After the war, Galloway returned to the *Avalanche*. He became a leader in the postwar southern white resistance to Reconstruction. He and his fellow editors "conducted a spectacular verbal fight against local Radical rule in 1867 and 1868, deliberately getting themselves cited for contempt by a notoriously corrupt Radical judge, then continuing publication from their jail cells." (Eventually the state supreme court ruled against the judge.) And, as will be seen, Galloway's resistance to Republican politicians and black equality was not always carried out through the courts.[39]

Keating was, by contrast, a quiet man. He enjoyed the theater and counted as friends many of the singers and actors whose shows toured Memphis. He liked horse racing. He liked serious music—a good thing, considering that his wife and daughter were both accomplished musicians. According to the author of an 1888 biographical sketch, "only silence and seclusion" gave Keating relief from the attacks of the "troublesome disease" that had necessitated surgery during the 1860s. When suffering, he turned to his books. He read a lot and accumulated an impressive library. He preferred serious literature and, above all, information—about history, science, theology, psychology. His biographer said that Keating "loves his books, next after his wife and children, and these after his God." One of his oldest friends commented that Keating "does not mix much with people, being a student and an editor, but he is charming," earnest, enthusiastic, and "full of gentleness and sympathy."[40]

What Keating and Galloway had in common was a fanatical commitment to the Democratic Party. Day in and day out, the *Appeal* traced the fortunes of the Democrats on the state, the local, and the municipal level. On the eve of July Fourth in 1878 the paper ran an analysis of who was likely to vote for whom in the upcoming municipal elections—the "negroes" being in with one faction, the Irish being out. His biographer expressed regret that a man like Keating, a person with so many varied interests, had become an editor: "It is painful to think of such a mind as an editor, for a newspaper belongs to the public, and he has contracted to please them. Worse still, the newspaper belongs to the party, and the editor must give up to the party what belongs to mankind," suppressing "the rising thought" and concealing "the honest admission." It seems very doubtful that Keating felt the same. His entire life testifies that he was as fascinated by the play of politics as he was by the ideological foundations of political belief.[41]

When Keating assumed ownership of the *Appeal*, Tennessee had completed the process of Reconstruction, but Arkansas and Mississippi, both within miles of Memphis, had not. The *Appeal* became the voice of southern white opposition to Reconstruction in those states. Keating and Galloway excoriated all factions of the Republican Party, from the so-called Radicals in Washington to the "carpetbagger" state governments to the newly empowered former slaves. They advocated white supremacy, opposed giving black men the right to vote, paid obeisance to the Lost Cause, and supported states' rights. Somewhere in the confusion of war and Reconstruction, J. M. Keating acquired the courtesy title of Colonel.

As the 1870s rolled on and Reconstruction ended, the Memphis Democrats learned to court black voters and the *Appeal* became less strident. Keating, in particular, seemed ready to focus on economics: "We want to be let alone. We want to make money; we want the prosperity that comes of strict attention to business, and we don't want any more scares or excitements."[42] Although the *Appeal* still stood for the Democratic Party, Keating's pro-business boosterism may have given the paper a greater appeal to the city's multiethnic business class. Northern-born businessmen advertised heavily in the paper.

By the mid-1870s the *Appeal* had pulled ahead of all other Memphis papers in circulation. As managing editor, Keating supervised forty people, all of them engaged in the work required to print and distribute five thousand papers per day. Only three were what might now be called "content providers": a city editor, a river editor, and a reporter. These three, plus Keating and Galloway, wrote all the local copy for the paper or edited the wire service reports. (The *Appeal*'s front page typically featured state, national, and international news from the Associated Press wires.) Four men worked in the counting room, taking money for subscriptions and advertisements. The rest of the staff did the technical work. The *Appeal* employed eighteen compositors, who turned the copy to type at a rate of roughly one line per minute, working in the blaze of lamps deep into the night. After a page was set, it was placed in a small proof press and a sheet was "pulled" so that the editor could check for errors. If one was found, that line had to be corrected. Once proofs were deemed acceptable, the forms went down to the pressroom. Sixteen pressmen fired up the furnace under the steam boiler, set the page forms in the press, and began the run. By dawn, freshly printed papers, their ink still damp, would appear on doorsteps all over town.[43]

For an editor like Keating, the entire day's work culminated in the rattle, swoosh, and thump of the press. After that, he was briefly free from the constraints of deadlines, and he could go home—in Keating's case, probably to an empty apartment. (Carrie had musical talent and Neil wanted to be a painter, so for several years Josephine Keating moved with them to New York, where they could obtain better educations than they could get in Memphis.) Then it was sleep, breakfast, and back to the office again, even on the Fourth of July. After all, another paper had to appear on the morning of the fifth, full of news of the day's festivities. However, the biggest event of the day traditionally received only minimal coverage: the "colored people's" parade.[44]

FOR YEARS AFTER the end of the Civil War, former Confederates and their children ignored Independence Day. (Fondness for the Fourth of July resurfaced only in the 1890s, in the burst of unified patriotism that characterized the Spanish-American War.) In 1869 a Memphis newspaper reported that only blacks and Germans celebrated the day. Similar sentiments could be found in local newspapers as late as the 1880s, but if white Memphians did not want the Fourth of July, their black neighbors were happy to adopt it as their own.[45]

In 1878 black Memphis celebrated the Fourth in the city's streets, as had been the practice since 1865. Over the years the celebrations had become ritualized: benevolent and fraternal organizations marched down Main Street through the business district and the white neighborhoods to one of the town's parks, where the assembled crowd listened to the reading of the Declaration of Independence.[46] The parades also prominently featured the city's black militia troops, the McClellan Guards and Brown's Zouaves. Armed black men marching through the streets of the city demonstrated that the community had the capacity for self-defense. In Memphis, that statement had particular resonance. Many of the men and women cheering the McClellan Guards in 1878 could remember all too well a time when blacks in Memphis had desperately needed defenders and found none.

THE ECONOMY OF ANTEBELLUM Memphis was heavily dependent upon the cotton that slaves produced, and on the slave trade itself. The city was a center for the traffic of slaves between the Upper South and the cotton lands to the southwest. Memphis was located in Shelby County, which had 16,953 slaves in 1860. But Memphis itself was overwhelmingly white, with a slave population of only 3,882 out of a population of 22,600. That changed when the Union army occupied the city. By 1865 the city's black population had grown to at least 15,000, most of them residing in South Memphis near Fort Pickering, which was garrisoned by black Union troops.[47]

The Freedmen's Bureau, a federal agency created in part to facilitate the southern transition from slave to free labor, had an office in Memphis. In 1866 a Freedmen's Bureau agent described "a bitterness of feeling which has always existed between the low whites & blacks, both of whom have long advanced rival claims for superiority, both being as degraded as human beings can possibly be." This was augmented in Memphis by "an especial hatred among the city police" for the recently discharged black soldiers, "which was most cordially reciprocated by the soldiers."[48]

When the Third Heavy Artillery, the last black military unit in Memphis, disbanded on April 30, 1866, inebriated soldiers celebrated in the streets. On May 1 a fight between discharged soldiers and Irish policemen set off the Memphis Race Riot. Memphians told conflicting stories about how the riot began and progressed, but after a day of street fighting between the soldiers and the police, the Memphis mayor requested that federal troops be sent to restore order. Having dispersed the crowd, the troops returned to their garrison. That night, according to a historian of Memphis, "many white Memphians, emboldened by false rumors of black depredation, swarmed into South Memphis and slaughtered every African American they saw."[49]

A U.S. House of Representatives committee investigating the riots took testimony from witnesses later in the month. Although the police force appears to have been at the center of the riot, the reports indicated that the mob included native white southerners and prominent businessmen. According to a Memphis resident, city recorder John C. Creighton told a crowd of men, "Boys, I want you to go ahead and kill the last damned one of the nigger race, and burn up the cradle," adding, "God damn them, they are free, free indeed, but God damn them, we will kill and drive the last one of them out of the city." Other witnesses reported similar statements from Creighton. A Republican newspaper editor blamed the riot on the *Avalanche*'s incendiary editorials, arguing that the Irish were used as "cat's-paws." Matt Galloway's testimony before the committee indicated that he was, as he put it, "with the crowd" in South Memphis. While white rioters pillaged Memphis's black neighborhood, the Union general in command at Fort Pickering gave orders that the discharged black troops be confined to base and denied access to weapons. He did not intervene to effectively quell the riot until May 3. White mobs burned out ninety-one houses, four churches, and twelve schools. Five black women were raped. Two whites and forty-six blacks were killed.[50]

Although many blacks fled Memphis in the immediate aftermath of the riot, the community soon recovered and continued to grow. A developing black middle class organized churches, schools, mutual aid societies, and fraternal organizations. In 1869 black voters aligned with white radicals (and aided by the state's disenfranchisement of former Confederates) elected Edward Shaw to the Shelby County Commission. Shaw, a freeborn black man who had moved to Memphis from Kentucky in 1852, became black Memphis's most radical leader of the Reconstruction period.[51]

As BLACK MEMPHIS REBUILT, white Tennesseans joined in the South's resistance to Republican politicians, black equality, and federal power. The resistance took different forms in different places but is remembered now for one organization created in Tennessee: the Ku Klux Klan. All evidence indicates that when six young Confederate veterans of Pulaski, Tennessee, created the Klan in December 1865, they intended to form a fraternal organization, chiefly for purposes of fun. Older, more powerful men turned the club into a terrorist organization.[52]

For that transformation, Tennessee's Radical governor William Parson Brownlow deserves partial credit. In April 1866, at his behest, the state legislature disenfranchised former Rebels. It may seem strange that the Rebels, having fought a long, bloody war against the United States, should think that when the war ended they could go back to the status quo antebellum and participate in the politics of the nation as if nothing had ever happened. Yet when you read the historical materials from this time period—the letters, memoirs, and newspapers—it is clear that the former Confederates did believe exactly that. They thought losing the vote was not fair. Plus, in a political system that equated voting with manhood, losing the vote symbolized not just disfranchisement, but emasculation. Then, in February 1867, the state legislature gave black men the right to vote, and Republicans began to organize southern branches of the Union League to get the new voters to the polls.

In April, leaders of the Tennessee Democratic Party met with Ku Klux Klan officers in Nashville and together reorganized the Klan as a secret political organization. Memphis Democrats, including Matt Galloway, were at the head of the movement, and Nathan Bedford Forrest became the first grand wizard. Throughout the South, the Klan and similar groups used violence to keep black and white Republicans from voting. In Memphis, the Klan targeted Edward Shaw for assassination. In November 1868 Klansmen attacked a black political meeting Shaw was attending. He and others at the meeting had come prepared. They drew their weapons and fought back, driving the KKK away. In 1869 Forrest ordered the KKK to disband, but the organization continued to terrorize blacks and white Republicans throughout the South until the U.S. Congress passed the Ku Klux Klan Act of 1871, empowering the federal government to use military force and the power of the law to suppress the organization. Although white violence against blacks did not disappear, the Klan as an organization faded away. (The modern Klan's roots lie in twentieth-century cinema and mass marketing techniques. D. W. Griffith's 1915 film *The Birth of a Nation* made heroes of the Reconstruction-era Klansmen. An Atlanta entrepreneur capitalized on Griffith's film by forming a new KKK, but the revived Klan really took off in the 1920s when organizers began selling memberships on the pyramid scheme.)

Organized white terror in Memphis diminished after electoral victories by conservatives led to an end of state Reconstruction in 1869. Under the new regime, former Confederates regained the right to vote and the state legislature repealed laws that had banned racial segregation in public transportation. However, a new state constitution created in 1870 mandated universal manhood suffrage, so black men were not disenfranchised. In Memphis, this put black voters in a position of considerable power, and in 1874 they formed an alliance with Irish and Italian voters, electing an Irish mayor and placing six black men on the city council. Ed Shaw was elected wharfmaster, with duties including collecting fees from shipping. Before the next city election Memphis's white elites took steps to woo black voters. Playing off of Shaw's unpopularity among some members of the community, Democrats encouraged black leaders to break with Shaw and side with them. In 1876 the president of a popular black fraternal organization invited white political leaders to speak at a July 5 rally. When Nathan Bedford Forrest took the stage to

address the crowd, a young African American woman presented him
with a bouquet of flowers as a token of racial reconciliation. The former
head of the Klan gallantly accepted not just the flowers but the giver's
status as a lady, referring to her as Miss Lewis and noting, "If there is
any man on God's green earth who loves the ladies, it is myself." He assured the crowd that the former Confederates wished them well: "We
were born on the same soil . . . why should we not be brothers and sisters." In the municipal elections, half the black electorate helped vote in
a slate of white southerners. This seeming rapprochement with southern whites did not mean that black men had given up politics. In 1878
two black men were elected to the city council.[53]

Looking at their community and the city as a whole, black political
and social leaders had reason for optimism in 1878. On the other hand,
no ambitious black man could have doubted that the potential for white
supremacist violence still existed. Nathan Bedford Forrest had died in
1877, but former Klansmen abounded in all aspects of Memphis's public sphere, from the courthouse to the press. The men who had burned,
raped, and killed still walked the streets of Memphis, and the survivors
still bore the scars.

ROBERT REED CHURCH had a dent in his skull deep enough to insert a
finger. In 1866 white rioters shot him, left him for dead, and trashed his
saloon. When the House Select Committee came to town to investigate
the riot, Church testified that the mob stole his cash—"two hundred
and fifty dollars in big bills and about fifty dollars in small change"—
and drank all his whiskey. After he finished his statement, the committee chairman asked, "How much of a colored man are you?" Church
replied that he did not know: "My father is a white man. My mother is as
white as I am." The chairman asked, "Were you a slave?" Yes, Church
said, "but my father always gave me everything I wanted," although he
"does not openly recognize me."[54]

Charles B. Church was a steamboat captain. He owned Robert's
mother, Emmeline, a seamstress who lived in Holly Springs, Mississippi.
Church was born there in 1839, named Robert, but always called Bob.
When he was twelve, Emmeline died and Captain Church came to claim
his son. Years later Bob told his daughter that Captain Church had been

"a good father" to him "all my life. He raised me from a little boy." The captain installed his son as a cabin boy on his riverboat and later promoted him to steward.[55]

A young man in the Mississippi riverboat hospitality trade could learn a lot about the economics of pleasure. Bob Church's father, a jovial, burly man, aimed to transport people in comfort. His kitchen was legendary. According to one Memphis woman, the captain's concern for detail paid off: "To sit at the Captain's table was a distinction, and no admiral presided with greater courtesy or hospitality than he, while the guests were served from sterling silver, elegant china, and glassware." Bob Church's first job was to wash the dishes.[56]

Captain Church "ran the river" between St. Louis and New Orleans, and young Bob went with him from port to port and ashore as well. In 1855 he and his father survived one of steamboating's frequent disasters. Heading to New Orleans with 130 passengers and 4,500 bales of cotton, Church's boat, *Bulletin No. 2*, was tied up at a landing when the cotton caught fire. Bob ran to the front of the boat, where a crew member was helping women passengers escape, but then turned back to find his father. Captain Church was rolling cotton bales off the boat and urging passengers to jump from the deck to the bales. The fire destroyed the *Bulletin*, but Captain Church received a silver service from the people of Memphis inscribed with thanks for his "noble efforts to preserve the lives of his passengers." The whole adventure made a lasting impression on Bob.[57]

People who met Bob Church while he was working on his father's boats may not have known that he was the captain's property. His father told him not to act servile: "If anyone strikes you, hit him back, and I'll stand by you. Whatever you do, don't let anyone impose on you." Years later, a friend from the riverboat days was shocked when he learned that the young man he had worked with had been enslaved. He wrote to Church, "I never heard of you being classed as a slave." A slave he was, nonetheless, and subject to his owner's commands. Captain Church ran the river down to New Orleans regularly, and Bob went with him. In New Orleans, Bob met a woman who belonged to one of his father's friends, and in 1857, with their respective owners' permissions, they married and had a daughter. But when the captain retired, he kept Bob with him in Memphis, and that was the end of Bob's marriage.[58]

We cannot know why Captain Church did not emancipate his son,

*Robert Church as a young man. (Papers of the
Robert R. Church Family of Memphis, Special Collections,
University of Memphis Libraries)*

but had he done so, Bob would have had a new set of problems. Under
Tennessee law, emancipated slaves had to leave the state. In 1854 a new,
more draconian law had been passed requiring masters who freed their
slaves to pay for the slave's transportation to Liberia. Enforcement was
unreliable. Some freed people were forced to leave the state, others allowed to stay. By keeping Bob as a slave, the captain made sure that his
son would not be exiled.[59]

For the younger Church, 1862 was a momentous year. He got married to Louisa Ayres, a Memphis woman who, like him, was owned by
her father. (This marriage had no more legal standing than Church's
previous one, but it served to validate his connection with Mollie, the
child Louisa gave birth to in 1863.) He left the river under most dramatic circumstances. When the Civil War began, Captain Church's fleet
was confiscated by the Confederacy and became part of the Rebel navy.

In 1862 Bob was working as a steward on the *Victoria*, at that point a Confederate troop transport. The Union navy captured the boat during the Battle of Memphis, and in the confusion he literally jumped ship and swam to shore. By doing so, he freed himself, not so much from the loose ties of slavery that bound him to Captain Church as from the institution as it existed in the Confederacy. Although slavery remained legal in occupied Memphis, the Union army showed little enthusiasm for enforcing the laws that supported the institution, and slaves in the city began to act as though they were free.[60]

Many freedmen found the transition from slavery to liberty fraught with difficulty. By all accounts, Church did not. His wife, an accomplished hairdresser, helped support the family, and Church soon managed to open a saloon. Under existing state law, an establishment with a billiard table had to have a municipal license, but only whites were allowed to obtain such licenses. Early in 1866 Church was indicted for operating without a license. He fought the indictment in municipal court, arguing that under the newly passed federal Civil Rights Act, the racial discrimination implicit in the state law had become illegal. On April 16 the county criminal court judge ruled in his favor.[61]

Then came the race riot. The shot to the head left Church subject to violent headaches but did not otherwise chastise him. If anything, he became more defiant. He made money and acquired property. He and Louisa had a son, Thomas. On Sundays he took Mollie to visit his white father, who patted her head, praised her, and sent her home with treats. Bob made friends, among them John Overton, grandson of Memphis's founder. He purchased expensive toys, such as a sleigh. What, his friends asked, did he want with a sleigh in Memphis? But when it snowed, Church harnessed up and sailed down Main Street.[62]

The picture that emerges is of a proud young man who expected to be treated as the equal of any other man and generally managed to make that happen. This took a great deal of courage and an evident willingness to meet violence with violence. In 1868 or so, Church took Mollie with him on a train trip. He bought them first-class seats, then left Mollie while he went down to the smoking car. A white conductor accosted the five-year-old, asked whose little nigger she was, and tried to force her from the first-class carriage into the Negro car. One of Church's white friends fetched him back from the smoker. He and the conductor squared off in the aisle, both with their hands on their pistols, and cursed at each other until the passengers managed to separate them and calm them down. Mollie remembered her father promising that he would "make trouble for this road." Mollie and her father stayed in the first-class coach.[63]

ON JULY 4, 1878, the day's amusements—the parades and military drills, the shopping and eating and drinking, the horse races and picnics—concluded with a fireworks display. Some thirty thousand people lined Front Street to watch Peter Tracy's fireworks display coruscate above the river. Orphans from St. Peter's Catholic Church, the Episcopal Church Home, and the Leath Orphan Asylum were transported downtown, courtesy of the streetcar company, and seated on stands specially constructed so that they could get a good view. Judging by the write-up in the next day's paper, the show was spectacular. The crowd especially applauded the Tomb of the Pharaohs, "showing in its pyric combustion that monument of antiquity, an Egyptian Pyramid," and the Crown Jewels, a "figure of matchless splendor" dedicated to the ladies of Memphis. In the evening's final illumination, fireworks formed an arch in the evening sky spelling out "Memphis, July 4, 1878."[64]

A careful reader of the July 4 *Appeal*, one willing to wade through the Independence Day promotions and the business news, would have found a short paragraph on the topic of yellow fever. On July 3 the city council had met to consider Dr. Mitchell's proposal for quarantine. They voted against it. A week later Dr. Mitchell resigned from the board of health. "As the position I held as president of the board of health was unsalaried, I took it with only one motive—to improve the sanitary affairs of Memphis," he said. "Every year since 1870 the city has been exposed to the yellow fever from New Orleans, and in 1873 we suffered a major epidemic. I have strongly urged quarantine. The council, urged on by some of our leading physicians, has refused. I have no choice but to resign with the earnest belief that if we ever have yellow fever here again it will be our own fault for not taking the known, necessary precautions against it."[65]

TWO

Yellow Jack

AFTER THE FOURTH, MEMPHIS SETTLED into summer doldrums. In the cotton fields of Tennessee, Arkansas, and Mississippi, white blossoms gave way to gradually burgeoning bolls. Soon the bolls would open into fluffy balls of fiber, turning the fields as white as snow. Each August, the region's farmers, tenant families, and hired hands began the harvest, dragging long fabric sacks down each row and handpicking each boll of cotton. Memphis factors anticipated the arrival of the first bales of cotton in mid-August, but cotton picking continued well into the fall. Meanwhile, downtown merchants laid in stocks in preparation for the postharvest flush times.

The big news was the weather: hot and hotter. For days, afternoon temperatures reached the high nineties. Men and mules collapsed in the streets, felled by heatstrokes. The trolley line outfitted its mules with head shades made of tree branches, and people put cabbage leaves in their hats to stay cool. In the privacy of their homes, women stripped off their heavy clothing and approached what the *Appeal* referred to as "the fig leaf wrapper, the Paradise style of summer wear." Men in public life had to suffer. The *Avalanche*, the *Appeal*'s greatest rival among the city's morning papers, commented that a fancy man in kid gloves was now looked on as a miracle of fortitude. People filled the seats around the Court Square fountain from morning to night, seeking relief in the oasis of water-cooled air.[1]

Memphis is always hot in the summer. What made 1878 different was not the summer's heat, but its duration. Heat waves in July are expected, but summers that begin in March and continue into September are not. Each day, people trudged along Memphis's dirty streets, sweating under the blazing sun. Nightfall brought little relief. Heat built up in houses and apartments during the day. Unable to sleep in stifling bedrooms, suburban Memphians carried their pillows out to porches and terraces. In the center of the city, people dragged chairs out onto the sidewalks. Along Main Street from Overton to Beale, the length of the city, they sat fanning themselves until the hours just before dawn. They also slapped and swore at mosquitoes. The high-pitched whine and bite that annoyed sleepy people on the city's sidewalks came from *Anopheles*, the malaria carrier. Endemic in the Lower South, malaria was one of the accepted trials of life, a familiar and commonplace affliction. The disease's connection with mosquitoes would not be discovered until 1897.[2]

During the daytime *Ae. aegypti* mosquitoes flitted through the city's streets. Memphis's water supply system functioned as a habitat for the yellow fever vector. Lacking municipal water, people collected rainwater in cisterns dug into the ground and lined with brick. *Ae. aegypti* avoided marshes, swamps, and all such places commonly associated with mosquitoes, preferring containers of still, clean water. Although *Ae. aegypti* has been known to lay eggs in vases, jugs, rain barrels, and even baptismal fonts, its predilection for cisterns was so marked that Americans called it the common gray cistern mosquito. There were more than four thousand cisterns in Memphis, each capable of housing swarms of mosquitoes, each mosquito a potential virus carrier.[3]

Female cistern mosquitoes are not strong fliers, having a usual range of about fifty yards. Within that range they must find the blood meal they need before they can lay eggs. In Memphis they bit housewives and maids drawing water from backyard cisterns. They fed on people walking down the street, sitting on porches, hanging out laundry. They drew blood from children playing in the yard. They did all this in the bright sunlight. Unlike *Anopheles*, the cistern mosquito feeds by day. Old and young, rich and poor, respectable and raffish, black and white, it mattered not to *Ae. aegypti*; all human blood was the same.[4]

The long summer contributed to a bumper crop of cistern mosquitoes. *Ae. aegypti* lies dormant at temperatures lower than 50 degrees and will not feed at temperatures less than 60. It becomes most active, and most voracious, between 70 and 90 degrees. In 1878 the early spring gave the cistern mosquito an unusually lengthy reproductive season. In addition, the intense summer heat may have sped up the mosquitoes' development from egg to adult, reducing the time needed from about forty days to as little as fifteen. As the new generations emerged, mated, bit people, and laid eggs, the cycle accelerated. The *Appeal* commented on the proliferation of gray cistern mosquitoes and advised rubbing onions on the bites to reduce the itching. Getting bitten by the gray mosquito was as much a part of summer as fireworks on the Fourth of July and, until an infected human transported the yellow fever virus to town, just as harmless. Once that happened, however, the extra mosquitoes vastly increased a person's chances of being bitten and infected.[5]

While Memphians scratched mosquito bites and talked about the weather, in New Orleans the city's medical authorities used carbolic acid to "disinfect" the streets around the buildings where the *Emily Souder* crew members had sickened and died. Carbolic acid, now known as phenol, is an extract of coal tar. In the 1860s the British surgeon Joseph Lister developed a system for preventing infection in wounds by washing the wound in carbolic acid and wrapping it in bandages soaked in the same compound. The acid irritated the skin but killed bacteria. Lister's system transformed surgery. It also helped popularize the use of carbolic acid as a preventative disinfectant for many different diseases. In vain did an 1875 conclave of physicians point out that carbolic acid had been used in New Orleans in 1867, 1871, 1872, 1873, 1874, and 1875 but "failed to arrest small-pox, scarlet fever and yellow fever." In the 1878 epidemic, carbolic acid would be sprinkled on surfaces, swabbed on others, placed in bowls in sickrooms so that its fumes could clean the air, and used in quantity to disinfect streets and houses.[6]

In New Orleans, weeks passed with no new cases. A young man did come to the Touro Infirmary with an illness resembling yellow fever, but when he recovered, his physicians decided they had been mistaken. The city's doctors relaxed. Then in mid-July suspicious cases began to appear in clusters around the infirmary and in areas corresponding to the locations of the original *Souder* patients. An outbreak on Constance Street seemed inexplicable until the authorities discovered that a tugboat captain who lived in the neighborhood had docked his boat at the Calliope Street wharf recently vacated by the *Emily Souder*. By early July, several of the captain's family had fallen ill, and shortly thereafter the neighbors began to exhibit symptoms of yellow fever.[7] Despite growing evidence that yellow fever was in the city, the Louisiana Board of Health

did not tell the public about the outbreak until July 24, when they announced that fourteen people in New Orleans had contracted the disease
and seven had died.[8]

New Orleans natives had complacently believed that they and their
children were immune to the Strangers' Disease. Looking back from
the perspective of 1898, a French physician explained why. "Yellow Fever is exceedingly mild in children if disturbing treatment is not resorted to," wrote Just Touatre, former chief physician at the French
Society Hospital in New Orleans. "This benign type of the disease is
what had led to the belief in the immunity of children born in New Orleans. Every year up to 1878 there were a few or many cases of Yellow
Fever. Children became acclimated by taking the disease during in-
fancy; the attack of fever lasted one, two, or three days without alarming
symptoms and caused no uneasiness to the family. Children nearly always recovered, and the cause of the indisposition was unrecognized. It
was really Yellow Fever, however—acclimating fever, attenuated Yellow
Fever." According to Dr. Touatre, "the grave or fatal cases were credited
to malaria and a new morbid entity had even been invented for the occasion, Hemorrhagic Malarial Fever, which existed and was observed only
at times of epidemics of Yellow Fever and which was nothing else than
Yellow Fever in the Creole, accompanied by black vomit."[9]

Creole immunity was "dogma," Dr. Touatre said, "the fixed opinion
of all the most distinguished physicians of that city," until the 1878 epidemic, "when the disease attacked a large number of children, and was
observed by means of the thermometer by all physicians." When the
natives of New Orleans found out that most of the cases—and most of
the deaths—had been among young children from relatively nice neighborhoods, the news created a panic unprecedented in the city's history.
Forty thousand people fled New Orleans in the next few days.[10]

ON FRIDAY, JULY 26, the Memphis morning papers carried the news of
the New Orleans outbreak. A frisson of dread spread through the city.
The population was all too familiar with epidemics, having suffered from
smallpox in 1873, cholera in 1873, and yellow fever in 1867 and 1873. Over
a thousand people had died in the most recent epidemic, more than
enough to convince people that yellow fever was a serious matter. Yet
aspects of the 1873 epidemic may have given some Memphians a false

sense of security while fueling the fears of others. As noted above, in that outbreak the disease had been generally confined to one section of town, a slum inhabited mostly by people Dr. John Erskine had labeled "a low class" of Irish. Based on that experience, Memphians might have hoped that their neighborhoods would escape the disease. On the other hand, Erskine had hypothesized that the 1873 outbreak occurred where it did because the neighborhood was so dirty. If you believed that yellow fever was connected to filth, then the condition of the city in the summer of 1873 was enough to scare you half to death. J. M. Keating summed it up: the Nicholson pavement was rotting, the soil was saturated with sewage, the bayou into which toilets drained had become a stagnant pond in which decaying animals bobbed along, the cellars of houses along the main streets exuded noxious gases—"every affliction that could exaggerate a disease so cruel seemed to have been prepared for it by the criminal neglect of the city government, who turned a deaf ear to the persistent appeals of the press." Attempts at cleanup were already under way, directed by Dr. Mitchell's replacement as president of the board of health and funded by donations from the business community. These efforts were not enough to reassure the fearful. Keating said that "the whole population were worked up to a point of dread, in some cases bordering on insanity," before the municipal government finally consented to quarantine.[11]

Dr. John Erskine had opposed quarantine in June, when there was no official confirmation of yellow fever in New Orleans. Now that the presence of fever had been confirmed, Erskine and his colleagues on the health board became, according to Keating, "anxious" for quarantine. The board of health sent the city government an official letter requesting quarantine, and the mayor ordered it established. Designated the city's quarantine officer, Erskine put as much effort into enforcing quarantine as he had into fighting it a month previously. A smiling, cheerful man, so very straight and tall and strong that Keating described him as physically perfect, he expended copious energy in an attempt to prevent an epidemic in Memphis. Erskine established three quarantine stations: one on the Memphis and Charleston Railroad twelve miles east of the city at Germantown, one on the Mississippi and Tennessee Railroad eight miles south of the city at Whitehaven, and, for river traffic, a station at the southern tip of President's Island.[12]

Since physicians believed that letters, baggage, clothing, or any form of freight could carry yellow fever, Memphis's quarantine plan stopped all inbound railroad freight several miles outside of town. Freight cars were to be unloaded and cargos disinfected and held for ten days. Doctors and detectives were stationed at the checkpoints, with instructions to detain people who appeared to be sick and send them to the city hospital. Sick or not, if you came to Memphis, your luggage would be impounded. In the first week of August the health board made the quarantine tighter. On August 1 the board resolved that "no passengers or baggage from New Orleans or Vicksburg, by steamboat or railroad, will be permitted to enter the city of Memphis, until further notice." As of August 3, shipments from New Orleans and Vicksburg were simply returned. A Citizens' Sanitary Commission, organized by Memphis merchants, funded the railroad detectives and bought a small cannon for the quarantine station on President's Island.[13]

A Memphis correspondent to the *New York Times* described the "rigid quarantine" on the river but concluded that it was "all humbug," since refugees from New Orleans arrived daily in Memphis by all the rail routes. The *New Orleans Times* ran a story describing the mechanism used to get around the quarantine. Refugees from New Orleans would travel by train to a station along the line to Memphis, then buy another ticket there. When they arrived at the quarantine station outside Memphis, their tickets gave no indication that they came from the city quarantined against. Refugees also arrived by water, smuggled in by rowboat, and landed under the bluff. The board of health did manage to stop freight entering from New Orleans, unless it was freight that people in Memphis particularly wanted, like the thirty cars full of sugar, coffee, and hardware that sat at the Whitehaven quarantine station until city merchants successfully pressured the authorities to waive the quarantine and let the train through.[14]

If quarantine failed, the second line of defense was sanitation. Although generations of observers had noted that some clean cities suffered outbreaks while some filthy cities escaped, this made little impact on people's deep-seated belief that filth caused illness. Memphis needed a good scrubbing. But to clean the streets required work crews, and the city did not have enough money to pay them.[15]

Memphis's business and professional class included men who had built railroads, smuggled cotton, commanded troops in battle, organized political campaigns, and, almost certainly, ridden with Forrest in the

KKK. When a group met with Mayor Flippin on the last day of July, their disdain for the municipal government was obvious. The question at hand was the funding of the board of health's sanitation measures. The suggestion that the Howard Association, a private philanthropic organization, might be able to lend the city money for sanitation provoked indignant denunciations: the suggestion was "beneath contempt." Judge Henry G. Smith asked why the city had not done more already. He proposed that the assembled businessmen should raise funds for the cleanup, since the municipal government lacked both the will and the capacity to do so.

Nathan Menken, a prominent merchant, was one of the Union veterans in the room. He pointed out that "the proper way to raise the amount needed in the current emergency was by taxation." Then Menken cut to the heart of the matter. He asked the mayor to state the amount needed, and he pledged five hundred dollars, "or one thousand dollars if needed." By the end of the meeting, twelve men had pledged funds for sanitation. A crew of about a hundred men and boys went to work and by August 4 had cleaned Poplar, Front Street between Beale and Madison, and parts of the center city. Worried residents took precautions on their own, burning camphor, pine tar, and other smoky, odorous substances to fumigate their premises.[16]

The Memphis Howard Association contributed funds to the cleanup. Howard Associations, named in honor of the British prison reformer John Howard, were founded in many antebellum American cities to support philanthropic work of various sorts. A group of young New Orleans businessmen organized a Howard unit in 1837 specifically to help during yellow fever epidemics, and their example spread. In Memphis, as in other southern communities, the Howard Association existed solely to help the victims of epidemics. The Howards, as they were universally called, drew their funds from community donations. By 1878 they had developed a system that could be put into place quickly when an epidemic struck. They divided the city into wards and stationed a volunteer in each. The Howard volunteers did not wait for people to ask them for help, but instead went into stricken neighborhoods, sometimes door-to-door, to locate the sick. They hired physicians and nurses as needed for all victims, regardless of religion, class, or race. Providing funding for street cleaning was a gesture toward warding off a yellow fever outbreak.[17]

In late July the fever began to spread up the Mississippi Valley like a slow-moving tidal wave. Memphians could look at a map and say, now it is here and here, but that is still a long way from us. Yet the fever leaped disconcertingly from city to city. Vicksburg, halfway between Memphis and New Orleans on the Mississippi River, reported its first fever cases on August 9. Four days later, fever broke out in Hickman, Kentucky, thirty-six miles south of Cairo, Illinois.[18]

As fear increased, public dread fastened on the unfortunate towboat *John Porter*. A stern-wheeler steamer, the *Porter* hauled barges laden with coal from Pittsburgh down the Ohio River and into the Mississippi, one thousand plus miles downriver to New Orleans. Reaching New Orleans in mid-July, the *Porter* started back to Pittsburgh on July 18, towing behind it a number of empty barges, some of which had been at the docks for weeks. John Murphy had been added to the crew in New Orleans. On the first day out, he complained of a headache. By the time the *Porter* reached Vicksburg, Murphy and another crewman were so sick they were hospitalized. An additional crewman had what appeared to be "simple intermittent-fever," but he was considered well enough to proceed. About fifty miles north of Vicksburg the crewman died. The *Porter* turned back to Vicksburg, for reasons that were not clear to people at the time and are less so today. The suggestion has been made that they were returning the man's body for burial. At any rate, when the boat got back to Vicksburg, the captain discovered that Murphy and the other hospitalized crewman had died of yellow fever. The boat was "disinfected" and allowed to continue on its voyage. On July 27 the *Appeal* featured a story on the *Porter*, which was then chugging upriver toward Memphis.

As the *Porter* approached the city, crowds of people began to gather on the bluffs. Dr. Erskine took a tugboat out to the boat, and the officers insisted that they had no yellow fever cases on board. They attributed the crewmen's deaths to sunstroke. Erskine was not convinced. He told the officers they could not land, and the boat continued on its voyage up the Mississippi and then on to the Ohio, passing out of the gaze of worried Memphians and into the story of another river town.[19]

By the time the *Porter* reached Louisville, the captain, mate, chambermaid, pilot, cook, deckhands, and engineers—almost everyone on the boat—had contracted the fever. Louisville let the *Porter* land, and most, but not all, of the sick crew were dismissed. A couple of men who seemed to have mild cases of "intermittent-fever" stayed on board. New crewmen were added, and the boat, with a crew of thirty-seven, set off for Pittsburgh on August 13. Yellow fever spread rapidly through the new crew.

Cincinnati refused to allow the boat to land. So did other, smaller towns. Finally, laden with the sick and dying and beset with mechanical problems, the *Porter* wound up anchored about two miles downriver from Gallipolis, Ohio, with a guard posted to keep the sick from coming ashore. Poverty was a better guard, however, as most of the crew stayed on board until the owner sent them their final wages on August 20. With money in pocket, everybody capable of walking escaped from the plague ship. Yellow fever broke out in Gallipolis on August 28. During the *Porter*'s long voyage, twenty-six of the crew contracted fever and fourteen died. In the village of Gallipolis today, the broken rocker shaft of the *John Porter* tops a memorial to the sixty-six townspeople who died.[20]

In the second week of August, people in Memphis began to hear rumors of an epidemic in Grenada, Mississippi, a hundred miles south on the Mississippi and Tennessee Railroad. Telegraphed queries elicited replies insisting that there was no yellow fever in the town. That pretense crumbled during the weekend of August 9–11. Over the three days from Friday to Sunday, Grenada officials telegraphed to confirm the presence of the fever. Memphis Masons, Odd Fellows, and Knights of Phythias also received telegrams from their Grenada lodge brothers. The Howards met on Monday, August 12, and dispatched twenty-one nurses to Grenada by the afternoon train. Butler Anderson and W. J. Smith, president and vice president of the Memphis Howards, went to Grenada to supervise the work.[21]

Modern technology helped spread Yellow Jack farther and faster than ever before, but as the case of Grenada illustrates, new technologies could also be used to sound the alarm and bring help. In the 1870s, telegraphic messages passed between city and city, person and person as quickly as e-mail does today. The Associated Press had correspondents, usually local journalists, in towns throughout the Mississippi Valley. The stories they filed were picked up by newspapers across the country. Thus the Sunday, August 11, *New York Times* ran a dispatch from Memphis: "News has just been received that seven deaths occurred in Grenada to-day, and that 15 or 20 new cases were reported."

In Houston, Texas, an experienced yellow fever nurse wrote to her sister, "I cannot read these accounts, and appeals for help, and turn a deaf ear. I start tomorrow." Fifty years old, well educated, and accepted in

Houston as a lady, Kezia DePelchin taught school, gave music lessons, and, during Houston's repeated yellow fever epidemics, served as a volunteer nurse. Having had the fever as a child, she was immune. DePelchin believed that caring for the sick was a Christian duty, and being free of familial commitments, she intended to work without pay for as long as her money held out. Her friends feared for her. "They come in to bid me goodbye as if I were going to execution," she wrote.

Her social circle included members of Houston's wealthy upper class. They contributed funds for the trip, and she had some money of her own, so she set off for Grenada with more than fifty dollars. DePelchin took with her a valise of medical supplies, a basket, a watch, a brooch containing a precious lock of hair, a knife, a tin cup, and a big straw hat. In a small trunk she packed three calico wrap dresses, slippers for quiet footsteps in the sickroom, and warm clothes for the trip home. The epidemic would not end until the weather turned cold, and she knew that Houston authorities would not lift their protective quarantine and allow her to return until assured that the danger was past.[22]

"No apprehension is now felt by sensible citizens that any yellow-fever will appear in our city this season," said the August 11 *Appeal*. In the days since the *John Porter*'s passage upriver, the news from New Orleans had heightened public fears. According to Keating, street-corner Cassandras spread wild rumors all day long. Having supported quarantine, the editors of the *Appeal* now attempted to bolster public confidence that sanitizing the city would stave off the fever. The editor officially discounted scaremongering, but the *Appeal* published the New Orleans Board of Health's instructions for using carbolic acid to disinfect houses. The paper assured the public, "The work of the board of health is having a good effect."[23]

After the deaths began, when people tried to figure out where and when Yellow Jack had come to Memphis, it became clear that the fever had a foothold in the city before the quarantine went into effect. Post-epidemic accounts differ slightly in details; what follows is a synthesis of reports by Dr. R. B. Maury, a member of the Tennessee Board of Health, and by J. M. Keating. Both men agreed that (quoting Dr. Maury) one early "focus of infection" was "established about the 1st of August, in the houses 177, 179 and 181 Second Street, midway between Poplar and Washington." The property at 179 Second Street belonged to a lawyer, G.P.M. Turner, the Shelby county district attorney, who resided there with his family. Addie Robinson, an African American cook, lived in a small house in the backyard. On July 21 her husband had come home from a downriver trip complaining that he did not feel well. He had chills and a fever. His wife treated him with hot teas, and he recovered. Willie Darby, a young man who lived next door at 177 Second Street, habitually walked down the alley past the cook's house to his job at an oyster house. On July 25 Darby fell ill with fever. His aunt nursed him, and he survived. But Darby's aunt got sick. So did at least four other people who lived at 177. In the first two weeks of August, several died. The fever spread across the alley to 181 Second Street. One of the two people who died there on August 12 had black vomit, the most distinctive symptom of yellow fever. Meanwhile, Turner's two daughters came down with fever; one died. Dr. Maury noted, "The houses abovementioned are but two short blocks from the river front, and are midway between two great thoroughfares, Poplar and Washington streets, both running to the steamboat landing, and both these streets were infected along the whole length at a very early period of the epidemic."[24]

Although Dr. Maury was convinced that the Memphis epidemic began with Addie Robinson's husband on Second Street, he acknowledged two other foci of infection, one on Washington near Poplar, and one at 34 Alabama Street, at the house of Patrick M. Winters, justice of the peace and former chief of police for the city of Memphis. This outbreak was traced to the steamer *Golden Crown*, a confirmed yellow fever carrier. One of the passengers, William Warren, sneaked into Memphis but was caught, quarantined, and died of the fever on August 5. Some female relatives of the Winters family were smuggled ashore on August 2. Two days later they were caught and forced to leave the city. Although the women never fell ill, when people in and around 36 Alabama Street took the fever, the outbreak was attributed to them. Dr. Maury did not think that these three foci represented all the cases of yellow fever in Memphis by early August. As he said, *"After the 15th of July, when the fever was observed to be in New Orleans, abundant opportunities were occurring, almost daily, for its introduction into this city."* [Italics in original] Dr. Erskine's quarantine stations had closed the door too late.[25]

What conversations took place among Memphis physicians in the first two weeks of August? Perhaps there were debates as to whether the people dying on Second Street and Poplar and Alabama had yellow fever or some particularly malignant form of malaria. Perhaps health officer John Erskine was waiting for a case with symptoms so evidently those of yellow fever as to remove all doubt. On August 9 such a case emerged. Kate Bionda was an Italian immigrant. She and her husband ran a Front Street "snack-house" (a nineteenth-century equivalent of a diner or fast-food place) that served river men and wharf workers. When Mrs. Bionda became ill, Dr. E. Miles Willet detected signs of yellow fever. He called Doctors D. D. Saunders, president of the board of health, John Erskine, and Heber Jones, all of whom agreed with his diagnosis. Mrs. Bionda died on the morning of August 13 and was buried before sundown. The health board's announcement appeared in the morning papers: "Mrs. Kate Bionda, at 212 Front Row, is undoubtedly a case of yellow fever."[26]

To Dr. Erskine, the snack house epitomized the kind of environment hospitable to yellow fever, and Mrs. Bionda the kind of person susceptible. He judged her to be a hard drinker and a slattern who lived in the midst of "debris and trash." As health officer, Dr. Erskine immediately ordered the Bionda house fumigated and disinfected. He had barriers put up around the house and disinfected the streets around it. The *Memphis Avalanche* described men "with speed sprinkling walls, streets, and pavements" with carbolic acid and coal oil until "the sidewalk was black with carbolic acid, and from streets and walls arose the smell of tar and lime almost stifling." Erskine posted police guards to keep people away from the Bionda house. He issued orders to householders: clean your premises, dispose of your garbage three times a week, use a solution of carbolic acid to disinfect your privies and your yards, and stop throwing "dead fowls, rats, water-melon rinds, fruit parings, filth, slops, etc., in the gutters." The Wednesday, August 14, *Appeal* reported Mrs. Bionda's death tersely, in stark, clear terms, but then editorialized that a few cases of yellow fever did not an epidemic make. According to the paper, the health board believed "the present fine sanitary condition of the city" and "the ability of the board to meet and wrestle with the disease" with "all the aids of modern science" meant there was no reason to fear an epidemic in Memphis.[27]

The public was not reassured. Keating wrote, "The little company of panic-stricken residents was increased to a regiment." On Thursday,

August 15, the board announced twenty-two new cases; on Friday, thirty-three more.

On Friday, August 16, the *Appeal* reported the fever "raging on Washington and Poplar streets, between Fourth street and the market-house; on Alabama street east of the bayou; on Main, between Washington and Exchange streets; and on Commerce street between Front and Fourth streets." The city of Memphis dropped its quarantine. At that point it was useless to quarantine against New Orleans. Instead, Memphis had itself become a place to quarantine against.[28]

YELLOW FEVER COMES ON suddenly with dizziness, headaches, fever, and chills. One victim described his symptoms as follows: "Sharp, remediless pains began at the base of the brain and coursed their way down the spinal column, paralyzing in the effect produced, and followed by chills, aggravating the distress and inaccessible, or seeming so, to treatment." On the third day he described himself as "as yellow as saffron, and as haggard as death. My limbs were powerless, and if I attempted to recall the past my brain wandered or failed to respond." After about a week of this, most people begin to get better. The period of "remission," as it is called, can last for two days or two hours. If you are lucky, the fever is done with you, and you recover as quickly as you might from a mild bout of influenza. Unfortunate people have a brief respite before the fever comes back with a vengeance. It is this second stage of the fever that kills.

The disease's nature as a tropical hemorrhagic fever begins to manifest itself as the patient goes into "intoxication." Victims develop jaundice. Their noses bleed. Their gums bleed. They have stomach pains. If they are capable of bowel movements at all, they pass tarry stools, indicating the presence of blood in the intestines. They vomit coagulated blood, the infamous *vómito negro*, which looks like coffee grounds suspended in dark liquid. Although most people considered black vomit a signal of approaching death, people did survive it. Dr. Erskine correctly singled out a different symptom as an indicator of mortality: the inability to produce urine, signifying renal failure. Some patients exhibited what modern physicians call "psychomotor agitation": they flailed about and had to be held down. In the final stage of the disease, victims slipped into a stupor, followed by coma and death.[29]

Observers associated yellow fever with a specific set of odors. In the earlier stages of the disease, yellow fever victims smelled like rotting hay—corruption overlaid with sweetness. By the end, the victim's blood-spattered sickroom stank like a slaughterhouse. If you have never passed by an abattoir, you can perhaps grasp what they were talking about by remembering the smell of hamburger gone bad. One victim described the smell as disgusting, adding, "It cannot be described; it must be inhaled to be properly appreciated, and once inhaled can never be forgotten."[30] By August 14 the odor of yellow fever had begun to waft through Memphis streets.

The impulse to run from infection is deeply embedded in Western culture. Medieval Europeans had a bit of Latin that served as advice for the wise during epidemics: *fuge cito, vade longe, rede tarde*, i.e., "flee early, go far, and stay late." Memphians had delayed too long to flee early, but they fled fast.

Keating watched the stampede: "Men, women and children poured out of the city by every possible means of escape . . . Out by the country roads to the little hamlets and plantations, where many of them were welcome guests in happier days; out by every possible conveyance—by hacks, by carriages, buggies, wagons, furniture vans, and street drays; away by batteaux, by any thing that could float on the river; and by the railroads." In three days, more than twenty thousand people left Memphis. Observers had never seen anything like it, even in cities evacuating ahead of enemy armies.[31]

Desperate people mobbed Memphis's railroad depots. Men with guns forced their way aboard already full railroad cars. They forced windows open and crawled through, falling into the laps of scandalized female passengers. Refugees filled the aisles and packed the platforms. One of the Howards described how "women wept and begged, and men cursed and fought, in their efforts to be first." He said, "Ordinary dangers seemed to have no terror, and men would leap upon the platform, or cling, swinging, to whatever offered a hand-hold."[32]

Keating thought that the panic fed upon itself until it infected the entire population and deadened "all human sympathy, all the kinder emotions of the human heart." Yet it was Keating's job—and the job of the other journalists in Memphis—to convince as many as possible to leave. The medical community of Memphis was still divided as to the nature of the disease confronting them, with some insisting that it was a particularly malignant form of malaria. (The *Appeal* commented drily, "It matters not what you call it, it kills.") The doctors agreed that the disease, whatever it was, would continue to spread as long as there were people to be infected. The yellow fever was like a fire. To stop it—and to save lives—the disease's human fuel had to be removed.[33]

NOT EVERYONE COULD or would leave. Some lacked the money to pay for transportation out of town or shelter elsewhere; others had family members who could not travel. The desire to protect property influenced some. Many African Americans did not fear the fever, believing that they were to some extent immune. And then there were the people who stayed to care for the sick and to protect the city itself. Motivated by faith in God or duty to humanity, they made the decision to risk their own lives to help others.

Among the most stalwart in this crisis were members of fraternal organizations. Bound by oaths of brotherhood, they mobilized relief and medical care in Memphis and throughout the South. Some lodges supplied insurance for members. Others undertook direct care of the sick and support for their widows and orphans. In Memphis, the Masons had the highest profile. Many of the city's most prominent, wealthy, and influential men were Masons. (As an example, the Masons among the gentlemen of the press included J. M. Keating, his city editor, the Associated Press correspondent, and the editors of the *Ledger* and *Avalanche*.) The brotherhood linked white men across some of the religious and political divisions of the period. Although long-term Catholic opposition to Freemasonry meant that no Catholic priest would join the Masons, Memphis lodges included the Anglican priest George Harris; the pastor at Central Baptist Church, Sylvanus Landrum; and the secretary of Beth El Emmeth synagogue. The aged editor of the *Masonic Jewel*, A. J. Wheeler, refused to leave the city, saying that his duty as a man and a Mason required him to stay and help. Many of the relief leaders were Masons. Although most could have fled to safety, they chose to stay.[34]

Having lived through epidemics before, J. M. Keating decided to stay in the city. However, there is no evidence indicating that his family was in Memphis during the outbreak. Given that Josephine and Carrie lived in New York part of the time anyway, it seems unlikely that they would have chosen to stay in Memphis during the yellow fever season. Records do not indicate that Neil was present in Memphis either. Keating's partner Matt Galloway left Memphis for the duration, devoting his time to fund-raising for the relief effort.

Nathan Menken and Dr. William Armstrong both chose to stay. On the surface, the two men had little in common. Menken was Jewish, a merchant, and one of the richest men in town, while Armstrong, a devout Presbyterian, was a middle-class physician. Yet both had been formed by their experiences (on opposite sides) during the Civil War, both were dedicated family men, and both felt a duty to help the weak and suffering. This sense of responsibility, toward family, community, and humanity in the largest sense, led both men to stay in Memphis.

Nathan Menken worked in his family's dry goods store on the corner of Main and Court. Born in Cincinnati to a wealthy and prominent Jewish family, Menken and his brother Jacob had volunteered for the Union cavalry, the most romantic, dashing branch of service. As captain of Company A, First Ohio Cavalry, Nathan had seen action in thirty battles and skirmishes in western Virginia. In the summer of 1862 he commanded General John Pope's escort during the Northern Virginia Campaign. Pope botched that campaign badly, as Menken had reason to know. He was there when Pope led his troops to ignominious defeat in the Second Battle of Bull Run, and he barely escaped death when his horse was shot from under him. Perhaps Nathan got tired of war, or of incompetence; perhaps the family claim weighed heavier than the Union. With Jacob and Nathan gone, the family business in Cincinnati had failed. In December 1862 Nathan resigned his commission, and in 1863 Menken Brothers opened a new store in occupied Memphis.[35]

The Menken brothers were among many newcomers who came to the Bluff City to capitalize on the opportunities created by the Civil War. They were moving to a town with a settled, prosperous (and often pro-Confederate) middle-class Jewish community—one that had just passed through a most traumatic event. In 1862 Memphis was the center of a lively trade in cotton and contraband goods. White southerners, northern businessmen, Union officers—the black market pulled in all varieties of people, including a number of Jewish traders. Irritated by this illicit commerce, General Grant targeted for punishment not smugglers in general, or even Jewish smugglers in particular, but the entire Jewish population of the military Department of Tennessee (consisting of Kentucky, Tennessee, and Mississippi). On December 17, 1862, Grant issued

General Order Number 11, expelling all Jews from those three states. Some of Grant's subordinates seem to have enforced the order only against northern newcomers, while others ignored the order altogether, but a few officers took it quite literally and forced people to leave their homes and board trains for the North. When a Jewish delegation brought the order to President Lincoln's attention, he immediately rescinded it. The experience left a long shadow. Lincoln became a hero to the Memphis Jewish community, but when Grant ran for president in 1868, the rabbis of Memphis organized a mass meeting that passed a resolution declaring him unfit for the office.[36]

Nathan and Jacob Menken were staunch Union men, charter members of the Military Order of the Loyal Legion, a patriotic brotherhood formed by Union officers in the wake of Lincoln's assassination. Nonetheless, they adapted quickly to Memphis. Their store proved profitable, and they were able to pay off with interest the debts outstanding from the Cincinnati store failure. Nathan married Sallie Edwards, daughter of a prominent Memphis Jewish family, in 1869. They had six children and lived in a house in the suburbs. Possessed of a surplus of what people in the 1870s called "nervous energy," Menken was generous, outspoken, and impetuous—still at heart a cavalryman, eager to charge into battle.

When the epidemic began, Memphis's Jewish community numbered around three thousand. They decided to send as many people as possible out of town. Nathan Menken bought tickets for several poor families. He put his wife, Sallie, and their children on the train out, planning to join them in a few days. But, as Memphian Jacob Kohlberg wrote after the epidemic, "To our utter dismay we found every avenue leading to the city densely packed with Jewish families." It appears that in this moment of fear, Jewish families from outlying towns made their way *into* Memphis, seeking aid from the region's largest Jewish community. Perhaps the arrival of these new refugees influenced Menken to stay; perhaps he was convinced by the Howard Association's plea for volunteers. He wrote to a friend, "I saw that so few would stay to help and so much help was needed. I could not leave."[37]

Service in the Confederate Army brought Dr. William James Armstrong to Memphis via Mississippi and a wartime romance. Having read medicine with a doctor in his native Maury County, Tennessee, and obtained a medical degree from the University of Nashville, in 1862 the

Memphis, Tenn
Aug 17th, 1878

My dearest one –

I do hope you &
the little flock got safely through, and
are well – I have thought so much about
the dear little pig – if she was still sick
that night &c – is she well now? – I know
Grandpa & her Aunts cannot help falling in
love with her – You cannot conceive of
the desolation of our good city – I do not
suppose that one fifth of the white population are left in the corporation – on our
Street counting even as far out as Mrs
Cochran's, there is no one left, until you
would reach the poor families near Finnie's,
except Mrs Fithian's family & myself – poor Mrs
Nelson stood watch over me, according to her
promise to you, one day, and she left last
night, perfectly demoralized, leaving me

"My dearest one." This letter from William Armstrong to his wife, Lula,
appears to be the first he sent from Memphis after evacuating his family in
August 1878. (The Letters of William J. Armstrong, Health Sciences Historical
Collections, Health Sciences Library and Biocommunications Center, the
University of Tennessee Health Science Center, Memphis)

"Beauty" in charge, as a special protection —
Little Beulah Tatum was taken down on
yesterday — but I hope will prove a mild
case — Peter Tighe is no better & the result
looks gloomy — I have reason to think from
the reports of the last 24 hours, that the
disease will not be long-lived — Much decrease
in the number of cases — I do hope you
& the dear little ones will keep well & that
we may not be separated long — Kiss
them all for me, & do make them behave
properly in their absence from home —

Your husband —

Mary gave me a very poor breakfast —
I am afraid she is not a good cook —

twenty-four-year-old Armstrong went off to serve as a Confederate army surgeon under General Gideon Pillow in Mississippi. There he met Miss Louise Hanna, a Memphis merchant's daughter who was staying with friends in Artesia while her mother worked as a nurse for the Confederate army. He fell for her hard and fast, courting her with long, detailed, and increasingly romantic letters from their first meeting in March 1863, moving quickly from "Dear Miss Hanna" to "My darling Lula." They married in December, on Lula's sixteenth birthday.

Fifteen years later he had a medical practice at 249 Second Street and a house at 286 Alabama, next to the Presbyterian church. He and Lula sometimes disagreed about religion—she was a Methodist, he a Presbyterian—and he worried about money, as a man with many children might reasonably do. He had stayed in Memphis during the 1873 epidemic and was apparently convinced that the disease was not contagious. He was one of the doctors who signed Erskine's petition against quarantine. When the epidemic began, Lula was twenty-nine and had just given birth to her eighth child. Dr. William Armstrong got Lula and the children out of town to Maury County as quickly as possible and went to work for the Howards.[38]

"My dearest one," he wrote on August 17, "I do hope that you and the little flock made it safely through, and are well." The neighbor who had promised Lula to watch over the doctor had lasted one day: "She left, last night, perfectly demoralized." He said, "I do hope that you and the dear little ones will keep well and that we may not be separated long. Kiss them all for me and do make them behave properly in their absence from home." A few days later Armstrong described what was happening to Memphis. "You cannot imagine the desolation in the city. For squares, you will only see a family, now and then." Armstrong was willing, even eager, to draw his pay for seeing patients; eight children and a wife require a lot of support. However, he was not optimistic. "This is the most terrible fever that ever invaded any country before. I do not know of a single recovery, so far."[39]

MOST OF THE CITY'S WHITE Protestant ministers joined the general evacuation—a fact that was to cause much comment in weeks to come. Catholic priests stayed, bound by their duty to administer last rites to the sick. The city's Anglican priests stayed; leading Methodist, Presbyterian, and German Free Protestant ministers stayed. But by the end of August the Reverend Sylvanus Landrum of Central Baptist was the last white Baptist minister in the city.[40]

The Reverend Henry Sieck, pastor at Trinity Lutheran Church, was one of the clerical refugees. He had planned a trip to a church dedication and a conference in Arkansas on August 16. His pregnant wife, Pauline, would stay at home. Then the board of health announced the presence of yellow fever in the city. On August 14 his physician came to tell him that he and his wife should leave. Dr. Hewing worried that Sieck would contract the disease while visiting stricken parishioners, and he warned that if Pauline got the fever, it would kill her.

"Dr. Boecher was also at the house and argued to the contrary—that preachers and doctors should NOT leave at this time," Sieck wrote. "To which Dr. Hewing replied: 'I am leaving tonight with my family, to save them, and Mr. Sieck should do the same. Why should he stay? He can't do anything!'" When Dr. Boecher pointed out that the pastor could "talk to the sick and give them consolation," Dr. Hewing retorted, "'Oh sure, consolation! Give a man consolation when he is already unconscious with yellow fever! Mr. Sieck, you HAVE to go!'" That very morning Sieck had received a free railroad pass to his church dedication. He surmised that "perhaps this was the way our Lord was trying to direct me," bought a ticket for his wife, and boarded the train for Little Rock.[41]

Little Rock quarantined against Memphis on the day after Kate Bionda's death. A post-epidemic report explained that although state legislation set quarantine limits at five miles, the Little Rock Board of Health ignored the rule, "as it was apparent at the commencement, that unless the great highways of communication were controlled at the entrance into the State all local restrictions would only afford the city a very limited protection." Therefore Little Rock ordered the Little Rock and Memphis line not to make its usual run from Memphis. The railroad ignored the edict and sent out a train loaded with passengers, including Reverend and Mrs. Sieck. Officials halted the train ten miles outside Little Rock and quarantined the 130-odd passengers for the next twenty-one days.[42]

"The hot sun beat down on the railroad cars," Sieck wrote. "The children were crying for food and drink, and there was not even good water available." Sieck and his wife left the train. They unsuccessfully importuned neighboring farmers for food, but finally found a black woman who fed them a meager breakfast and, later, a more substantial lunch. The Siecks fortified themselves with cognac, the pastor having had the foresight to bring along a bottle. Meanwhile, back at the train, hungry children cried.

Eventually Sieck and another refugee hired a black man to carry their families to the Mohr Hotel in Argenta, a small town across the Arkansas River from Little Rock. From there he contacted local Lutherans. They arranged for transportation and housing and helped the Siecks evade quarantine. They were luckier than most. Many passengers to Little Rock wound up camping out in the forests. The pastor made it to his conference and was honored to be asked to read his sermon on the Reformation to the delegates. On August 30 he wrote to Dr. Boecher that he would not come back to Memphis unless it was absolutely necessary. Sieck and his wife survived the epidemic.

As the Siecks discovered, refugees from Memphis faced outright hostility throughout the region. T. L. Turner was a fifteen-year-old living in Milan, Tennessee, about a hundred miles northeast of Memphis. A half century later he still remembered the trains from Memphis. People hung from the windows, "blackened tongues protruding from their cracked lips, and pleaded for water, but fear was greater than pity." Men with shotguns stood on the platforms to keep people from leaving the train. Finally, the town of Milan placed tables in the Obion River bottoms about four miles out of town and loaded the tables with food and tubs of water. When the train stopped, men, women, and children ran to the tables and plunged into the water. Townspeople gathered on a hill about a mile away to watch. The passengers, having been fed and watered like cattle, were then driven back onto the train at gunpoint. Refugees who already had the fever died on the roads out of Memphis, Keating said, "like dogs, neglected and shunned, as if cursed by God."[43]

Despite the horrors of the journey, most of the city's white middle class joined other well-to-do refugees from the region in a rush toward cooler climates. The farther a person could travel, the more likely it was that he or she could find unquestioning sanctuary. Just how far north would be safe, however, was debatable. Some twenty thousand Mississippi Valley refugees made their way to Louisville, the one major river city that accepted travelers from points south. Louisville's refusal to quarantine drew sharp criticism from Cincinnati, which refused all baggage from the South and made refugees submit to examinations from physicians. Cincinnati's health department actually required all trains to halt thirty miles out of town so that doctors and policemen could get on board and check out the passengers as the train approached the city. If they found anyone who looked sick, they made sure that person stayed aboard the train rather than disembarking in Cincinnati. In Louisville, however, the local medical faculty thought the city was too far north, too high, and too clean for the fever. Louisville's kindness was rewarded with a minor fever outbreak, during which twenty-eight people died. St. Louis split the difference between the two other river cities. There, city authorities allowed refugees admission, but employed special health wardens to locate any suspected cases of fever and confine the infected persons to a quarantine hospital ten miles outside the city. The St. Louis health police found eighty-eight cases of fever; forty-two people died; and the fever spread to the hospital staff, killing nine. But St. Louis itself escaped an outbreak.[44]

The *Avalanche* described post-stampede Memphis on Sunday, August 18: "The sun blazed in a cloudless sky, and the silent walls hurled back the dazzling light and its reflection met and broke into an awful intensity of heat. A coatless man smoking in a shady doorway; a mule crawling along with an empty street car, a dog limping toward the alley, were the only signs of animal life." Although no byline was given, the writer was probably Herbert Landrum, one of Reverend Landrum's sons. Herbert's father was one of the two Protestant ministers holding service in Memphis that Sunday.[45]

The people left in Memphis had some reason for optimism. The 1873 epidemic had begun in poor and dirty neighborhoods, just like this epidemic, leading some to hope that it too would be geographically limited. So far, the fever seemed to be confined to the "infected district" downtown, but people were leaving that district for healthier neighborhoods in other parts of the city. Anti-contagionists hoped that they would leave the fever behind. Instead, on August 22 the *Appeal* reported that the fever had "jumped the line" into the rest of the city. On August 23 the board of health announced that yellow fever was epidemic in Memphis. The next day the news was even worse: 106 new cases.[46]

People who had waited through the previous week's stampede now panicked, precipitating the last stage of evacuation. Keating encouraged people to leave: "The less food for the fever the less chance there is of the physicians and nurses breaking down. Our strength in that direction must be economized or we are lost indeed." After the dust settled, Keating calculated that some 25,000 people left Memphis in the first two weeks of the epidemic, most of them in the first wave. An additional 5,000 moved out to the countryside, leaving 20,000 people in town, 14,000 of them African American and 6,000 white.[47]

For two weeks Dr. Erskine had tried to stop the epidemic by disinfecting houses and scrubbing streets. He had failed. While the Howards cared for the sick, the board of health tried to prevent the disease from spreading by disinfecting outbreak nodes. Dr. Erskine rode his horse from district to district as the reek of carbolic acid filled the air. J. M. Keating did not blame Erskine or the modern science that had informed the quarantine officer's efforts. He thought that sanitation had never had a fair trial in Memphis. In an August 25 editorial he castigated Memphis's elected leaders for walking away from promises made after the 1873 epidemic. They had cut the board of health's appropriation from $40,000 to $8,000 per annum, "with which pitiful sum Dr. Erskine and his co-laborers commenced the sanitary work of this year, most of which has been done within the past two months, want of funds preventing an earlier beginning.

"And now we are paying for it," Keating wrote, "pay for it in the loss of life, in anguish of heart, in great sorrow, in woes unnumbered and sufferings so painful as to appall the stoutest heart. The poor laborer at his work, the clerk at his desk, the mechanic at his trade, the servant in her kitchen, the physician waiting beside his patient, women in the perils and pains of childbirth, fall victim to the pest which might have been kept far from us by the enforcement of those sanitary measures which the experience of 1873 had pointed out as essential to the public health."[48]

An Irish proverb says "Beware of the anger of a patient man." In the long run, Keating's passionate anger would help change Memphis for the better. The fact remains that he was wrong about the fever's causes. Erskine could have scoured the streets with laundry soap and swabbed out the gutters with carbolic acid without any appreciable effect on the fever. According to the best medical science of the time, when Erskine's cleaning crews entered the homes of fever victims, they were surrounded by fomites, breathing infected air, up to their elbows in contamination. In fact, they were most at risk when they went out into the yard for a drink of clean water from the mosquito-infested cistern. Once bitten, they would take the virus with them to other cisterns, wells, buckets, and rain barrels where squads of *Ae. aegypti*, proliferating in the un-naturally early spring and hot summer, waited to be infected. Like wild-fire raging through tinder-dry forest, the fever jumped ahead of all efforts to stop it and swept across the city. People got the fever fast, and they got it bad. The news from New Orleans had been correct: this summer's version of Yellow Jack was ferocious.

MAJOR W. T. WALTHALL of Mobile was something of an expert on yel-low fever epidemics. As a member of the Can't Get-Away Club, a medi-cal relief organization founded to combat a 1839 yellow fever epidemic in Mobile, he had survived multiple Gulf Coast outbreaks and had vol-unteered for the 1873 Memphis epidemic. Late in the evening of August 26, Walthall arrived in Memphis again.

"Entering Memphis at night, as at a similar stage of the great 1873 epidemic, the contrast was startling," he wrote. In 1873, when the fever had been mostly confined to the slums, Walthall had been surprised to find the churches open, the usual "loiterers" around the hotels and newsstands, and women and children enjoying the shade in the parks. "*Now*, on the contrary, the streets were dark, deserted and silent." Noth-ing seemed to be open but the Peabody Hotel, one saloon, and some drugstores. The Howard headquarters, however, was bustling, and the major's "comrades" from 1873 were very glad to see him. He was compe-tent, experienced, and above all acclimated. They needed him badly; in the weeks to come he would organize two Howard infirmaries, one for whites and one for blacks, and also supervise the forty-nine nurses sent to Memphis by the Can't-Get-Away Club.

Walthall thought that the evacuation, while necessary, had intensi-fied the fever's impact on the city. Businesses were closed, trade nonex-istent, the remaining people destitute, and medical personnel lacking. "The scarcity of physicians is a great evil, but that of skilled nurses is a greater," he wrote. "One of the most distressing things in daily experi-ence is the necessity of turning a deaf ear to the piteous appeals for a doctor, a nurse, or some other help." More medical help was on the way, but Walthall worried that it would not be enough.[49]

Howard Association president Butler Anderson, sent to help Grenada, contracted the fever and died; his co-worker W. J. Smith survived a very serious bout of fever and was incapacitated for weeks. Therefore the

Howards organized under the direction of A. D. Langstaff, the hardware-store owner who served as the association's vice president. Born in Canada, Langstaff had come to Memphis in 1865 and helped organize the Howard Association in the city in 1867. He had led the Howards through the 1873 epidemic. The *Avalanche* called him "as energetic, as clear headed a worker as ever steered so great a lifeboat among the shipwrecked."[50]

From their storefront headquarters at Main and Court, the Howards systemized the medical relief effort. Dividing the city into districts, the Howards sent out teams of "visitors," identifiable by their yellow silk armbands, to look for fever victims. Once they were located, the association dispatched physicians and nurses to the patients' houses. The vast majority of the sick were cared for in their homes, not hospitals. Visitors returned periodically to check on patients, make sure the nurses were doing their jobs, and drop off medicine and food.[51]

The *Avalanche* reporter described the scene at Court Square: "A railing blocks out all but visitors on business of life or death. They walk up to the second railing, where their wants are heard and promptly attended to." Nurses sat on benches between the railings under the eye of John Johnson, the former mayor, who served as supervisor of nurses. When a nurse was needed, Johnson called him forward, gave him a yellow badge, and sent him out to the case. In the background, Howards prepared "medicine, disinfectants or stimulants in parcels ready for distribution."[52]

Nathan Menken had a saying, repeated so frequently that it became a kind of motto: It is not what you believe that matters, it is what you do that the recording angel notes. He had intended to work for the Hebrew Hospital Association, but neither he nor, apparently, anyone else in that organization wanted to restrict their help to Jews. Keating reported that the members of the association made no difference as to religion, going from house to house asking, "Is help needed?" By August 28 Menken had joined the Howards. As a visitor at large, he filed reports on cases from all over town. In the *Appeal*, Keating commented that Menken, "one of our wealthiest merchants, is one of the most untiring of the Howard workers. He is a whole team in himself."[53]

DR. ROBERT MITCHELL had urged the city to enact quarantine. That failing, he had resigned from the health board, publically stating that if yellow fever came to Memphis, its people had only themselves to blame.

As the epidemic worsened, the Howards asked him to take charge of their medical corps. His service would make him famous. A month later, with the fever raging up and down the river from Cairo to the Gulf, Mitchell received a telegram from the U.S. surgeon general asking him to join a national yellow fever commission at the princely salary of $500 per month, travel expenses paid. Mitchell replied, "Thanks for the honor, but duty to the suffering people binds me here."[54]

Inside the Quarantined City

THE DEFINING DELUSION OF THE HUMAN ANIMAL *is control over nature. In its service we engineer cities, study meteorology, concoct medicines, enact religious rituals, and observe superstitions. Through means low and high, we try to get things to happen the way we want them to happen. By the nineteenth century, people in the modernizing Western nations had wrested a modicum of agency from the natural world, and they looked forward with confidence toward attaining more. Nowhere was this feeling more evident than in the United States of America, where the transformative powers of new technologies of communication, transportation, and production made life easier and more comfortable in so many ways.*

Nineteenth-century Americans were for the most part optimistic, can-do people. When a disaster happened, their tendency was to rush busily to save people, clean up, rebuild, bicker about what human failure allowed this to happen, and (encouraged by insurance companies) cogitate on how to keep it from happening again.

INSIDE QUARANTINED MEMPHIS, *people formed volunteer groups to save people and safeguard property. Keating was one of the first to blame the outbreak on poor sanitation and demand reform. These responses, useful and well meant as they were, did not give Memphians control over the epidemic. They did not agree on the causes of the disease. They could not cure the sick. They could not stop the disease from spreading. In the face of nature as expressed through the yellow fever virus, they were as helpless as sheep in a blizzard.*

They could make choices about their own actions and, in doing so, act out of their own deepest values or sense of self. And they could watch what other people did. Thinking about the fever itself was not helpful; the mind might wear itself out running through causes, preventatives, and cures without ever reaching a conclusion. So sitting at the bedside of the sick, patrolling the empty streets, sorting medicines at the Howard offices, they thought about big things: politics and governance, faith and morality, good and evil, the nature of manhood and the role of women. Survivors testified that the epidemic made them question what they believed, and wonder.

THREE

Siege

THE PANIC WAS OVER BY THE LAST week of August, J. M. Keating said. The weather was still very hot. He thought that the continued heat exhausted the body while the destruction wrought by the fever wore on the mind and the heart, and there was no relief. "An appalling gloom hung over the doomed city," he wrote. "The silence was painfully profound," and at night there were times "when the solemn oppressions of universal death bore upon the human mind, as if the day of judgment was about to dawn." Keating believed that "animals felt the oppression; they fled from the city. Rats, cats or dogs were not to be seen." Perhaps dogs could trot off into the countryside, but the people in Memphis were now trapped. "Shot-gun quarantines were by this time (the 26th of August) established at nearly all points in the interior, as well as upon the river; and, without leave, license, or law, trade was embargoed and travel prohibited."[1] Memphis was besieged, not by a hostile army, but by public fear. You could come to Memphis—individuals did, throughout the epidemic—but getting out was difficult indeed.

What happened in Memphis was going to be up to the people left there. Within days of Mrs. Bionda's death, Memphians had to deal with a breakdown of public order as the elected officers of the city fled. Members of the city's white elite organized to direct the relief effort. Before the end of August they established refugee camps outside the city, rallied national support for Memphis, and obtained enough food to keep the population from starving. Fearful that the impoverished, frightened people of the city might rise up against their authority, they turned for help to the black community. Meanwhile, organizations and private individuals put into effect their own plans to help the sick. But while they dealt with these concrete problems, people also attempted to find some meaning in the catastrophe.

Most of the city council left town with the first wave of refugees. This was not unexpected. The same thing had happened in 1873. In that year, a Citizens' Relief Committee had taken charge of city government, the fifty-man police force had remained at their posts, the firemen had doubled as sanitation workers to clean the streets, and the Howards had managed to care for the sick with seventy nurses. As bad as the 1873 epidemic had been, it was a medical rather than social catastrophe. In 1878 the fever was worse and the city government even less capable of coping. When the epidemic began, policemen's salaries were four months in arrears. Rather than expose themselves to yellow fever, disgruntled officers quit and took their families out of town. Mayor John Flippin stayed in Memphis. So did police chief Patrick Athy. They were brave exceptions among the general rout. Without effective government and policing, Keating feared riot, chaos, and fire. He envisioned thousands dying "on the streets, perhaps in the flames of their burning dwellings."[2] Even as the city council ran away, a group of Memphis businessmen stepped up and assumed control of public order.

Thursday, August 15, was a beautiful day, the sky a brilliant Mediterranean blue, the streets jammed with fleeing people. Keating spent the day helping to organize an impromptu city government. As the evening's glorious sunset faded into a cool night, compositors at the *Appeal* set into type an announcement: all those who planned to stay in Memphis should meet at the Greenlaw Opera House at eleven on Friday morning "for consultation and action with regard to assisting each other through the scourge and providing ways and means for removing from the city to a place of safety such of our people who are pecuniarily unable to do so without assistance."

Cotton factor Charles Fisher's name was printed below the announcement, as was that of Herbert Landrum's boss, *Avalanche* owner R. A. Thompson, who as postmaster was the most significant representative of the federal government in Memphis. Keating's name was farther down in the list, along with the hardware-store owners, the print shop operators, representatives of the Memphis and Tennessee Railroad, the local agent of R. G. Dun's Merchantile Agency, and D. T. Porter, a cotton factor who also headed the city's most prestigious insurance agency, Planters' Insurance. However, most of the signatories were cotton factors.

The president of the Memphis Cotton Exchange was one of the people calling for a community meeting.[3]

A large crowd of men, black and white, arrived at the Greenlaw Opera House on Friday morning. Although the meeting opened with general discussion and a rash of resolutions that did not pass, what followed indicated that the meeting's leaders were well organized. In short order they got the crowd to vote for a motion approving a nominating committee to choose men to lead a citywide relief effort. Fisher chaired the nominating committee, which included Nathan Menken and former mayor John Loague. While the crowd considered a motion authorizing Mayor Flippin to borrow money to pay city workers, the nominating committee caucused. They quickly returned with a list of twenty-two well-known names, including clergy, insurance men, cotton factors, merchants, and professionals assigned in pairs to each ward of the city, with Mayor Flippin and merchant L. D. Eiseman as committeemen at large. The rapidity with which the committee produced a completed list indicates that it was composed before the meeting convened. All that remained was to get the crowd to vote in favor of the list. Once that was accomplished, the Citizens' Relief Committee (CRC) could proceed, empowered and legitimated by "the people," as represented by the men attending the meeting at the opera house. Fisher then immediately asked the general meeting to authorize their newly elected leaders to choose "one colored man from each ward to serve on said committee, having the same authority as those above named." This resolution also passed.

The men who called the meeting knew what they wanted, and they got it. They placed on the executive board of the Relief Committee men they trusted, all of them white, and then required the board to enlist black men in the city's emergency government. These black men would be chosen by members of the city's white elites, not the public at large—and certainly not directly by the African American men at that meeting.[4]

The committee met at noon on Saturday, approved a list of African American members, and elected Charles Fisher as president. Their first major task concerned the large number of poor people, black and white, still in the city. The best medical knowledge of the time suggested that the quickest way to end an epidemic was to remove its fuel by evacuating people without immunity.

Earlier in the week, Dr. Paul H. Otey had proposed that the poor be relocated to camps established in the countryside, housed in U.S. Army tents, and fed with army rations. Dr. Erskine strongly supported Otey's proposal. Postmaster Thompson and the city's federal revenue officer telegraphed Secretary of War G. W. McCrary for tents. Although doubtful of the constitutionality of such aid, McCrary quickly ordered that a thousand tents be dispatched from Evansville, Indiana. A later request for food produced forty thousand rations, including flour, beans, rice, coffee, and twenty thousand pounds of bacon. The War Department made fourteen such shipments to beleaguered southern cities that summer, including additional ones to Memphis.[5]

Most of the men who headed the CRC had served the Confederate States of America. As Democrats, they were committed to limited government, states' rights, and a strict interpretation of the Constitution. The logic of that political position would have inclined them to agree with Secretary McCrary: there was no provision in the Constitution allowing for the kind of emergency aid they requested. The CRC members were willing to put aside what Thomas Jefferson called metaphysical subtleties (interpretations of the Constitution that clash with what you want to do). The former Confederates begged the Republican administration of Rutherford B. Hayes for help. Their former enemies sent the needed supplies without hesitation.

The CRC took on the task of finding a place to pitch the tents shipped by the War Department. On Saturday, CRC members Charles Fisher, Rev. Sylvanus Landrum, Luke Wright, and a group of doctors took the train into the countryside south of the city. Flamboyantly red-haired, Wright was to become one of the CRC's indispensable men. He and the other members of the delegation were there to check out a potential campsite for Memphis refugees. They found one at the "Webb place," four miles out of town, but the land was rented by a black farmer. The *Appeal* reported that "Mr. Price, a respected, old, and intelligent colored man" had "cheerfully" agreed to let the CRC have the land. Whether Price received any compensation other than being flattered in print is not clear. His farm became the first refugee camp and was named after a physician martyr of 1873, Joseph J. Williams.[6]

Although Mr. Price seems to have bowed to the wishes of the CRC, the black farmers in the neighborhood were much less welcoming. They did not want an "invasion by a possibly fever-bearing rabble," as a national magazine noted, and they drove out the doctor working at the campsite. The CRC sent the Bluff City Grays and the McClellan Guards out to the site. The militia remained there for the duration of the epidemic—as did the camp.[7]

While the CRC made hurried plans to evacuate the people left in town, a crime spree underlined the city's precarious position. At least two hundred robbers moved in on the city, attracted by the thousands of unoccupied houses stretching down streets where, Keating said, "not a living thing was to be met with by night or by day." Thieves pillaged houses. They slept in the owners' beds, ate their food, and drank their liquor. Targeting the residences of the sick, the robbers stole the Howard Association's yellow badges, presented themselves as nurses, and took what they would. Memphis's much-diminished police force could do little to stop the looting, and public outrage led to cries for summary justice on the gallows. As early as August 18 Nathan Menken roused applause at a public meeting by saying that he was personally willing to "shoulder a musket and assist in hanging to the nearest lamp post anyone caught committing depredations."[8]

The Citizens' Relief Committee averted mob justice by authorizing police chief Pat Athy to hire twenty-seven new men, thirteen of them black. The August 20 *Avalanche* reported, "The colored men were picked for good character, muscle and pluck, and chief Athy believes they will make good and efficient officers." A week later, deaths and resignations had reduced the force again. This time the CRC told the chief to fill vacancies immediately and promised to pay as many as thirty-five new men. The committee also requested that the chief create a ten-man mounted patrol for night duty, and it supplied funding for hiring horses. Whether deterred by this show of force or afraid of the fever, most of the thieving strangers disappeared from the city. Some died of fever in the houses they were robbing, leaving corpses to be discovered that October by returning householders.[9]

The CRC had started by naming black men as ward representatives, a dramatic gesture in the context of the times, but one that assumed black subordination to white leaders. On August 24 the committee added one black man to its executive board. J. A. Thompson had experience with city government, having been elected a city magistrate in 1876. However, Memphis's black citizens soon took action that indicated they wanted more than token representation. Mostly former slaves, blacks had moved off plantations into Memphis, got jobs, bought houses, started businesses, and built a community. Their property might not have been worth much, but it was all they had, and they could not afford to lose it. Their sense of ownership would prove to be the city's major bulwark against anarchy.[10]

A week after the CRC was organized, two dozen of the city's leading black citizens called a public meeting to discuss their community's duty during the epidemic. They specifically invited a number of white leaders, including the mayor, the police chief, the president of the board of health, CRC chairman Charles Fisher, and Luke Wright, who had helped pick the site for Camp Joe Williams a few days earlier. Wright, a prominent lawyer, was well known in the black community. These white guests saw the meeting as an opportunity to urge blacks to leave the city.[11]

With African American political boss Ed Shaw presiding, the meeting quickly chose a committee to consider how black Memphis could cooperate with the whites in protecting life and property. While the committee caucused, Mayor Flippin asked the meeting to approve a resolution calling for the depopulation of Memphis. The resolution urged the jobless to go find work elsewhere and proposed to send the sick and destitute to camps. The final part stated that all people, black or white, in similar circumstances, should receive "at the hands of the municipal authorities and the relief organization similar treatment in this our day of distress." One of the black men at the meeting seconded the proposal, and it was put to a vote. An uproar followed, with about half of those present voting for the resolution, half against. As chair of the meeting, Ed Shaw ruled that the resolution had failed.

Ex-mayor Loague stood to support the resolution. He told the assembly that if the board of health wanted the people to leave the city, they should do so. Apparently the crowd did not appreciate his speech. The resolution was reintroduced and failed to pass by a much bigger margin. Dr. Saunders, president of the board of health, warned the crowd that they were in danger from the fever and urged them to move to the safety of the camps. Congressman Casey Young made a speech appealing to the crowd's reason. Then people began to call for Luke Wright. The former attorney general was apparently trusted by people in the community. He spoke in favor of evacuation. Finally, on the third try, the resolution passed.[12]

If the white men at the meeting thought that black Memphis had just committed to evacuation, they were mistaken. The committee appointed at the start of the meeting returned with a resolution recommending that all classes of citizens accept "the offer of the citizens' relief organization to remove those who are not able to leave to a place of safety, furnishing them with comfortable shelter and abundant and wholesome sustenance." This statement did three things. It suggested that the CRC's evacuation plan applied only to the destitute who could not afford to leave, it put into writing the committee's expectation that black people who did evacuate would be treated well, and it pointedly failed to support the notion that the unemployed should go find work elsewhere. However, evacuating the city was not the committee's highest priority. Protecting property was.

Opening with the statement "we offer our services to protect the property of all, and the lives of those remaining in the city, with the assurance that we will not shrink from any danger that may be incurred in carrying out this object," the committee praised Chief Athy for hiring blacks as special policemen. The resolution promised Athy "every assistance in our power to guard and protect the property left to the care of the city authorities." The committee then proposed a list of black men, three for each ward of the city, "selected for the purpose of cooperating with the white people in enforcing law and order." The meeting approved the resolution.

And so was born the African American relief committee, called simply the "colored central committee" in the CRC's records. T. R. Morgan, a dentist, served as president, with J. H. Sayler and W. P. M'Farland as vice president and secretary, respectively. They sent a delegation to the CRC's Monday meeting to offer cooperation in "relieving the wants and protecting the property of the city." The CRC referred the delegation to Luke Wright, now chairing the general working committee. Then William Porter, who served with Ed Shaw as Fifth Ward representative on the African American committee, stepped even further out of the subordinate role usually assigned to black men. Rather than listening to white men tell him what his race should do, he made what the CRC minutes called "a strong and sensible speech, urging the cooperation of the whites and colored people for relief and protection."[13]

The CRC's actions indicate that its leaders did not know much about the black men and women who lived all around them in Memphis. Although willing to admit black men into their ward committees, they did not move to incorporate blacks into the governing executive committee until the very day of the black meeting at Greenlaw Opera House. They may have thought that the relief effort would concentrate on whites because they believed that yellow fever was principally a disease of whites; they may have simply assumed that as white men, it was their right and their responsibility to make decisions for women, children, and blacks. However, nothing in what they said or did suggests that they understood that black Memphians had a lot to lose if the city slid into anarchy.

NATHAN MENKEN THOUGHT he understood the differences between men and women. In a letter to his Sallie, the former cavalryman praised her as a wife worthy of a soldier. "I'm proud of you, especially when I hear of men saying their wives wouldn't let them stay and they had to skip," he said. "A man ought to be a man, and what he recognizes as a duty should be done. And his wife should be a woman, not a ninny, a plaything. Man is made for strife, woman for beauty, to gladden his heart with her smile and voice, and cheer him in his struggle . . ." Menken expressed ideals that were widely held by men and women in the educated middle class. A man had rights and privileges not given to women, but he also had the responsibility to live up to his role: in short, to be a man. When Keating referred to one of the heroes of the epidemic as a manly man, he was not setting up a joke; he was describing a quality of character the people of his time deeply admired.[14]

Men ran the relief effort in Memphis. The streets were guarded by policemen and militia units, all men. The pastors and priests who stayed in Memphis were men. The journalists and telegraphers who informed the nation of the city's agony were men. The doctors were men. The Howard Association recorded the names of 526 nurses who came to Memphis from other locales; 362 of them were men.[15] These men had many opportunities to live up to their society's concepts of true manhood. Significantly, they used martial metaphors to describe their situation. The epidemic was a war, and they had enlisted for the duration. Although terrified, the brave held their ground. Those who died fell with their faces toward the enemy. Fighting the epidemic, like fighting a war, was a matter of manhood.

There were heroic men in Memphis, but heroism from men was expected—commendable, but not news. Yet by the end of August, Memphians were coming to recognize that courage did not always coincide with manhood. The men doing relief work were shocked when other men proved to be arrant cowards. Keating reported the most astonishing examples. There was the man who refused to come to the hospital to nurse his wife: "If I goes, who takes care of my dog?" Another man, a widower, moved to Louisville but left his children in Memphis, where they died.[16]

In one comfortable middle-class Memphis home, a wife told her husband to save himself. She would stay and nurse their little daughter. Her husband moved to supposed safety in a house across the street. The child worsened; he never crossed the street to help. The wife fell ill, and he stayed away. Finally, both died. He watched from across the street as strangers carried out their bodies and took them away for burial.[17]

Courage, or the lack of it, lay at the heart of the Donovan scandal, the first of many in fever-plagued Memphis. Big John Donovan, a burly Irish politician, had been out of town when the epidemic hit. He delayed his return, stopping at Brownsville, about fifty miles away. The pregnant Mrs. Donovan, still in Memphis with their children, caught the fever. Contacted, Donovan wired back asking that his family be cared for. Yellow fever causes internal organs to hemorrhage, making it especially dangerous to pregnant women. Twelve hours after the onset of the fever, Mrs. Donovan gave birth to a stillborn child. She died shortly thereafter. One of the Donovan children died that same day. Donovan sent instructions for their funeral but stayed in Brownsville. The surviving children were eventually evacuated to Nashville, where they were reunited with their father, weeks later.

Newspapers in Memphis condemned Donovan as a villain, and his name became a byword throughout the nation. A *Chicago Tribune* writer mentioned Donovan's name to introduce his readers to a story about someone just as bad, the owner of a cotton gin, "a bachelor and a man of wealth, sporting diamonds and fast horses." This man fled in the first rush, leaving his sisters and father behind. After one of the sisters died, the others wrote to him asking for money so that they could leave the city. He sent them five dollars "and an order on Flaherty and Sullivan, undertakers, for a coffin."[18]

Such cases left Keating "dazed with amazement that human beings can be so cowardly." When the epidemic started, he had urged the men of Memphis to buck up. "There is no use being rattled in the face of the enemy. 'Screw your courage to the sticking place,' and you'll not fail."

When one of the men who had deserted a sick wife let it be known that he was considering suicide, Keating said publically, in the *Appeal*, "If he isn't dead, somebody ought to kill him." The moral cowardice displayed in Memphis made him wonder if Memphis was sliding back to the days of the London plague. Only the thousands of cases of heroism gave him hope for modern civilization.[19]

At the Memphis *Avalanche*, young Herbert Landrum was holding the fort. In his early twenties, Herbert was a preacher's kid, the son of Rev. Sylvanus Landrum of Central Baptist Church. In normal times, he was a bright, witty young man with a gift for writing and for friendship. At work and at play, he and his friends Robert Catron and Ed Worsham formed an inseparable triumvirate. All three had chosen to stay in Memphis after the fever hit. Now Catron, the Associated Press agent for Memphis, filed dispatches twice a day at the Western Union telegraph office. His stories ran in papers throughout the country. Catron also filled in as needed on the city's newspapers. Although young, Worsham was already a prominent Mason, and he took a leading role in his lodge's relief efforts. Worsham wrote to a friend on August 26, "The fever is not abating. Very many people have left, and there is much destitution. There are a few of us who are willing to stay and do the best we can." As for Landrum, he continued to publish the *Avalanche* as his co-workers fell ill, died, or fled.[20]

At midnight on August 29, with a steady drizzle soaking the dark streets, Herbert Landrum tried to explain to the outside world what it was like in Memphis. "We are doomed. It is hard, as we write in this dark, dismal night of death, not to realize the full meaning of that brief sentence." He described relief workers' vehicles rattling along the wet pavement outside the *Avalanche*'s Monroe Avenue offices. "Else is silence, deadly and awful, with naught but the rattle of the water from the roof into the tin gutter, and that has the ominous gurgle of a death rattle in the human throat." At least ninety-two people had died by fever that day. People said that city undertaker Jack Walsh was storing corpses in his stable until he had enough for a wagonload for burial in Potters Field, but he protested that he simply could not keep up with the death rate.[21]

The "horrors of the hour cannot be told," Landrum wrote. "They are horrors such as make a hell on earth, such as make life almost a burden." In his darkness, Landrum found one group most worthy of praise: the women of Memphis. The faithless were men, the so-called stronger sex. Shining in contrast, "the faithfulness of woman, as a devoted mother, as a patient attentive wife, as life-risking daughter, sister, friend."

> By the bedside of the burning body, inhaling the poison of the sick room, foul with that odor which tells the nature of the dread disease, performing service which none other will do, wearing a smile while the heart is breaking and lifting up the head when in the last agony, her person is befouled by that most repulsive and horrible of all substances—black vomit—she sits and watches, and nurses and cares for her loved one till he lives again or passes beyond her aid. The penalty of her service of love is generally death.[22]

ON THE EVENING of August 17 a priest stood at the doors of Trinity Infirmary in lower Manhattan to give his blessing to two nuns on their way to Memphis. Sisters Constance and Thecla taught at a girls' school in Memphis run by the Sisters of St. Mary. Vacationing at their order's convent in Peekskill, New York, when news of the epidemic arrived, they had hurried to the infirmary to pick up medical supplies and now sat in the carriage that would take them to their train. The priest later told his congregation, "I have seen no braver sight."[23]

Catholic nuns earned plaudits from the nation for their care of the sick in the Memphis epidemic. However, the two nuns setting off for Memphis were not Catholics, but Episcopalians. The Episcopal Church is a branch of the Anglican Communion, created when Henry VIII took England out of the Roman fold and, in the process, dissolved English religious orders and confiscated the properties of monasteries and convents. For three hundred years Anglicans abjured religious orders as vestiges of papist practices. In the nineteenth century, however, some Anglicans began to move toward an increased stress on the church's pre-Reformation roots. In mid-century, these "high church" Anglicans began to found religious orders, the first such in their communion since the sixteenth century. Among the new orders was the Sisters of St. Mary, founded in 1865 in New York.

The very idea of Protestant monks and nuns was deeply disturbing to many Episcopalians and to other Protestants as well. When Kezia DePelchin, a Methodist, visited St. Mary's Episcopal Cathedral in Memphis, she was shocked. "Lo! The inmates were dressed like nuns; dress of coarse black stuff, cape collar and cuffs of white linen, each wore a cross." The women "called each other sister, thus Sister Constance, Sister Thekla [sic], etc." DePelchin remembered that as a child in Madeira, she had seen "nuns, in sable gowns, greet their friends through iron gratings." To her, "such communities, were relics of the dark ages, that I thought forever swept away from the pure church of Christ, by the mighty power of the Reformation. What would Martin Luther say?" The Sisters of St. Mary had to prove to their own church (as well as to skeptical Methodists) that their order should exist. Led by Mother Harriet Starr Cannon, the sisters persevered. The order founded St. Mary's Free Hospital for children in Hell's Kitchen, and a convent in Peekskill. The Episcopal bishop of Tennessee, Charles Todd Quintard, and Mother Harriet had both grown up in Connecticut and were old friends. At the bishop's request, in 1873 the order took charge of an Episcopal girls' school in Memphis.[24]

The sisters' convent, their school, and the rectory where Rev. George Harris, the cathedral dean, lived with his wife and children all clustered around St. Mary's Cathedral, a small wooden structure with aspirations toward church Gothic. The Episcopal compound occupied the triangular space where Alabama Street ran into Poplar. Neighbors included Alabama Street Presbyterian Church and the residence of Dr. and Mrs. Armstrong.

Mother Harriet had placed Sister Constance in charge of the convent and school. Born Caroline Louise Darling to a Unitarian family in Medford, Massachusetts, Sister Constance had struggled against family disapproval of her conversion and profession. She was young, sweet-faced, well educated, a talented artist, well equipped to make friends and supporters among Memphis's upper-class Episcopalians. Sister Thecla, a Georgian, and Sister Hughetta, a Memphis native, provided southern voices for the endeavor.[25]

The new project got off to a rocky start. The sisters arrived in Memphis just in time to help nurse during the 1873 yellow fever epidemic. However, with the support of Memphis's elite, St. Mary's School began to grow. Within a year they had eighty paying pupils. Sister Hughetta remembered the years prior to 1878 as a wonderful time, full of work and hardship but also achievement: the nuns had built "probably the best Church school in the southern states." Hughetta especially treasured the memory of spring commencement: "scores of white-gowned girls with huge bouquets of flowers and scores of little girls running about with the flower baskets of the seniors, of dignified fathers and happy mothers smiling upon their children, while in and out of the crowded rooms moved the stately darkey waiters carrying ice cream and cake on large silver trays—the fine trays being the property of rich and kindly neighbors." Devout Episcopalian women affiliated with the sisters worked as associates. They taught in the girls' school and in a separate school opened for poor children. Bishop Quintard had founded a Church Home for orphans in the late 1860s. The first sister sent to run the home died after a year in Memphis; the second had to give up the work because of ill health, but in 1877 Mother Harriet sent young Sister Frances to Memphis to manage it.[26]

In early August, Constance and Thecla had traveled to the order's Peekskill headquarters for a retreat. Two weeks later George Harris, dean of the cathedral, sent them word about the outbreak. He asked if the order would send additional sisters to Memphis. Mother Harriet told them no. She could not send the young postulants, and the convent's associates were married women with family responsibilities. Constance and Thecla left for Memphis immediately.[27]

The sisters had come to Memphis to run a school for girls. They had no special training as nurses, nor were they accustomed to hard physical labor. But the cathedral was in the infected district, and people turned to the priests and nuns for help. Charles Parsons, rector of Grace Episcopal Church, moved into the rectory with Harris, both men having sent their dependents to safety in the country. They were joined by Belton Mickle, civil engineer and railroad man. In the convent, Constance, Thecla, Hughetta, and Frances were supported by their associate, Nannie Bullock. Dr. Armstrong served as the community's physician.[28]

In late August, as fever swept down Alabama Street toward the cathedral, Constance began to keep a diary, scribbled on loose pieces of paper at rare moments of leisure. Her journal of the fever summer describes work without rest, struggle without victory. Called to help a family, Constance and her companion went to their house, where they found a young girl "in mourning," the parents dead, one on the sofa, one on the bed, and the girl's brother in bed, delirious, rocking back and forth. The atmosphere was foul. There was a crowd of black people around the gate of the house. They refused to offer any help. "I told them of the danger of their standing there—general scattering," Constance wrote. "I sent for undertaker and promised to come back. Came out desperately sick and hurried on . . . (searching for nurses all the way) . . ." Disturbed as she was by what she had seen, Constance could not go home to rest. Before the day was over, she had supplied another sick family with beef tea and, with the help of two Howard nurses, put up a new bed for the father of the family. On their way home, the sisters were stopped by a black man, who called to them, " 'There's an *Episcopal* sick in here.' We went into a dirty grocery, found three sick, two in one bed. I just crawled home and fairly dropped into bed, first time for three nights."

The next morning, Sister Thecla was called out to help some patients before the rest of the nuns were up. After making her confession, Constance hurried out to see her patients. On the way, she passed two corpses. She wrote, "horrible sight and air fearful; complained to Board of Health; got policeman to bring undertaker." After that, she was called to the home of "Mrs. A." She found her down with fever. There were four children in the house. Constance wrote, "baby starving, drove all about for milk. Sent Sister Thecla to her; sent Mrs. Bullock for nurse." In the midst of the emergency, a domestic inconvenience: "The horse has lost all his shoes, no blacksmith in the city."[29]

ANNIE COOK WAS A FIXTURE of the Memphis demimonde, a woman with a (most likely deliberately) shadowed past. Memphis historian Franklin Wright did extensive research into the madam's personal history but was unable to state authoritatively whether Cook was her birth name, married name, or neither. Said to be of German ancestry, she worked as a domestic in Louisville before the Civil War. She may have been married at some point. In 1858 she had a son. During the 1860s she apparently began working as a prostitute and in 1872 moved to Memphis. Four years later she moved her establishment to the Mansion House on Gayoso Street. She rented the three-story building from William Duff, attorney-at-law. When Cook redecorated in the spring of 1878, she purchased new velvet rugs, chandeliers, a piano, chromolithographs, and beds. In addition to Cook's rooms and the ground-floor parlor, the house had twelve rooms, gaslights, and indoor plumbing.[30]

When the epidemic began, Cook sent all her prostitutes away except Lorena Meade, a Louisianan who presumably was acclimated. The two of them turned the Mansion House into a hospital and began nursing yellow fever patients. Wright believes that they rolled up the carpets in the parlor and turned it into a ward, using cots instead of placing patients on expensive mattresses that would have to be burned. Cook's brothel-hospital received press coverage up and down the Mississippi Valley, combining as it did sin and redemption in one elegantly furnished package. In a culture with a bad case of virgin/whore syndrome, Cook was catnip: a prostitute behaving like a nun.

Court Square was the epicenter of the Memphis relief effort, with the CRC headquarters on one side of the square, the Howards on the other. Each day, Keating walked a block from his rooms in the Planters' Insurance building to the *Appeal* offices overlooking the square. On the way, he could confer with Dr. Mitchell about the latest lists of the sick and the dead. He might encounter Dr. Erskine as he hurried through on his way to patients or on an errand for the health board. He could talk to Nathan Menken, whose store was nearby. He might have tipped his hat to the prostitute Lorena Meade, on her way to pick up supplies for Annie Cook's hospital. Morning and evening, Court Square was the best place in Memphis to collect news. At the end of August, however, the conversations took a new and ominous turn.

The 1870s were great years for all manner of class-based social upheaval, from the Paris Commune of 1871 to the Great Railroad Strike that had paralyzed the U.S. transportation system in 1877. Generations of Americans had prided themselves on the nation's freedom from European class conflicts. The 1870s put paid to that notion. Upper- and middle-class Americans shuddered at potential threats to life and property from "the mob," that dangerous aggregation of individual working-class Americans. In Memphis, fears of riot and mob violence arose over the most basic of issues: food.

Normally, Memphians bought fresh vegetables, fruits, eggs, poultry, meat, and fish at the city's markets and butcher shops. It was clear that as the epidemic progressed, farmers would stop bringing produce and livestock into the town. As noted above, Memphis asked for and received army rations from the federal government. However, to feed the city, more would be needed than the secretary of war had agreed to supply, and it would have to come from private sources. Congressman Casey and Mayor Flippin sent telegrams to the mayors of New York, Boston, and Baltimore asking for assistance. Robert Catron, the Associated Press

*Court Square. This recent photograph of the small park in the heart of Memphis
shows the fountain that provided a much-enjoyed cool oasis in the summer of
1878. Court Square was the epicenter of the relief efforts. The Howard headquarters
was on one side of the square, the Citizens' Relief Committee's commissary on
the other, with African American troops bivouacked close by.*

stringer in Memphis, used his connections to the nationwide newspaper
network to send out a general plea for help on August 19. Though ultimately generous, the response took time.

Middle-class Memphians probably had larders stocked with food-
stuffs that would keep: ham, bacon, flour, sugar, crackers, coffee, and tea,

plus canned goods. Many had backyard gardens. Some kept milk cows. Just the same, shortages were irksome. As early as August 24, Dr. Armstrong groused to Lula about the food situation: "no butchers stalls—no groceries—no food stores—we live on bacon—coffee & milk." On the other hand, the poor lived day to day, sometimes literally hand to mouth, on the money earned by that day's labor. With no money to buy what few groceries were left, they went hungry. Soon, finding, guarding, and distributing food became the CRC's major task.[31]

At the end of August the rations sent by the secretary of war were all that stood between the poor of Memphis and starvation. That, and the CRC's distribution system. The federal government had given the Citizens' Relief Committee forty thousand rations, and the committee had at hand about $10,000 in cash to spend on relief. With those resources, they fed the sick, supplied rations for the camps, paid for transportation out of town, and funded Chief Athy's new policemen. They did not think they could feed all the destitute in Memphis, nor did they wish to do so. CRC members wanted to make sure that only the deserving poor received charity. According to Keating, they were not running "a free lunch establishment." They also thought they could use food as an enticement to evacuate. Therefore they announced rules that required people seeking relief to apply to their ward committee, which would investigate each case prior to approval. If you were sick, you qualified. The committee would also feed adults (but no more than two) who were nursing a sick person. If you were not sick and not caring for the sick, the CRC's position was that you should evacuate to one of the camps, and if you chose to stay in Memphis, your ward committee would not give you papers and you would receive no food from the CRC.[32]

Every day about noon a crowd of about five hundred people, most of them black, gathered at the Court Square commissary. They carried baskets and clutched authorization papers from their ward committees. The crowd sat on the curb and in the street in front of the commissary door, waiting. Finally a black man climbed up on a box and began to call the names on the list of those allowed to have food. As a woman held her basket to be filled with food for her and her family, a CRC representative entered her name and the amounts drawn in a ledger. The CRC kept meticulous records. Keating praised the commissary workers for their "order and precision, notwithstanding the clerks died so fast."

Indeed, the cost of accountability was high: five men died keeping books at the CRC commissary. The CRC's insistence on regulations and record keeping assured donors that their contributions were used as promised, but the laborious process seemed discriminatory to some observers. To be fed, you had to have papers from your ward committee certifying that they had investigated your circumstances and considered you eligible for aid. A black minister said that the process of getting rations was so difficult that many blacks "get out of heart before they reach the end." If you were ill, the simple task of standing in a long line could be too much for you. A white northern missionary described how blacks, too weak to stand in the relief lines, sat on the streets until night fell, then went home to die without help.[33]

The rations distributed did not come in the form of modern Meals, Ready-to-Eat. In August the CRC doled out fifteen thousand pounds of bacon, plus much smaller amounts of ham, beef, flour, bread, crackers, rice, grits, lard, and sugar. The only vegetables handed out were canned tomatoes, dried peas, and beans, 111 barrels and 2½ pecks of potatoes, and 61 barrels of onions. They had 1 pound of apples, most likely furnished locally, and 27 barrels of lemons. It says much about priorities to note that the rations included more than a thousand pounds each of grain and roasted coffee. Among the remaining miscellany were tea, salt, pepper, vinegar, ice, soap, a dab of mustard (1 pound), and supplies for animals: 38,000 pounds of hay. The people who received rations sometimes complained about the quality of the food, but no complaints have survived concerning the quantity. However, only 4,042 people received CRC rations in August, and there were about 20,000 people left in the city.[34]

Unable to get jobs, increasingly hungry, angered by the CRC's rules, working-class Memphians soon served notice that they were not going to sit passively and starve. On August 29 the *Appeal* printed the following anonymous letter to the editor:

A Fair Warning to Memphis. Editors Appeal.—We, the poor class of Memphis, are well aware of the fact that the government has sent provisions for us, and we can't help the distress of the city. We desire to make an honest living, and if something is not done for us we will take the law in our own hands. We can't starve, and don't intend to as long as there is anything to eat in Memphis. If we could get employment, we wouldn't ask it of you. Give us something to subsist upon, and Memphis shall be at peace; and if not, we will turn her up side down, if possible. IRISH AND NEGROES.[35]

Veterans of opposing Civil War armies put their heads together to consider tactics: How could they defend the CRC commissary should the mob rise? The city's most prestigious militia company, the Chickasaw Guards, got out of town early in the epidemic. The sons of the Memphis elite spent the late summer and early fall elsewhere, participating in drill competitions and putting on drill exhibitions in major midwestern cities to raise money for yellow fever relief. The Bluff City Grays had been detailed to keep the peace in the camps. The answer was obvious: the CRC would have to call on black troops. The McClellan Guards were out at Camp Morris Henderson, but Memphis had another black militia company under the command of Captain Raphael T. Brown, a barber by trade. Brown's Zouaves set up an encampment close to Court Square, and detachments began standing guard at the CRC commissary. In 1866 Memphis whites had rioted when federal black soldiers resisted the city's Irish police force. Now the police force was largely African American, and black soldiers protected the rations upon which the destitute Irish depended.[36]

FOR WEEKS THE BOARD of health and the CRC pushed for evacuation, urging everyone, black and white, to move out of the city. "Depopulation is the forlorn hope, and to that end all the influences of begging, persuasion, and even compulsion must be turned on," the *Avalanche* said. "These people must be gotten out of the city, must be, and the fever stamped out through lack of material for its ravages." Before the epidemic ended, the CRC had taken on the direct supervision of at least six camps. They also furnished supplies to a camp founded by a Catholic priest. Among them, these camps sheltered approximately thirteen hundred people.[37]

The largest of the CRC facilities, Camp Joe Williams, was located on a rise about five miles from Memphis. It had fresh water from springs, excellent drainage, and a commandant who despised the refugees sheltering there. John F. Cameron wrote later, "Very few worthy people inhabited the tents of Camp Williams." The former Union cavalry colonel described his charges as "mechanics, tradesmen, laborers, women of *industrious* habits, of indifferent morality, Catholics in faith . . ."[38] Cameron ran the camp as a military installation. It was laid out neatly in streets named after CRC members; shipping labels were used to number each tent. The colonel ordered reveille sounded each morning at five, taps each night at ten. Inhabitants received wood and water daily, rations every other day. The camp's two bakers supplied bread; the butcher portioned out beef, fresh and salted. Cameron required all able-bodied men to join one of the details that policed the camp twice a day.

Men moved their families to the camp, then went back into Memphis every day to work, check on property, or (according to Cameron) drink and plunder. They apparently believed they would be safe as long as they got out of Memphis before nightfall. This peculiar commuting pattern had a predictable result: fever broke out in Camp Joe Williams. Cases also appeared among the black farmers who had protested the camp's creation in the first place. The camp hospital cared for the sick. Because people were too afraid of fomites to use tents previously occupied by yellow fever victims, Cameron had the tainted tents and bedding burned in a deep fire pit. He attempted to reassure the refugees by setting up his personal tent a few yards from the hospital. Later he moved into a shack previously used to store corpses. To keep order, Cameron depended on the Bluff City Grays and the McClellan Guards, stationed, as he put it, in the heart of the camp.[39]

Most of the people who had stayed in Memphis did not move out to the camps. Historian Khaled Bloom suggests a number of reasons for their recalcitrance: fear that their property would be lost, a sense of responsibility to the sick or the community at large, fatalism, destitution, stupidity, and the desire to make the most of opportunities for looting.[40] It also seems likely that at least some had heard about the rigor of daily life under Colonel Cameron's command and preferred to avoid it.

The majority of the city's African American population refused to leave the city. Their decision to stay in Memphis reflected current ideas about the nature of yellow fever. Whites believed that people of African descent either did not get the fever or, if they did, had very mild cases, and the people of African descent believed that too. Despite news reports that blacks were contracting the fever and dying of it, blacks in Memphis did not react to the epidemic with anything like the level of stark terror demonstrated by whites, and they formed a minuscule part of the camps' residents.

The CRC created a camp specifically for black Memphians and put that camp under the control of the officers of the McClellan Guards. Camp Morris Henderson was named for the African American minister of Beale Street Baptist Church who had died in the 1873 epidemic. The new facility allowed the CRC to segregate refugees by race, but by placing the camp under the control of black officers, the CRC was also assuring that black refugees would be protected by black soldiers. Camp Henderson was a short walk from Camp Williams. If Colonel Cameron's assessment of the white people in his camp was accurate, the few black refugees who chose to stay at Camp Henderson may have appreciated the presence of a black militia unit.[41]

The only major camp not run by the CRC was founded by Father William Walsh for members of the Father Mathew Society, an Irish temperance organization. When the epidemic began, members of the society wanted to hire nurses and care for their own. Father Walsh did not believe that his Irishmen were up to that task. Instead, he suggested that the society evacuate members and families to its own camp. With the CRC furnishing tents, the Father Mathew Society pitched camp in a wooded area outside of town.[42]

AT ST. MARY'S EPISCOPAL CATHEDRAL, the days passed and the workload increased. Sister Constance's diary entries became shorter. The weather was rainy and damp, enlivened by periodic gunpowder explosions set off to clear the air. (Not everyone in Memphis had given up the hypothesis that miasma caused the fever.) Constance described nights lit by "burning bedding everywhere, leaving black piles in front of the houses." At the end of one exhausting day she wrote, "One cares so much for the lovely weather, the evening light: one sees such exquisite pictures everywhere. It seems almost heartless to care for them!"[43]

Rev. George Harris and his colleague, Rev. Charles Parsons, were caught up in the relief effort. Like so many in Memphis, they were Civil War veterans. Harris had been a Confederate chaplain. A West Point classmate of George Armstrong Custer, Parsons had served in the U.S. Army artillery.[44] On August 20 Harris and Parsons sent out an appeal for help addressed to the people of New York. They described the desolate city and outlined their plans:

> First—To feed the hungry, who can earn nothing.
> Second—To provide for the barest necessities of the sick.
> Third—To minister to the dying.
> Fourth—To bury the dead.
> Fifth—To take care of the children who are made orphans by the
>   ravages of the fever . . .

Taking care of orphans became a major project for the Episcopal cadre. Although the city ran the Leath Orphan Asylum, in the last week of August the Citizens' Relief Committee decided to take over the Canfield Asylum, normally for black children, and turn it into a home for children orphaned during the epidemic. They asked the Sisters of St. Mary to run it. Rev. George Harris served on the CRC, and he may have suggested that the Episcopalians could care for the orphans. Since the Roman Catholics ran their own orphanage, the Canfield orphans would mostly have been from miscellaneously Protestant families. At the cathedral the Episcopalians had two priests and four nuns, more personnel than any other white Protestant group in Memphis could muster. At any rate, the CRC took over the Canfield Asylum, announced that it would be open for all, and put the sisters in charge. On the evening of August 28 Constance and her sisters met collectively for the first time since she and Thecla had returned from New York. Dr. Harris and Rev. Charles Parsons joined them. "We made list for the Asylum," she wrote. "Curious how cool we all were."

Constance asked the motherhouse in Peekskill for more nurses. The sisters already had charge of the Episcopal Church Home. She wrote to Mother Harriet, "They sent us the orphans so fast that we cannot keep them in the one outside room we dare to use here. And we have taken the Canfield Asylum and are fitting it up roughly for them as a sort of quarantine house, carrying them over to the Home as fast as we dare. They brought in six this morning—miserable dirty little things—one only ten months old." She added that she would have to send help out to the Church Home, where Sister Frances was making a slow recovery from the fever.[45]

In a later message she explained why additional help was so important and described the community's experiences. "Cases that are nursed seldom die," she said. "Most of the dead have died of neglect or utter ignorance on the part of their attendants. The panic is fearful today. Eighty deaths reported, and half the doctors refuse to report at all. We found one of our nurses lying on the floor in her patient's room down with the fever, another is sickening." She was worried about Reverend Parsons, who had a chill: "I really believe that Dr. Harris and I and the two negro nurses are the only well persons anywhere near."

Dr. Armstrong was now working with the sisters, the Howards having added care for the orphans to his already heavy workload. Constance wrote, "Dr. Armstrong has shut himself up for the night declaring himself worn out . . . This is the dreariest night we have had." She was exhausted. "The calls for food and wine are incessant. I have been on my feet almost the whole day, for our old cook would not do a thing if one of us did not stay with her, whenever we could be spared from the sick." A nurse came by to say he wouldn't stay in a house anymore if someone didn't remove the dead woman who had been there for two days. "We are absolutely forbidden to touch the dead even if a coffin could be found. Dr. Harris is all that earthly strength can be to us, but he is far from strong. I do not think he even hopes to get through."

On August 31 Harris fell ill, and two days later Parsons followed. With both priests sick, the sisters could no longer take daily Communion, and they felt bereft. Constance despaired for Harris's life. She told one of the nurses working at the asylum, "We have almost no hope."

IN THE LAST WEEK of August, members of the relief community began to realize what they were really up against. Like Constance, they approached despair. The fever was not abating, as they had hoped. It had spread past the original infected neighborhoods and was now breaking out in the suburbs. Dr. Armstrong told Lula that the disease was not yellow fever as it appeared in 1873. "It seems to be a plague sent upon our southern people possibly for their past wickedness." Armstrong and the other Howard Association doctors stayed on the road, going from house to house. The *Appeal* said, "It is blood-curdling to listen to the details of heart-rending incidents encountered by the visiting nurses in various parts of the city."[46]

One night in August a Howard visitor walked through the dark-shadowed streets by the light of a full moon. In the still night he heard a voice singing a lullaby. On impulse, he followed the sound to a cottage. Through the window he could see a woman holding a child, pacing back and forth and singing. He opened the door and spoke, but she ignored him. Her appearance was wild, her eyes wandering. The visitor went back out into the street and asked a black woman to help him. Together the white man and black woman returned to the cottage and coaxed from the singer the decomposing body of her baby.[47]

As authorities scrambled to organize the city's response, no one noticed that Dr. K. P. Watson was missing. When his colleagues realized that they had not seen him for some time, they simply assumed that he was working in another part of the city. Sergeant McElroy of the U.S. Army Signal Corps, stationed in Memphis, was walking down Second Street when people told him that something was wrong at one of the houses. The sergeant broke down the door and found Watson's partially decomposed body on an old mattress on the floor. No one in the neighborhood knew how the doctor came to be in the house. Keating thought that "the condition of the corpse and surrounding circumstances told the story too truly. He had been seized with a violent attack of the fever, and during the attendant delirium, he had crept into the place, where he may have lingered for days, or it may have been only for hours, finally dying unattended by nurse or physician, not even a friend to smooth his dying pillow." It was a story to be repeated many times in the weeks to come. The *Appeal* reported Watson's death on August 31.[48]

Keating wrote, "If the awful sights and experiences of the past two weeks are to be repeated, we may make up our minds to die, every one of us." The epidemic lasted for eight more weeks.[49]

HOWARD OFFICERS FINDING THE DEAD BODIES
OF MOTHER AND CHILD.

*Enacted in Memphis, New Orleans, and smaller towns in the
Mississippi Valley, this scene is nowhere near as harrowing
as stories reported in the Appeal.*

FOUR

The Destroying Angel

SEPTEMBER BEGAN WITH A "ripple of riot."[1]

The Citizens' Relief Committee trusted the black militiamen bivouacked on Court Square no more than they trusted the poor of Memphis. If a riot broke out, would these troops fire on people of their own race? The CRC members were doubtful. Therefore the inner circle made a plan. If a riot began, someone was to ring the fire alarm bell three times. Then the trusted white men—about a hundred in number—would rally at the Southern Express office on the north side of Court Square. What they thought they would do at that point is not clear from the historical record, but it probably involved holing up in the Express office until reinforcements could arrive. In preparation, they ordered a train held in ready at Camp Williams to bring the Bluff City Grays to Memphis. The Chickasaw Guards were told to await orders at Grand Junction, Tennessee, on the Memphis and Charleston Railroad line. Two neighboring towns volunteered to bring their militia units if needed. Significantly, the black militia unit at the CRC camps—the McClellan Guards—were not included in the contingency plan.[2]

On September 2 the Zouaves were on guard at the commissary. A crowd waited for rations. Among them was a black man, Alf Watson. According to an eyewitness quoted in the *Appeal*, Watson had brought his pistol with him with the stated intention of killing "some damn negro." Watson got into an altercation with one of the militiamen, slapped the soldier, and cursed him. When a black policeman told him to behave himself, Watson cursed him and said, "No d—n negro can arrest me." The policeman called the guard to help him. Watson started running,

Luke Edward Wright was sixty-three when Gerard Barry
painted this portrait, but it captures some of the force of personality
he displayed at age thirty-two, in the summer of 1878.

but stopped to pull out his pistol. The soldier shot him in the leg. As
Watson's woman wailed, the crowd seethed, and the Zouaves rushed to
reinforce their line.

Luke Wright was in the commissary at the time. He came out to the
front of the building and immediately praised the black militia for their
action. Then Wright spoke to the mob. He warned them of the consequences of disorder. He told them that the CRC could bring military

Illustrations from Frank Leslie's Illustrated, *September 21, 1878. Although Leslie's Newspaper occasionally refers to "our correspondent" in Memphis, there is no evidence that the newspaper actually sent anyone to the epidemic-stricken regions. These pictures do not necessarily represent actual scenes sketched from life. Instead, the illustrations correspond closely to news stories of the epidemic. It is probable that Leslie's artist used wire accounts and imagination.*

CITIZENS FLEEING FROM THE STRICKEN DISTRICTS INTO IUKA, MISS.

Of the exodus from Memphis, Keating wrote that people went "out by every possible conveyance—by hacks, by carriages, buggies, wagons, furniture vans, and street drays . . ." Kezia DePelchin described the Mississippi countryside as "covered with refugees—wagons piled with furniture for camping out—cats, chickens and children in loving confusion."

HUNGRY CITIZENS SEEKING FOOD AT THE COMMISSARY DEPOT, MEMPHIS.

*The artist correctly shows that most of the waiting people were African American,
but focuses our attention on a white woman, posed in the middle of the frame.
In the front row, what appears to be the artist's conception of a German Jew,
possibly representing the city's immigrant population.*

VICTIMS OF THE FEVER AWAITING BURIAL AT ELMWOOD CEMETERY, MEMPHIS.

*This generic graveyard scene captures what Herbert Landrum
called the wholesale burial business, but shows the workmen digging
individual rather than trench graves.*

force against them. He stood there for roughly an hour, a red-haired white man haranguing an angry crowd, and the Zouaves stood with him. Their presence and Wright's speech averted a potential riot.[3]

In a pattern common to southern history, the white leaders of the relief community blamed black discontent on a white agitator, Mike Pyne, who had urged the crowd at Court Square to take by force the food the government had sent. Pyne disappeared. Keating said baldly that he "was, it is said, soon after 'lost.' He has never been heard of since." The implication is that he was murdered or, as the CRC might have seen it, executed.[4]

The September 3 *Appeal* announced that the CRC had put Luke Wright in charge of all available militia forces. Wright already headed the organization's working committee and had been tasked to liaison with the black relief committee. Called "General" because of his previous tenure as the city's attorney general, General Wright now took command of the CRC's efforts to keep public order.

EPIDEMICS GRADUALLY BUILD to a crescendo and then slowly diminish as the people subject to the disease contract it, die, or recover. In September the number of cases, and deaths, rose rapidly. On September 1 the *Appeal* reported 152 new cases. A week later the paper published a table comparing deaths in the first twenty-six days of the 1873 and 1878 epidemics. The 1878 epidemic started a month earlier than the 1873 epidemic, and by the first week of September the daily reported deaths were around ninety. No single day in 1873 had reported death totals higher than eighty-one. The comparative table showed "how much more rapid and fatal the fever this year has been than in 1873. Counting from the twelfth of August, and including the three cases that occurred between then and the first, we have for the first twenty-six days the awful total of 1,051 deaths, against 558 for the same number of days in 1873."[5]

Relief workers felt the pressure as the epidemic picked up speed. Charles Fisher, head of the CRC, took a moment to write a short note to his sister: "Fever terrible over 400 new cases to day getting worse and worse."[6] Just before he fell ill, Reverend Charles Parsons reported to his bishop. "People constantly send to us, saying, 'Telegraph the situation.' It is impossible. Go and turn the Destroying Angel loose upon a defenseless city; let him smite whom he will, young and old, rich and poor, the feeble and the strong, and as he will, silent, unseen, and unfelt, until his deadly blow is struck; give him for his dreadful harvest all the days and nights from the burning midsummer sun until the latest heavy frost, and then you can form some idea of what Memphis and all this Valley is . . ."[7] Keating headlined a story THE CITY A CHARNEL HOUSE, and later estimated the death toll in early September at two hundred per day.[8]

THE TIDE OF DEATH was too much for Jack Walsh, the city undertaker, and his colleagues. For some time people had complained of the stench coming from bodies hidden in houses. Now unburied bodies lay in the city streets. The CRC set the police to watching the undertaker in an effort to get him to work faster, and they created a corpse-hunting squad of two policemen for each ward. The relief committee also funded a thirty-man gravedigger squad, to be commanded by two black men. On September 4 furniture wagons (the 1870s equivalent of moving vans) filled high with coffins rumbled back and forth to the municipal Potters Field all day long, but at nightfall sixty bodies still awaited burial. Luke Wright and Charles Fisher sent gravediggers to the Potters Field. Herbert Landrum described them digging like army sappers all day long and into the evening, by "the pale light of a new moon . . . like body snatchers, among the weird shadows of the night."[9]

HAVING CHOSEN TO STAY in Memphis and care for patients during the epidemic, Dr. William Armstrong was working for the Howard Association medical corps. By August 24 he was seeing thirty patients before noon, fifteen after. He still found time to write to his wife, Lula, several letters each week, sending news about neighbors, family, and friends, including the neighbors Mr. and Mrs. Benjamin Fithian and daughter Mary. Mrs. Fithian and Mary moved into the Armstrong house to take care of the doctor. (Normally surrounded by family, Armstrong was afraid to sleep in the house alone for fear that he would fall sick during the night.) As the epidemic worsened, the Fithians planned to leave, much to Armstrong's regret. However, Mrs. Fithian fell ill, then Mary, and the Fithian family stayed on Alabama Street for the rest of the summer.[10]

As the days wore on, Armstrong's letters reflected his growing anxiety.

"I feel sometimes as if my hands were crossed and tied, and that I am good for nothing, death coming upon the sick in spite of all that I can do." Although he despised the "cowardly" physicians who fled, he contemplated doing the same. He decided that to run would be folly, as he would probably take the disease with him and get sick in some place where there would be no experienced doctors to treat him. If he stepped out of the house, people instantly grabbed him and dragged him off to see yet another patient. "Poor people," he wrote, "I feel sorry but cannot help them." Four days later he wrote to Lula, "The fever is assuming a most fearful form, and no sign of abatement, in fact it looks more and more gloomy every day." By the last week in August the caseload he shared with another Howard physician had grown to 127. Despite all his anxiety, Armstrong stayed and did the best he could to help his patients. On September 1 he wrote to Lula, "I never was, in all my life, so full of sympathy and sorrow for suffering humanity."[11]

AMERICAN PHYSICIANS HAD DEVELOPED a basic regimen for treatment of yellow fever: at the onset of the fever, try to get the patient to sweat by covering him with blankets and giving him a warm footbath. (Some preferred to add mustard to the bath to increase the warming effect.) Give the patient a purgative to empty the stomach, an emetic to empty the bowels. Sponge baths will help lower the patient's temperature. Keep the patient hydrated with small but frequent sips of tea, ice water, or champagne. As the patient recovers, introduce light foods like broths, rice water, milk, and other bland substances. Above all, keep the patient quiet. Dr. Choppin, head of the Louisiana Board of Health, had prescribed this regimen; it was also the gist of what was termed the "Creole" treatment.[12]

To this simple course of treatment, physicians added embellishments of their own. Dr. Mitchell prescribed a treatment that followed the basic tenets described above, but he also drew from the increasingly old-fashioned "heroic" medicine tradition of the early nineteenth century, when doctors used various dangerous chemicals to induce vomiting and defecation. He purged his patients with calomel (a compound of mercury) and oil, sweated them, dosed them with quinine, advised sponge baths of cold water and whiskey for temperatures above 102 degrees, and prescribed various chemicals, including bicarbonate of potash, chloride of potash, and spirits of niter as diuretics. He also advised keeping the patient quiet for five days after the onset of fever. He said, "I do not permit any one to go in the sickroom but myself and nurse; in fact, the world closes on the patient until I turn him loose; he sees nothing, hears nothing, and remains perfectly quiet in bed."[13]

Although physicians boasted that their treatment would save the patient, there was no cure for yellow fever; there is no cure today. In 1878 Dr. Choppin of New Orleans wrote, *"We know of nothing in the way of remedies which will check the disease. I know of none.* Every kind of treatment meets with about equal success, or the results vary very little. Of course, common sense in the application of the treatment will do more than could be obtained without its exhibition. *Yet we are at a loss to know how to check the ravages of the fever* when it attacks the human body."[14]

Small wonder that people devised their own treatment regimens or that they sent Keating letters suggesting all manner of nostrums for the sick in Memphis. He published the letters without comment. In truth, medicines prescribed by graduates of the best southern medical schools were no better than the remedies worked up by Creole grannies. Sometimes the patients got better, and sometimes they died.

Most of the Memphis doctors had served in Civil War medical corps. They could perform surgery and use anesthesia to make it bearable for patients. They could deliver babies, although both mother and child might have been safer under the care of a midwife. They did not know what caused infection, but some of them understood the uses of carbolic acid to prevent it. They could set bones, remove bullets, or amputate injured arms or legs. But they could not cure yellow fever. A yellow fever victim's body was a battleground in which the virus strove against the patient's immune system. In that struggle, the patient's best ally was not a doctor, but a good nurse.

Today the word "nurse" immediately conjures an image of a woman clad in traditional starchy whites or the modern patterned scrubs, a professional conversant with medical science and modern technologies. Memphis's nurses were nothing like that. Of the nurses imported into Memphis during the epidemic, most were men. Few had any formal training. The nation's first schools for nursing, all in the northern states, had been operating for only a few years. However, the Civil War had given many Americans experience in simple nursing. Our image of the Civil War nurse is Clara Barton, later founder of the American Red Cross, but the poet Walt Whitman also served as a Union army nurse during the war. So did many other men, it being the practice to employ the walking wounded as nurses for those more seriously injured. Women learned nursing of a sort in the same way they learned to cook, sew, clean, and perform other household tasks.

For either sex, the Memphis epidemic offered opportunities. Anyone could call himself a nurse, come to Memphis, and collect pay from the Howards for sitting at the bedside of fever victims. The city's fraternal organizations also hired nurses for their members. Creoles or acclimated Anglos from the Gulf Coast were more experienced and more likely to survive than nurses from the West or North. Shreveport, Savannah, Charleston, Houston, and other cities sent nurses. Some were funded by their city of origin, others came for the pay.[15]

Although most were native-born Americans, Memphians called the nurses from elsewhere "foreign nurses." The newcomers did not have a good reputation. In the first place, black Memphians resented them as interlopers who poached jobs rightfully belonging to them. Others in Memphis focused on the character, or lack thereof, exhibited by the foreign nurses. A physician quoted in a Louisville *Courier-Journal* story said that the city's need for nurses drew to it "an invasion of cut-throats, thieves and prostitutes of as bad a type as ever trod the earth." Human vultures, the reporter called them, come to Memphis to pick over the leavings of the sick and dying.[16]

Since physicians prescribed champagne for yellow fever and used such spirits as brandy for rubbing alcohol, sickrooms contained copious amounts of free booze. This proved too great a temptation for some medical attendants. As Kezia DePelchin noted, too many of her colleagues took the alcohol intended for external application to patients and applied it internally to themselves.[17]

People who "made of the epidemic a carnival" infuriated Keating. He described how one nurse, "stupefied by wine and brandy, allowed a poor woman to leave her bed, naked as when born, and wander out into the country, on an inclement night, calling as she went, for her husband who had preceded her to the grave by a few days." Relief workers found two male nurses, half naked, passed out on the floor beside the dead body of their patient.[18]

Keating told the latter story in the context of an extended diatribe on the sexual misbehavior of nurses. He could not understand how anyone could be interested in illicit sex while nursing yellow fever victims. "There was nothing in the surroundings, or in the life, which was hurried forward with such rapidity to death, to prompt or encourage lewdness; on the contrary, there was everything to forbid and repel it." As far as he was concerned, it took a "propensity deliberately nursed" to stage orgies in the midst of a yellow fever epidemic. Apropos of one thief and her "paramours," he said primly that they had fallen "victims to the fever which they invited by their debauchery, and hastened by their excesses." Whores, thieves, drunks: the status of "foreign" nurses in Memphis was not high.[19]

Being from Houston, Kezia DePelchin struggled to maintain her dignity in the face of Memphians' ever-ready suspicion of foreign nurses. She refused to let patients call her by her first name, as if she were a servant. When one woman insisted that saying "Mrs. DePelchin" was too hard, she was grateful for once to have the first name of Kezia, which was not any easier to pronounce. Too short to be imposing, she was also far from being a beauty by the standards of the time. Rather than doe eyes, bow lips, and an expression of insipid innocence, she had deep-set eyes and a wide mouth curved toward a smile. At one point during her Tennessee adventures she noted that what she had done that day would be most romantic if one were young and pretty, which she was not. Heroines—or heroes, for that matter—are not expected to have a comic turn of mind or a self-deprecating sense of humor, traits amply exhibited in DePelchin's correspondence. But like her contemporary J. M. Keating, DePelchin had a life full of unexpected turns and intense drama.[20]

The nurse from Houston was born in 1828 on Madeira, a small island off the coast of Portugal most known for its fortified wines. Her father, an Englishman, had come to Madeira for the wine trade, but in the 1830s he decided to move his family to Texas. His wife having died, he sent his children off to the frontier under the supervision of their governess, Hannah Bainton. In 1837 they landed at Galveston in the brand-new Republic of Texas. Kezia's father, Abraham Payne, rejoined his family two years later, and in the summer of 1839 he married the governess, making her the children's legal mother and guardian. When a yellow fever hit Galveston that September, two of Kezia's siblings died. Her father, much weakened by the disease, lived until June of the following year. For the rest of her life Kezia retained a tender sympathy for the orphaned. Left alone in a strange land, Kezia and Hannah moved to Houston. A well-educated

Kezia Payne DePelchin. This photo, captioned "From an old photograph,"
appears in Harold J. Matthew's biography of DePelchin,
Candle by Night.

woman, Hannah quickly found a job as a teacher. She also tutored Kezia in reading, writing, arithmetic, German, French, and Latin and taught her to play piano on a paper keyboard until a friend supplied an actual instrument.

In 1843 Kezia Payne's life took another major turn. When Judge Benjamin Buckner, a wealthy, politically powerful jurist, lost his wife in childbirth, he asked the cultivated Hannah Payne to take care of his baby girl. Cordelia Buckner grew up to be a grand lady, daughter of a civic leader and married to a prominent man. Kezia and Hannah, although more than a notch above the average southern lady in education, were always working women, teaching school and giving music lessons to earn their living. One of their students later described Hannah as a "gentle, gray-haired English woman," and Kezia as "homely" but "exceedingly charitable" and fond of children. They were poor. But Hannah was the only mother that Cordelia Buckner Morris had ever known, and Kezia was

"Aunt Kizzie" to her children. Through Cordelia, the English governess and the orphan had connections to generations of Houston's upper class.[21]

During the Civil War, Kezia married a Belgian musician, Adolph DePelchin, seven years her junior, a widower with a small son. The marriage was a disaster. Years later her friends in Houston referred to him as a "little French dude" who "wasn't worth killing." He lived off Kezia's money but resented her going out to work. After a year she threw him out. A brief reconciliation in the 1870s produced the same results: Adolph took all her money and left. Nonetheless, they never divorced, and Kezia used her married name, Mrs. DePelchin, for the rest of her life.[22]

DePelchin's dear stepmother died in 1870, leaving her alone but also free of familial responsibilities. Now middle-aged, officially married but practically single, she could spend the meager income she earned through teaching however she pleased. She could travel, and she made a trip to the Centennial Exposition in Philadelphia in 1876. She did a great deal of charity work, funded in part by her upper-class friends. She was immune to yellow fever and had nursed in several epidemics, and when the Houston papers reported the impact of the fever on Grenada, Mississippi, she was free to go.[23]

In the last week of August, DePelchin took a five P.M. train from Houston for the fever zone along the Mississippi River. The following afternoon they pulled in at Little Rock to the music of a band assembled on the station platform to see off twenty volunteer nurses on their way to Memphis under the leadership of Dr. Edward T. Easley. All traffic from Little Rock to Memphis having been halted, the train took a circuitous route up to Charleston, Missouri, over the river into Kentucky, and down to Humboldt, Tennessee, where Dr. Easley telegraphed Memphis for passes permitting them into the city.[24]

On this long trip DePelchin found out that only three of the twenty Arkansas nurses had acquired immunity to the fever. She was horrified and did her best to convince the Arkansas volunteers to turn back. "No, they would not hear of such a thing. I was in hopes that even in the last, they would not be allowed to enter Memphis. The impulse is noble, to come to help suffering humanity, but it is like someone who cannot swim, plunging into a foaming torrent to save a drowning man . . ."

The train reached Memphis on August 31. To get to Grenada, DePelchin should have stayed on board. She didn't know that and got off the train in Memphis. Later she mused on how little things like misunderstood railroad schedules can alter the affairs of men—"and women, too, sometimes." Circumstance had put her on the train with the Little Rock contingent, and now a mistake about timetables led her to fall in with the rest of the nurses and follow them to the Peabody Hotel, where Howard president Langstaff met them. She had dinner and went to her room. It was clear to her that Memphis needed nurses now as much as Grenada did. She prayed for guidance: Should she stay in Memphis or go on to Grenada?

At nine P.M. there was a knock on her door. A man had come to the Peabody to get a nurse for a sick woman, but all the Howard volunteers were already out on cases. Would she go? Although she had intended to work without pay, Dr. Easley had explained to her that with Howard Association credentials she would receive essential organizational support. She and the young man went to the Howard office on Main, where she got a Howard badge, the 626th issued. As they walked on, her companion explained that he was a watchman. The sick woman had a companion, another young woman, he said, but no relatives. They arrived at a large house, elegantly carpeted and lighted with gas. Upstairs in a "handsomely furnished" room DePelchin found her patient, Myra, and her friend Linda. "I've brought you a nurse," the watchman said, and then quickly left. Someone had piled blankets and comforters on Myra and built a fire in the fireplace. DePelchin did what she could to lower the room's temperature, made her patient as comfortable as possible, and sent the other young woman to bed.

DePelchin was puzzled. "These women, whoever they are, seem so friendless, no one comes to see them or inquire after them," she wrote. Here was this house, so fine that a watchman had to be stationed to guard the property, but the women had no money "to buy the necessities of life," and the only food in the house was a loaf of bread furnished by the Howards. The next morning she found an open grocery, bought some coffee and crackers, and prepared to camp out. Dr. Burroughs, the attending physician, told her that instead of getting rooms at a downtown hotel, she could stay in the house. Although she remained there to care for her patients, she did not collect her trunk and move in. The place made her uneasy. She wrote to her sister, "I want to know where I am."

Every morning and evening, carts filled with coffins passed by the house on their way to Elmwood Cemetery. Linda got sick too, so the

Howards sent a black nurse out to help. Myra was nervous, her restless sleep tormented by bad dreams of a woman who tormented her. "Don't let me die like she did," she cried out. "She died so dreadful." Awake, she begged DePelchin not to leave her, explaining that Miss Mag was always after her. Putting together Myra's delirious talk and comments made by the other nurse, DePelchin finally figured out where she was: "This was one of those houses whose 'way is to hell, going down to the Chambers of Death.'" Her patients were prostitutes, and the deceased Miss Mag was their madam.[25]

SUPPLY AND DEMAND made the late nineteenth century the golden age of American brothels. The harsh economics of an industrializing society sent a steady supply of young women into the trade. Prostitution paid better than most jobs available to an uneducated daughter of the working class. Attitudes toward male sexuality insured a steady demand for whores. Believing that men needed sex more than women and that the male imperative had to be satisfied some way, many Americans considered brothels a necessary evil. Without them, men might debauch and ruin virgins or lure wives away from the home. Even worse, they might masturbate, a practice condemned by moralists as unnatural and by physicians as a danger to mental and physical health. Through their degradation, prostitutes protected the home and saved men from ruin. Prostitution also enabled men to have sex with limited economic consequences. In the new urban America, a middle-class child was a drain on family finances. During the nineteenth century the fertility rate for white American women declined with every decennial census. (Statistics on black women were not compiled before the Civil War.) In 1800 the fertility rate for a white woman was 7.04. By 1870 it was 4.55. (By 1900 it would be 3.56.) The only reliable way to avoid having children was to stop having sex. For men who lacked that level of self-control, prostitutes provided an outlet. Adultery was never morally acceptable, but society did not ostracize men who strayed, as long as they were discreet.[26]

The impulse to rescue fallen sisters led American women to establish asylums and halfway houses for prostitutes in most major American cities. In Memphis, the Women's Christian Association demonstrated their understanding of the problem by the way they approached it. In addition to founding the Navy Yard Mission for the fallen in 1872, they

opened a job placement agency for women and also supplied food, clothing, and money to the destitute.[27]

In July of 1878 the Shelby County grand jury proposed the establishment of legal, regulated brothels to be located in designated districts.
A debate ensued in the pages of the *Appeal*. None of the participants
signed their actual names, preferring to use pseudonyms. "Fair Play"
condemned the concept that prostitution was a necessary evil. "Necessary to whom?" Fair Play asked. "Surely not to the female part of the evil,
for the female part suffer untold pain and penalties, as well as unmea-
sured degradation." The writer condemned the hypocrisy of men who
arrested and jailed the prostitutes they themselves patronized. To end
the social evil, Fair Play said, men should learn to control themselves.[28]

Two members of the grand jury wrote letters defending their position. "He says that if all men were celibates, and would control and gov-
ern themselves, that this evil would be suppressed," wrote grand juror
#1. "This is evidently true, but what do impracticable theories amount
to in dealing with a subject that needs a practical remedy?" The social
evil served to protect virtue and prevent rape. Grand juror #2 argued
that removing the prostitutes would get them away "from our wives and
daughters—and sons, too." As far as ending prostitution, however, that
would require divine intervention.[29]

Although appalled by their occupation, DePelchin did not desert her
patients. Other Howard nurses were not willing to stay with Myra and
Linda: "They said the place was not 'spectable and the women swore at
them." The sick women never swore at Kezia. Around her, they wept,
begged her not to leave, and evidenced contrition for their lives of sin.
She decided that if God spared them to repent, she would nurse them
while they were sick and help them leave the life afterward.[30]

FAITH GAVE BELIEVERS like Kezia DePelchin an explanatory matrix
that helped them understand their experience and invest it with meaning. Faith supported them and gave them comfort. At one point during
the epidemic DePelchin helped transport an Irish maid named Bridget
to the Market Street Infirmary. As the ambulance neared the building,
Bridget "crossed herself and gave thanks that a church was opposite, its
shadow would fall on the house where she was sick." DePelchin wrote,
"This faith was a comfort to her. I was glad she had it." But faith was not

always a consolation. If you believed that you had a personal relationship with God, you had to ask Job's question: Why me? What did I do to deserve this? Why is God so cruel?

One of the Texas nurses had to tell two small children that the rest of their family was dead. She told DePelchin that the little boy cried out, "'Don't tell me that my mother is dead. God wouldn't be so mean as to take her.'" DePelchin met a woman who had lost her husband and two children to the illness. When Kezia offered sympathy, the woman told her to "hush," not to say a word. "I would not have God hear me murmur for anything. He may take these two from me if I am impatient," she said, pointing at her surviving children. DePelchin wrote, "But it is thus the people of Memphis look on it. This epidemic is a scourge."[31]

Scourge: God's whip to drive his people from their sins. Houston physician W. L. Coleman, although a white southerner, wrote years later that he believed yellow fever originated in "the notorious 'middle passage' with all its attendant atrocious horrors," and he argued that the disease was a scourge of "retributive justice" for the sin of slavery.[32] For centuries Judeo-Christian religious leaders taught their followers that disease (and any other form of bad fortune) was the punishment of God for sins. Coleman's hypothesis at least attributes to the Almighty a grand and somber motive for smiting the South. Antebellum American Christians typically attributed epidemics to more individualized sins, such as drunkenness and debauchery. By the 1870s, educated religious leaders were more likely to suggest that ignoring natural law—which was, of course, God's law—created conditions ripe for disease outbreaks. As Reverend Landrum put it, cleanliness was indeed next to godliness: "If indifferent to this virtue, you may expect only pestilence." On the other hand, some people contended that God's wrath had fallen upon Memphis for the sin of celebrating Mardi Gras.[33]

The mother who feared God's wrath if she grieved, the Catholic girl comforted by the mere shadow of a church, and the historically minded Dr. Coleman were Christians, as were most of the religious people in the Mississippi Valley in 1878. However, American Christendom of the 1870s was much more a beleaguered, divided, and contested place than nostalgia might suggest. One of the strongest challenges came from Gilded Age "freethinkers," a term that corresponds roughly to today's agnostic. Robert Green Ingersoll, a respected Republican leader, drew large crowds (and earned high fees) for speeches defending science and free thought.

Ingersoll ridiculed the idea that God smote humanity with plagues and asked why, if it were so, would anyone worship such a being?[34]

Friction between American Catholics and Protestants was serious and lasting. It had been several decades since Protestant mobs had attacked Catholic churches and burned convents, but many, perhaps most, American Protestants preserved a visceral animosity toward the Church of Rome, seeing it as the ancient enemy of true religion and a powerful contemporary opponent of progress and liberty. Protestant suspicion was not allayed by Pope Pius IX's 1864 Syllabus of Errors. As Protestants read it, the encyclical condemned separation of church and state, free exercise of religious belief, and the idea that the Papacy ought to accommodate itself to progress, liberalism, and modern civilization.

American Protestantism had its own divisions. As an example, consider the household of Dr. William Armstrong. The physician adored his wife, Lula, but he was a Presbyterian and she a Methodist. In the letters they wrote during the epidemic they continued what must have been a long-term debate over religion. Armstrong did not think his wife took her faith seriously enough. A Calvinist, he wanted Lula to put more faith in Providence. When Lula wrote to promise that she would amend her ways, he applauded her resolve and added that he hoped she would "not let this be a Methodist outburst, but a solid, square, faithful promise." Armstrong did not indicate that he thought his wife was a lost soul, but he did clearly think his version of Protestantism was better than hers. Baptists and Presbyterians and Methodists adhered to different doctrines, they thought that those doctrines mattered, and they expected congregants to understand their denomination's stance on infant baptism, missionary societies, church polity, predestination, the role of the Holy Spirit, and biblical inerrancy. There were divisions within denominations as well. Baptists in particular had a tendency to splinter over doctrinal differences, but all the major Protestant denominations had split into southern and northern branches before the Civil War and in the 1870s were as yet unreconciled.[35]

If you found all this unbearably tedious and irrelevant, Gilded Age America offered other alternatives. After the Civil War, grieving women often turned to Spiritualism. Through séances, their dead spoke to them, bringing hope of a happy reunion in the afterlife. Christian Universalists believed that a loving God had sent his Son to bring universal redemption and salvation. For both movements, the doctrinal quarrels that had divided Christians for centuries were essentially irrelevant.[36]

In this competitive religious arena, members of different denominations scrutinized the behavior of others for signs of true faith and pointed fingers at those found wanting. When the Memphis press reported that almost all the Protestant ministers had left the city during the stampede, Keating noted that "no discordant incident of the epidemic gave rise to more general indignation or as bitter comment in the public press." As to the behavior of Catholic priests and nuns, Keating acknowledged that "there could be no greater contrast." For Catholics, absolution from a priest was "considered a requisite to an assurance of final happiness— hence the pleading demands upon the priests." Catholic priests had been "tireless in the administration of their sacred offices," he said. "They obeyed every call."[37]

As bishop of the Diocese of Nashville, Patrick A. Feehan had oversight of Memphis's five Catholic churches: St. Bridget's, St. Mary's, St. Patrick's, St. Peter's, and St. Joseph's. On the day when the newspapers announced the epidemic, priests from all over the diocese came to Feehan's Nashville offices to volunteer for service in Memphis. In the years after, the bishop was never able to speak of that day. The priests stationed in Memphis stayed at their posts and died. Those sent to replace them died. The Reverend Denis Alphonsus Quinn, a mission priest based in Memphis, later wrote about the epidemic and about the men with whom he served. The sketches below are drawn from Quinn's memoir.[38]

Father Martin Walsh of St. Bridget's liked a good laugh and never gave a beggar less than a dollar. He walked through the Irish districts of Memphis as if on the road from Tipperary, and rowdy crowds of men "would take to sudden flight at the first wave of his blackthorn." Just before the fever arrived, Walsh fell from his horse and broke his foot. His cousin Father Michael Meagher came from Nashville to visit him and stayed to help out during the epidemic. Walsh limped from house to house on his crutches until he was too sick to go on. Walsh died on August 29, his cousin Michael on August 30.[39]

Father Martin Riordan of St. Patrick's, vicar general of the Diocese of Nashville, read eighteenth-century English essayists and did calculus and geometry for amusement. His sermons drew Protestants who simply liked to hear him talk. The old Irish ladies loved him because he had been born in Ireland, had the Gaelic, and could hear their confessions in their mother tongue. Seriously overweight and in bad health, Riordan made his way on foot to carry the sacraments to the sick until, exhausted, he contracted the fever and died on September 17.

Father J. J. Mooney was an Irish patriot, always ready to discourse upon the oppression of his native land by the perfidious British. He sang Irish ballads and conversed with Riordan in Gaelic. He had worked for years at Christian Brothers College in Memphis, but in 1878 he was reassigned to Nashville. When the epidemic broke out, Mooney thought that his transfer had been God's way of saving him from exposure to the disease. But the bishop sent him back to the city, so Mooney wrote his will and ordered masses for his own soul. He died on September 27.[40]

The Franciscans maintained a friary in Memphis and provided priests for St. Mary's, the parish church for German Catholics. Letters from the friary wound up at Quincy College in Illinois and in 1977 were translated from the German and made available in typed format by the Reverend August Reyling, OFM. At the time when the epidemic broke out, Father Maternus Mallman was engaged in an attempt to get one of the brothers removed from Memphis. On August 14 Father Maternus wrote to his superior, "Father Herman is drunk from morning to night" and, he added, likely to make all the other priests die of sheer vexation.

For the next several days Father Maternus's letters alternated short descriptions of worsening conditions in Memphis, long descriptions of Father Herman's bad behavior, and brief statements of his own personal desire to be elsewhere than Memphis. Gradually Father Maternus became more concerned about the epidemic. "The Yellow Fever is making headway in a horrifying manner," he wrote on August 17. "All its victims die." After that, the file contains letters from Franciscans volunteering for service in Memphis. All the priests who stayed at the friary died, including Father Maternus, except Father Aloysius Wiewer. The son of German immigrants, Wiewer had joined the Franciscans in his early twenties and in 1878 was probably not yet thirty. Having contracted the fever in 1873, he was one of the few priests with immunity.

On September 27 Father Aloysius sent a letter to Father Herman, who had left the city at some point during the epidemic. After express-

Father Aloysius Wiewer, O.F.M. On September 27, he wrote,
"All persons around me are dying; I alone am spared." From
The Book of Three States: Notable Men of Mississippi, Arkansas and
Tennessee *(Memphis: Commercial Appeal Publishing Company, 1914).*

ing relief that Herman was still alive, Aloysius wrote, "We had, in our
Friary, six deaths within fourteen days." He added, "For the past four
weeks I am all alone here in the midst of a terrible epidemic. All persons around me are dying; I alone am spared." Thin, with a long, pale
face and wire-rimmed glasses, Aloysius walked through the filthy Memphis streets on sandaled feet, wearing the dark wool Franciscan robe
and hood in the summer heat. Father Quinn considered Father Aloysius
a living saint and argued that he had done more "priestly work" than anyone else in Memphis.[41]

At the end of the epidemic, Bishop Feehan stood at the altar of St.
Bridget's to preside over the funeral of twelve of his priests. No one
knows how many Catholic nuns died in Memphis. Father Quinn thought

that at least fifty had perished there in yellow fever epidemics during the epidemic years, but contemporary sources give different numbers. *Donahoe's Magazine*, an Irish Catholic publication, tallied the 1878 fever deaths by the diocese from which they came, not the place where they died. They counted 20 nuns from Nashville, 23 from New Orleans, 10 from Natchez, and 1 from Mobile. *Donahoe's* did not include the midwestern contingent. A German Franciscan nursing order, the Sisters of St. Mary, had found refuge from Bismarck's *Kulturkampf* in St. Louis. Mother Mary Odilia Berger sent thirteen nuns, one third of the congregation, to Memphis and to Canton, Mississippi. All of them contracted the fever, and five died.[42]

Kezia DePelchin, a Protestant and proud of it, could not understand why people thought she was a Catholic. She habitually wore a broadbrimmed straw hat, a calico wrapper dress, a leather belt, and a watch attached to her dress with a black ribbon; she did not wear a black robe, white veil, or cross. Finally a man explained it to her. Other nurses seemed most concerned about money, but Kezia did not care about money at all. Although many nurses refused to do household chores like cooking or cleaning, Kezia would turn her hand to anything that helped a patient or the patient's family. When an old Irishman worried about going hungry without a cook, Kezia went out to the kitchen and made him coffee, bacon, and a pan of biscuits. When a patient complained of chill, she took the wool petticoat she had shucked because of the heat and used it in lieu of a blanket. While on a nursing assignment in the Mississippi countryside she fed chickens and pigs. People thought that nurses who behaved like that had to be Catholic nuns.[43]

The Catholic priests who died in Memphis have histories. Most of the Catholic nuns do not. From wire reports, *Donahoe's* gleaned the names of Mother Alphonse, Josepha, and Mary Dolora, Dominican nuns who taught arithmetic, geography, botany, natural philosophy, rhetoric, history, and good English grammar at St. Agnes Academy, one of the oldest and most prestigious schools in Memphis. When the epidemic began, the sisters volunteered to help the sick. Keating wrote, "Unlike the regular nurses, they never suspended to revitalize their wasted energies . . . Tired nature, wanting the sweet restorer, broke under the strain. They went down before the reaper like ripened grain." Seven of the sisters died before the first week of September. *Donohoe's* also lists Vincentia and Stanislaus, Franciscans; and Maria Joseph, superior of the Convent of the Good Shepherd. Keating provided additional names: Mary Bernadine, Mary Veronica, Wilhelmina, Gertrude, and Winkelman. Since nuns then received new names on taking holy orders, the names tell us nothing about the persons. The Marys and Marias could have been erudite, fond of Shakespeare, good musicians, deeply loyal to Eire, or homesick for Bavaria. They could have been uneducated, superfluous children of the poor. Presumably individuals to their sisters and personalities within their orders, these obedient daughters of the church left little mark in the chronicles of the epidemic. That we know their names at all is due to Keating and the other journalists of Memphis.[44]

WHILE THE CATHOLIC CLERGY earned plaudits, the Protestant clergy failed to clothe themselves in glory. Catholic writers took pride in their priests and nuns while graciously excusing Protestant ministers from similar martyrdom in a way that made it clear how far a preacher was from a priest. Father Quinn explained that a dying Catholic needed a priest to hear his confession and "hand him over to his creator." (Quinn added, "Unfortunately, many Catholics defer half a century of repentance till the moment of death.") Protestant tenets did not require that the dying make confession and receive absolution. The New Orleans *Morning Star and Catholic Messenger* said, "A Protestant minister is not bound to sacrifice himself for his flock: he did not take vows to that effect on the day of his ordination, and his first duty as a man and father, is to himself and family." As to the accusation that Protestant clergy had deserted their posts, the writer asked, what posts? Noting that "a post implies duties," the writer listed the ways in which a minister was extraneous to the process of living and dying in a religious manner. All he did was "read a little, pray a little and sermonize a little." Since the minister knows "that his services can be performed by any layman, that he really has no help for the dead and dying, and having no duties to perform, how can he be accused of desertion, or blamed for a simple act of prudence?"[45]

BORN AND EDUCATED in Georgia, formerly pastor of the First Baptist Church in Savannah, the Reverend Dr. Sylvanus Landrum had no deep ties to Memphis. His decision to stay during the epidemic was based on his concept of duty. As he explained later, "There is no fixed rule in the matter of a minister's leaving. There are ministers who are not pastors; there are editors, business men or teachers, they can go. There are *exceptional* cases among pastors, as where a family is in such a condition that they cannot remain, and the husband is obliged to be with them. The general rule, however, is that *pastors must remain with their people during epidemics.*" Running from danger would bring disrespect to the cause of Jesus. When the fever broke out, Reverend Landrum said, "I went to the citizens meeting; aided in its organization; took my place on a ward committee and went to work."[46]

Reverend Landrum and his wife, Eliza Jane, had four children. His oldest son was pastor at a church in Georgia; his daughter had married a Georgia Baptist minister. The Landrums' two youngest sons, Herbert and George, were still at home. Herbert was twenty-two and, as we have seen, employed as an editor on the *Avalanche*, while George, nineteen, was a law student. When Reverend Landrum made the decision to stay in Memphis, Herbert insisted on staying too. Although George and Mrs. Landrum at first agreed to evacuate to the suburbs, Mrs. Landrum soon returned to the family home. The Landrums managed to get George out of town by assigning him to escort the children of a family friend to their relatives in Georgia. Herbert and his father went out day and night into the stricken city but returned to their home in a district free from fever until Herbert Landrum's boss, R. A. Thompson, editor of the *Avalanche*, came down with the fever. Herbert was devoted to Thompson and took responsibility for the older man's care. In order to nurse him, Herbert brought Thompson into the Landrum family home.[47]

"MY DEAREST ONE," Dr. Armstrong wrote. "Gloom impenetrable, through which there is no view to mortal eyes, hangs over our dear Memphis. The sights that now greet me every hour of the day are beyond the much talked of 1873, as that year was to me something new and beyond anything I had ever known." While Memphis's best people died by the dozens, he said, "we poor doctors stand by abashed, at the perfect uselessness of our remedies. What it is, what it is going to do with us all, is something that only God, in his wisdom, can reveal. It is appalling, startling, and makes the very bravest quake." He implored Lula, "Do take care of yourself and the children, as we want some of the human race left. Very few will be left here." Then he added, "Menken is dead."[48]

It is hard to avoid the conclusion that Nathan Menken saw the epidemic as something of a release from the tedium of commerce. His brothers needed him in the business, and by all accounts he was good at it. But the enthusiasm with which he dived into relief work, the joie de vivre he displayed in the charnel house suggests a man set free to be his preferred self. In Menken's case, that persona seems to have been a soldier.

The former Union cavalry officer wrote to his wife, "I am doing battle, and I feel as strong as a rock. I'm cheerful; I laugh, and my heart is firm, and when my children grow up let them do likewise. No running when duty calls, they can only die once, and let it be with their faces to the enemy." He told his sister that he would stay in Memphis "until the enemy pulls me down. I want to do all the good I can." Going among the sick and poor, he was able to make many people happy, something he thought a rare privilege. "People say I'm doing much good, and I'm well satisfied. I'm quite ready to fight the monster, as ready as I was to enlist in '61. Am well and cheerful, strong in my trust in God's love and protection, and if I fall I'm sure He judges right."[49]

His name runs through the chronicle of the epidemic. Here he is, putting up money for cleaning streets, volunteering to shoot looters, supervising a district for the Howards. Troubled to hear that people in Memphis were going hungry, he told Luke Wright to have a thousand loaves of bread baked and distributed, and send him the bill. A co-worker described him in those days: "Ah, how he worked and sweated, how he walked and ran and rushed from hovel to hovel, from sick-bed to sick-bed! What little heed he paid to the many letters and telegrams from relatives and friends [abroad] to leave the 'Hot-bed of pestilence.' "[50]

On the last Friday in August he worked all day, returned to his room in the Peabody Hotel, went to bed early, and never got up again. Keating wrote, "Everything that was possible to medical skill and the nursing of a devoted friend was done for him, but without avail." He died on Monday, September 2, and was given a large funeral by the standards of Memphis during the epidemic. One of the richest men in town went to the graveyard followed by one hack and three buggies.[51]

In addition to removing a mainstay from the lives of his brothers, his

children, and his wife, Menken's death took from the relief work an energetic, intelligent worker, a man Keating considered worth a committee by himself. In his illness Menken had been attended by Leopold
Iglauer, a Menken Brothers partner, and Samuel R. Meyer. The latter was
Menken's ward, taken in and employed at age eleven, now about twenty-
one. Exhausted by his efforts to save Menken, late in the epidemic Iglauer
contracted the fever and died. Meyer ran the Memphis store until the epidemic was over.[52]

WITH GEORGE HARRIS and Charles Parsons both gravely ill, Constance
took charge of St. Mary's Cathedral's local relief efforts and also served
as liaison with the northern communities that supplied critical financial
support. A church historian later wrote, "It was hers to overlook everything; to decide for others, and give them their orders; to keep the accounts
of three houses; to receive and disburse all moneys that came, to receive
and distribute the supplies; to answer letters and conduct the correspondence; to cheer her companions, to set them an example of courage—in
short she bore the weight of everything, and was the center and heart
of all."

Hundreds of requests for help poured in every day. Mother Harriet
sent Constance three additional nuns, but their presence did little to alleviate the overwhelming workload. The nuns ran from one crisis to the
next. Later, people would say that the sisters had worked themselves to
death and wonder why they had been so foolhardy, so lacking in wisdom. The need was so great that the sisters felt they had no choice but to
respond. In defense of Constance, one survivor asked, "How could she
hold back, from fatigue, or weakness, or wisdom!"

Sister Ruth, one of the nuns sent to Memphis at Constance's request,
wrote back to the motherhouse describing the situation at the Canfield
Asylum. As the city's orphanage for black children, the asylum was
staffed by an African American couple. As Sister Ruth saw it, the man's
job was to cook for "us," and the woman's job was to care for six black
children, one of whom was very sick. Ruth and two other white women
had charge of almost fifty children. "We are helpless and do not know
what to do nor how help can come," she said. "We have no clean clothes,
and it is utterly impossible to get any washing done. There is no one to
send for supplies, and no stores are open." She added, "It looks utterly

hopeless, and all we can do is to go on until each one drops. A box of clothing is at St. Mary's, but there is no way of getting it here; no wagons of any kind; and it would be just the same with provisions . . . Money is quite useless; there is plenty of money here, but it buys no head to plan, no hands to wash, nor the common necessaries of life."[53]

"I HAVE QUITE A HOSPITAL, in and around my house," William Armstrong wrote to Lula. It was September 6, and he had been parted from his family for three weeks. "Dr. Harris and Mr. Parsons both quite ill. Sister Constance and Thecla at the school. Jim Tighe's family in Collins' grocery—two sick at Goldsmiths—two at old Tighe's—and poor Mary Fithian taken down today." He was now the physician in charge for more than a hundred orphans under the care of the "kind and attentive" Sisters of St. Mary. The workload was heavy. "I wish I could go to some spot where there would be no burning heads and hands to feel, nor pulses to count, for the next six months—it is fever, yellow fever, all day long, and I am so wearied."[54]

FIVE

The Arithmetic of Sorrow

THERE WERE ONLY THIRTY-TWO HOWARDS, all male. This small group canvassed the city, visited the sick, doled out supplies, supervised volunteers, scheduled work for 111 doctors and a nursing corps that ultimately numbered 2,995, and ran an infirmary. As Howard Association president Langstaff pointed out, the Howards did not "anticipate, in the early days of the epidemic, that it would assume the proportions that it afterward did assume; that citizens would die at the rate of five and six score per day; that instead of providing two or three hundred persons with nurses and assistance, we would provide for twice as many thousands . . ." The workload would have stretched their resources had all been acclimated and immune, but they were not. Twenty-five of them contracted the fever. On any given day of the epidemic, someone in the Howards was likely to be down with the fever or recovering. Or dying: ten of the Howards perished in the epidemic.[1]

A Howard's duty necessitated close contact with the sick. Doctors could state categorically that yellow fever was not contagious, but that did little to allay a man's visceral reaction to walking into a room splattered floor to ceiling in black vomit, discovering corpses in unexpected locations, or finding dying parents lying in the same room as their child's maggot-ridden body—the emotional freight of such work was high indeed. Keating said that seeing so much suffering was "calculated to dull ones sense of realization, and what to us would hardly attract attention would curdle the blood of those less accustomed to them. Thus it is that we become more fearless, and are better fitted to endure the trying scenes that we are daily witnesses of." Weighed down with fear, grief, pity, and exhaustion, the Howards stayed on the battlefront.

Those felled by the fever came back to work as soon as they were able. Louis Daltroop, a young Jewish man, took charge of the Howards' own burial corps and interred the ten Howards who died.[2]

"WHO HAS THE HEART TO USE the multiplication table in the arithmetic of sorrow, and figure out the hearts broken, the lives embittered, the houses desolated?" Herbert Landrum asked. "Surely our cup of sorrow must be full."[3] In the first week of September, Landrum devoted much of his time to nursing R. A. Thompson, now lying ill with fever at Herbert's family home. Thompson had survived the first stage of the disease. He felt so well that he disregarded Dr. Mitchell's advice to lie still, and he reversed his position in the bed so that he could better read the morning papers. When the second stage of the disease hit Thompson hard, Dr. Mitchell attributed its severity to his reckless behavior. Sixteen hours after Mitchell found him reading papers and drinking tea, Thompson lay dying, Herbert Landrum by his side.[4]

That night, Herbert's father was called to the bedside of the family's physician. "I found him hopeless with the fever," Reverend Landrum recalled later. "Such quantities of black vomit as he threw up, I had never seen before." The dying man comforted his pastor, assuring him that his faith was secure, his mind filled with thoughts of Jesus and happy anticipation of joining his late mother in heaven. Landrum stayed with the physician until his death in the early morning. When he returned home at dawn, he found that Thompson had died during the night. His last service to his son's employer was to officiate at his funeral.[5]

The *Avalanche* published the following on September 4. Although no byline is given, both the writing and the subject matter indicate that Herbert Landrum was the author and that the piece was composed on the previous day as Thompson lay dying.

Break, break, break!
   Break on the cold, gray stones of hearts, oh sea of Sorrow and of Death!
   Monotonous as the breakers' surging moan, the tide of death moves solemnly up in the night of wo, and wave after wave, white-capped with the pallor of the graves, strikes the city and rolls over it. The living sits as the melancholy mourner by the sad sea-waves, watching the

tide's terrible work, scanning the faces of despair, up-turned and terror-stricken, in the flood, and giving a shriek of anguish as, swept by, appears one he loves. A moment, and the death-wave, receding, has borne that dear spirit off upon the boundless sea of Eternity.

Grief-stricken and tired, Herbert fell ill. People assumed that he had the fever, but soon he was back at work at the *Avalanche*, presiding over a much-diminished workforce and describing the disintegration of Memphis.[6]

KEZIA DEPELCHIN UNDERSTOOD the arithmetic of sorrow: "Oh when I look at the cart piled up with rough coffins, and think how some heart goes yearning out after each one, it fills me with a sadness I cannot find words to express." Yet her personal experience in Memphis began well. Myra and Linda, the two young prostitutes, were relatively easy patients. J. M. Trigg,[7] one of the Arkansas nurses contingent, delivered meals to the brothel when Kezia could not walk to the canteen. After the Howards sent out an additional nurse to help, DePelchin felt that her charges could manage without her at night. She took on another patient, spending a night nursing a woman who lived in an alley by the river in a Memphis slum so vile that the local nurse, a black woman, refused to enter it. When DePelchin returned unharmed at daybreak and chided the other nurse for her fear, the woman retorted, "You see, Miss, you don't know nothing about that neighborhood, and I does."

Taking a break during the daylight hours, DePelchin went to the Howards for a lodging ticket. She rented a "neat little room" at the Chambers House on Second Street, retrieved her trunk, much battered and broken in transit, changed clothes, and no longer felt like "a stray dog without home or master." She went back to visit her patient in the slums that night and realized that the woman did not have yellow fever. She was recovering from a beating administered by her husband for visiting her dying sister. The husband was not in the hospital, as DePelchin had thought, but in jail. DePelchin agreed to spend the night there, but after nightfall a Howard man came to take her back to her first patients. The nurse left there had deserted Myra and Linda. Although the Howards had sent a nurse to take care of the battered woman, she wanted her

husband back and asked DePelchin to intervene to get the man out of
jail. DePelchin wrote, "O woman! the same trusting fool everywhere."

Back at the brothel, Myra had taken a turn for the worse. She did not
recognize DePelchin and begged for the return of the woman who was
already standing at her bedside: "You are very good to me, but I love my
first nurse the best." At the end of the day DePelchin put on the dress
she had changed out of at the hotel, and Myra was finally convinced that
the "first nurse" had been there all along. Although DePelchin feared
that Myra would not live through the night—she was restless, nervous,
and had to be watched constantly—the young woman rallied and gradually improved.

On Friday night DePelchin had a piece of stale bread for supper, and
for breakfast in the morning some dry crackers. She ran out of coffee.
When the Howard visitor arrived, she told him to send a relief nurse, as
she was worn out. She went to her hotel room and to bed at noon on Saturday, slept for fifteen hours, and woke up in an optimistic mood. Her
first patients looked likely to pull through.[8]

ON THE AFTERNOON of September 5, one of the sisters found Constance resting on the sofa in the convent parlor. "I knew at once that she
was very ill," the sister later recalled. "She insisted that it was only a
slight headache, and would not listen to my entreaties that she would go
to bed, but continued dictating letters (acknowledgments of receipts of
offerings, goods, etc.) to Mrs. Bullock, who sat writing at her side. Her
face was flushed with the fever." Dr. Armstrong was passing the house,
and the sister called him in. Constance told him that she was not sick:
"It is only a bad headache; it will go off at sunset." Sent to bed, Constance refused a mattress. If she had the fever, they would have to burn
it. Later that afternoon Thecla came back from visiting a dying woman.
She told one of the nuns, "'I am so sorry, Sister, but I have the fever.
Give me a cup of tea, and then I shall go to bed.'"[9]

DEPELCHIN'S PATIENTS AT the brothel were well enough to leave with
less skilled nurses, so she went to the Howard infirmary to visit her
friend from Little Rock, J. M. Trigg, who had the fever. She found him

lying on a government cot in the infirmary, under the care of an experienced nurse from Charleston. All she could think to do to help was to leave her watch to be used for timing medicine doses. While waiting at the office for a new assignment, DePelchin encountered an old friend, a clergyman who ran toward yellow fever epidemics rather than away. The Reverend Dr. W. D. Dalzell of Shreveport had hired Kezia Payne as church organist when he was minister at Christ Church Episcopal in Houston in 1858. Born in Jamaica, Dalzell studied medicine and theology in Britain and held doctor of divinity degrees from the See of Canterbury and the University of the South. A physician as well as a priest, Dalzell had come to help out at St. Mary's Episcopal Cathedral, where his coreligionists were beset by troubles. How DePelchin's new assignment came about is not clear; perhaps Dalzell asked for her specifically, or perhaps the Howards thought that she might be sent to a nicer place after spending a week nursing prostitutes in a brothel. At any rate, shortly after meeting Dalzell, she was on her way to St. Mary's Episcopal. It was the beginning of her worst experience in Memphis.[10]

Kezia DePelchin was indeed an exceedingly charitable person. She did her best to be kind to persons of all creeds. However, her charity did not necessarily extend to the creed itself. DePelchin hated Catholicism with a fervor that suggests prejudice inculcated from childhood. Her first sight of the Anglo-Catholic Sisters of St. Mary puzzled her; the second provoked the indignant fulminations about dark ages and what Martin Luther would think that were quoted in a previous chapter. Fortunately for her and the sisters, she had been sent to the cathedral by mistake. Her job was actually out at the Church Home for orphan children run by Sister Frances. During the buggy ride out, she worried about the slippery slope from Protestant nunneries to Catholicism triumphant. She envisioned the "grey turrets of convent or monastery" frowning from every hill. "I dread to see these encroachments," she wrote. "I know in our fair island, they are not so much the homes of the peaceful shepherd of the sheep, but of wolves, who feed on them."[11]

At the Church Home, DePelchin was assigned to nurse eight children. She saw immediately that Lena, a German girl, was dying. "It is one of the peculiarities of yellow fever that the dying will try to get up, sometimes they will fight, anything to get away, and are very cunning in trying to get up when no one is looking at them." While DePelchin was occupied with the other children, Lena jumped out of bed, tried to get out the window, and even attacked the child in the next cot. She muttered continually through black lips. Her arms and legs were purple and trembling. After DePelchin put her arms around Lena and spoke to her in German, the child laid her head in DePelchin's lap. "She lasted a few hours, then her sufferings were over," DePelchin wrote.

The death of her first patient set the pattern for DePelchin's stay at the Church Home. Over the next few days, three children died. The surviving children were hard to manage. Dr. Armstrong barked at Kezia for following the instructions given by another doctor the previous day. The building itself was well lighted and pleasant, but fumes from the pans of carbolic acid that had been placed in each room made breathing difficult. DePelchin, citing her Houston experience, managed to get the amount of disinfectant reduced. When three Charleston nurses were sent out to the home, DePelchin took the opportunity to go into town for supplies and rest.

She walked in the rain to the Howard office, took care of her errand, and then went to call on the sick nurses in the rooms above the office. The news was all bad. "The best the only friend I had in Memphis, J. M. Trigg, was now gone," she wrote. "May God reward him for his kindness to those he nursed, and to me, a stranger." And she added that as she left, "I saw the cart piled with coffins, as usual, and almost wished that one was for me, so bitter was my life becoming."

Back at the Church Home, DePelchin found nothing to please her or alleviate her depression. She thought Sister Frances, just recovered from the fever, too ill and nervous to take charge of the situation. She disapproved of the way that nurses were shifted from child to child: "If I could have had the same ones all the time, I could have done better." Already disposed to frown on Sister Frances's habit, she was appalled yet again when she noticed that its buttons were marked with death's-heads. "I asked her how she could wear anything so horrid? I declare it put me in mind of that chapel of skulls in the Franciscan monastery in Madeira. I remember how we used to go on the other side [sic] the street when we went that way, and here was a Christian woman wearing Death's regalia from choice. I thank God for a brighter Faith."

That night was "a mixture of tragedy and comedy," she said. "Two of the children were very ill, one a boy eleven years was wild, he would jump out of bed the moment I left him to wait on the rest. If I turned round to administer medicine to the others, he was after me. I caught him round the waist and carried him back to bed at least ten times before midnight . . . and when I tell you I had but one bedpan for all these children you will appreciate my position." In the next room, a child named Charlie had a nurse to himself. Someone had promised the nurse a bonus of fifty dollars if Charlie recovered. DePelchin never learned the story behind Charlie's special treatment, but at one A.M. she found out that some of her patients knew about it and resented it. The largest child in the room had been sleeping and had missed a dose of medicine. When she woke up, she refused to take it because DePelchin had "waited on those little ones first." The girl kicked against the wall and woke all the other children. Pandemonium ensued. DePelchin feared that the noise would cost some of the children their lives. The twelve-year-old seemed especially angry at Charlie's special treatment, asking if he was better than she. Another child offered DePelchin her entire earthly fortune, fifteen cents, if DePelchin would cure her.

DePelchin thought that the Church Home had sufficient nursing staff to care for the twenty sick children in residence. What they lacked was a support system for the nurses themselves. No one prepared regular meals for the nurses; there was "not even a mattress to lie down on." Although DePelchin was on the night shift, Sister Frances objected to her going to town to sleep. "She thought a nurse ought to set up at least a week without sleep. I told her a Corliss Engine would want greasing in that time, and I was made of other material and had nerves that clamored for rest." DePelchin did not return to the home until after dinner. Meanwhile, Sister Frances had gone into the city.

DePelchin wanted to check on Fannie, a seven-year-old who had been severely ill the night before. No one knew where she was. Finally the African American cook directed DePelchin to the room where she had nursed the first night. On the porch just outside lay the body of a dead child. "The living one was inside alone, her hair was black, but not blacker than her mouth which was covered with flies, attracted by the blood that gurgled up to her lips; and not blacker than the heart that left her there to die." Fannie begged DePelchin not to leave her, saying, "I can't fight these flies." The room stank of blood and the excrement-filled vessel by the bed. When Kezia picked up the bucket to take it out, Fannie screamed, "Don't leave me, don't." DePelchin took off her hat and watch and told Fannie, you can see that I must come back for them. Clearly, Fannie understood that she had been left to die.

DePelchin set to work. She cleaned out the slops, got a fan to drive away the flies, gave the child laudanum via enema, warmed flannels and put them on her stomach, and rubbed her with whiskey. She built up the fire in the grate and improvised a bedpan from an old washbowl. About dusk a wagon arrived with three coffins—one for the corpse on the porch, one for another sick child, and one for Fannie, who was still alive. "Horrorstruck and bewildered," DePelchin wondered if Sister Frances had gone crazy: "I really believe the sight of so many dying had affected her brain." When Sister Frances came home at eight P.M., she sent for DePelchin to come and take charge of the room where she had worked the night before. Kezia refused to go. Sister Frances sent again, "saying the Howards sent me out there to nurse more than one. I again replied, if she wanted me she must send the sheriff, I would not leave for any other authority." Finally Sister Frances came herself, but DePelchin insisted that she would care for no one other than Fannie that night.

As the hour grew late, Mrs. Harman, one of the other nurses, came to the room to get some rest. She lay down on the floor, using Kezia's shawl as a pillow, and went to sleep. Fannie drifted off to sleep at dawn. When she woke, she took DePelchin's hand and asked that Mrs. Harman be called too. Fannie told them that she had dreamed of Paradise. "'I thought it was so beautiful. I thought I was walking there and you and Mrs. Harman were walking with me. Now let me go to sleep and dream that pretty dream again.'"

A child had been left alone to die, covered in filth and tormented by flies. When DePelchin walked out of that room in the morning light, she was ready for a fight. "You are angry," the cook remarked. DePelchin said, "I want to know what sort of people you have here. I thought I was coming among Christians. I believe I have stumbled among heathens." She confronted Sister Frances. Why was Fannie left alone? The sister replied that she had removed Fannie from the room where the other children were because she thought the child must die and she was concerned about the impact on Fannie's sister, who had just come down with the fever. That was all right, DePelchin said, but why did you leave her alone? Sister Frances replied that she thought Fannie was unconscious. She added that she had to get the children buried as soon as they died. She also had duties at the convent, where everyone was sick. Why did you order the coffins? DePelchin asked. "Fannie knew you thought she would die, now I think she will die." DePelchin continued, "I come from Texas, where you all look on us as a wild and reckless sett [*sic*], but I have yet to see such cruelty. A frontier Indian would blush through his war-paint at such a deed." Sister Frances "turned very pale and promised it should not happen again."

Assured that Fannie would remain under the care of Mrs. Harman, DePelchin left the home that morning, announcing that she would not return. She knew that her diatribe had made her presence disagreeable. Back in town, she tried to find Dr. Dalzell, but could not. She left word that a doctor must be sent out to the home and promised herself that she would speak to someone who could see that the children were not left as Fannie had been.

DePelchin's anger blazed through the last lines of her letter, in which she made comparisons between the Church Home and the brothel. "One the depth of sin and misery, the other claiming to be the abode of peace and holiness, but ah! Human nature judges too much by appearance. Christ reads the heart."[12]

Had DePelchin listened carefully to Sister Frances, had she been willing to put aside her prejudices and see the sister as what she was—a young woman, new in her vocation, worn down by illness, doing a job for which she was not trained in an alien city far from home—she might have had more charity. She might have listened when Frances said that she was needed at the convent because everyone was sick there. DePelchin did not know what was happening at St. Mary's Episcopal and by all indications did not want to know.[13]

ON THE EVENING of September 6 Dr. Armstrong wrote Lula a letter combining (characteristically) the mundane and the tragic. "Everything with me tonight is terribly blue," he wrote. The cook was sick, and how was he to get his coffee in the morning? He wanted to run away "like a coward," but he knew that his patients needed him. "I will lose Rev. Dr. Parsons tonight, and possibly one or two of the sisters—Mr. Harris with care will get well."[14]

Charles Parsons was not afraid of death. In the Civil War Battle of Perryville, he had defended a Union artillery battery with a single gun until the advancing Confederate infantry was within musket range. When the Confederate infantry commander ordered his men to shoot the Union officer, Parsons drew his sword and stood at parade rest, head high, face toward the foe. Impressed by this display of courage, the Confederate commander ordered his men to let Parsons retreat unharmed.[15] Parsons approached his death by fever with the same gallantry. No other Episcopal priest being available, he read for himself the last commendatory prayer in the Order for the Visitation of the Sick: "O Almighty God, with whom do live the spirits of just men made perfect, after they are delivered from their earthly prisons: We humbly commend the soul of this thy servant, our dear *brother*, into thy hands . . ." He died on the evening of September 6 and was buried in John Lonsdale's plot in Elmwood Cemetery.[16]

Constance faded away. She was not in pain, only so tired. She worried about the orphans and in her delirium rambled on about her accounts. Dr. Dalzell arrived from Louisiana on Saturday and the following morning celebrated Holy Communion in Constance's room. A friend had sent George Harris some white roses. He sent them over to the convent for Constance, and Dalzell laid them at the foot of the Communion chalice. "Sister Constance is dying tonight," William Armstrong wrote to Lula. He had been to see Constance and Thecla five times that day, once with Dr. Mitchell for consultation, but to no avail. (One of the sisters commented, "I never saw dear Dr. Armstrong so distressed as when he left.") As Constance's life ebbed, she recited prayers: "Oh God, make speed to save us; O Lord, make speed to save us," and then the Gloria, and finally one word, over and over: "Hosanna." She slipped into unconsciousness during the night and died the next morning. She was buried with Harris's white roses.[17]

When George Harris was informed of Constance's death, he wept like a child. He said that his work in Memphis was done, that the whole of Memphis was not worth the lives of Reverend Parsons and Sister Constance.

Sisters Frances, Ruth, and Clare (the latter two reinforcements sent from the motherhouse) and the convent housekeeper Mrs. Bullock walked behind Constance's coffin to Elmwood. Before the end of the month, all but Clare would be dead. So would Sister Thecla and the Reverend Louis Schulyer, a volunteer from New York. (Schulyer apparently sought martyrdom and quickly achieved it, dying four days after his arrival in Memphis.) Of the original Sisters of St. Mary in Memphis, only Hughetta survived.

In the midst of all this sorrow, Dr. Armstrong was much pleased to receive from the sisters an envelope inscribed "an expression of the affection and gratitude of the Sisters," within which were two fifty-dollar bills. "They are a very nice set of ladies," he wrote. Always worried about money, he had been warning Lula to watch her pennies. On September 9 he wrote to her: "My idea now is, if the weather becomes cool, before we have frost to let you buy some goods in Columbia, & not send anything from this poisonous atmosphere." Grateful at having been spared the fever, Armstrong wrote, "May He, who notes the fall of the sparrow, bless, guide and keep you in all peace, and grant us to meet soon, is your husband's prayer."[18]

EACH DAY, ROBERT CATRON sent out stories on the Associated Press wire. The news from Memphis appeared in papers throughout the nation and around the world and inspired the flood of charity that sustained the city through the crisis. However, the AP wire reports did not include enough of the information that Memphians, refugees or still in the city, wanted most: who was sick, and who had died. For that, the local papers were essential. The *Appeal* and the *Avalanche* ran long lists daily. Beyond that commonality, the papers continued to reflect the editors' very different personalities.

John McLeod Keating was a serious man and, given his life in the public arena, a reticent one. As an editorial advocate of positions political and social, he preferred to present his case in the voice of sweet reason rather than emotion, whether the case was actually reasonable or not. (His partner, Matt Galloway, was the office firebrand.) As a writer, Keating was much more buttoned-up than his junior colleague and rival, Herbert Landrum. On September 6 the *Avalanche*'s front page headline read like free verse:

The Mills of God
Grinding Us to Very Fine Powder.
The Stones are Whirling Faster and Faster,
While from Them Comes Shrieks of the Dying,
And Cries of the Sick and the Destitute.
Ninety-two Bodies Thrown Out
*   to the Grave,*

And Full Two Hundred Fresh
Material Laid Hold On
By the Omnipotent Miller who
Regulates the Mill Power.
In Other Cities the Same Awful
Monotony of Grinding
Goes on.
Grinding, Grinding, Grinding.

Keating's front page featured the closing rates for cotton and gold in Liverpool; a report from New Orleans sanitary inspectors that carbolic acid and sulfur fumigations had failed as disinfectants; an estimate of the current number of fever cases in the city; a list of contributions received by the CRC (a hundred pounds of zweiback from Fleishmann's Model Vienna Bakery, New York; six large coops of chickens from Knoxville; $25 collected by two ladies of Huntsville, Alabama; $1,000 from J. Pierpont Morgan on behalf of the New York Chamber of Commerce . . .); and stories from the stricken towns of the Mississippi Valley. Landrum told his readers what it felt like to be a young man during the plague, but for straightforward information—news, in other words—the *Appeal* was the anxious reader's best bet. Small wonder that people in Huntsville, Alabama, sat up until the midnight train pulled in just to get the latest edition.[19]

As the fever decimated the staff of the *Appeal*, the *Avalanche*, and the other Memphis papers, they turned for help to members of their craft. "Printers, to the outside world, are like actors, a queer set, apart from all the world, living within themselves, and after their own odd fashion," Keating said, adding, "but their hearts generally beat responsive to all the calls made upon them, and their money and their sympathies go out to the suffering as free as air." Printers were indisputably working class, so much so that in nineteenth-century cartoons the printer's folded paper hat (donned each morning to keep ink out of his hair) served as an emblem for Labor. But like actors, they usually worked night shifts and often spent considerable time on tour. Since a printer's skill was not bound to any particular locale, newspapers and print shops being found in every corner of the nation, most spent at least some time as "tramp printers." Alan Pinkerton, the nation's best-known detective and antilabor operative, commented that "a printer is normally considered 'no good' when he cannot definitely refer to this mark of graduation and proficiency, and there is not a newspaper or a job office in the world that has not its tramp-printer," cadging for a day's labor and sleeping at night on stacks of newsprint (or on the editor's couch). Having spent some time tramping as young men, printers built up connections in the trade. The brother-hood of printers came through for Memphis in 1878. The Memphis Typographical Union rented rooms and set up an infirmary, hired doc-tors and nurses, paid for medicines, and cared for the sick, the convales-cent, and their families. The typographers received almost $2,000 in contributions from union branches across the nation.[20]

Keating was not part of the web of kinship, lineage, and marriage that connected native-born Memphians. He had married a Nashville woman who spent months each year in New York, and their children comprised his only blood relatives in America. He knew scores of people in Mem-phis, from Democratic Party leaders, Masonic grand masters, and mer-chants on Main Street to the Reform rabbi and the waiters at the Peabody Hotel. He was by no means isolated. Nonetheless, the *Appeal* staff was functionally his family. He recorded each one's illness and kept track of their family members as well. He wrote, "No newspaper was ever better or more faithfully served than by these gentlemen for whom we sorrow as brothers."[21]

The *Appeal* employed approximately forty people. Eventually only two remained who had the technical skills to run the presses: Keating and the compositor, Henry Moode, who spent much of his time nursing his fellow workers in the typographer's infirmary. Left alone in the office, Keating drew upon the skills he had learned as a child in Ireland. It had been twenty years since he left the back shop for the front offices, but he picked up a composing stick and stood to his cases, as compositors said. Letter by letter, word by word, he set into type the news from Memphis, and with Moode's help ran the presses. The *Appeal* shrank to two pages and did not appear every day, but publication never ceased. Between the paper and his CRC work, Keating put in sixteen-hour days.[22]

When one of the telegraphers received a disturbing bit of news from a comrade in Boston, he took it to Robert Catron, who brought it to Keat-ing: "Memphis people living in Boston laugh at the reports of the panic which the Associated Press has sent north. They say things are not nearly so bad."

The message from Boston came as the epidemic reached its peak. A week earlier Keating had written, "If the awful sights and experiences of the past two weeks are to be repeated, we may make up our minds to die, every one of us." Shortly after that, he set into type the story of Mary Frankland, found dead in a house on Commerce Street, her baby still trying to nurse from her cold breast; J. Riviere, found lying at 81 Main Street, "alone, stark naked and literally covered with flies." His co-workers, friends, and acquaintances were dying. The idea that Memphis refugees laughed at such news provoked Keating to make a personal response in print. Published on September 10, in its cadence, irony, and cold anger the editorial is perhaps the most Irish thing he ever wrote.

We would give worlds, he said, to know which of the refugees "mock at the pangs and suffering of 3000 sick, laugh over the 1200 dead men, women and children, who sleep in Elmwood and Calvary cemetery and in Pottersfield, and deride the needy widows and orphans, and hungry, unemployed laborers, who clamor for the food doled out to them day by day . . ." Charity fed Memphis, charity from people who had never been to Memphis or met any Memphians but were moved by Robert Catron's accurate reports. The refugees in Boston might laugh, Keating said, "but we, who are here, are daily, hourly in tears" for the men and women who stayed to help the less fortunate "and have fallen in the cause of humanity." But surely there has been some mistake, he wrote. Surely none of the people who have fled would laugh at reports from Memphis, "surely there is not one so lost to shame, to the commonest decency, as to laugh while all the world is serious over our sorrow . . ."

The statistics alone were enough to make a man weep, Keating said. But the tales of individual sorrow were worse. "Lisping childhood, hoary and venerable old age, the vagrant and the merchant, the man of God and the unbeliever, all are taken, all are claimed alike by the awful pestilence." The disease struck at all ranks of society. "The cry of the fatherless is heard every hour, claiming the pity, the sympathy, and the tears of the most hardened veteran."

Then Keating told the world what the epidemic had meant to him. He described the fever's impact on the *Appeal* staff and said, "This is our personal measure of the dread epidemic, and surely it is a sad one. It has moved us to tears many a time in the past ten days, although we are not used to the melting mood." He had lived through five previous epidemics, but none approached this one in horror. Parents, children, husbands had deserted their dependents. Children begged food from dead mothers. Women died giving birth. Ministers on their way to help the sick were stopped by the "pestilence, that walks in the noonday as at night." Priests and nuns, caring for those whose families were far away, died before anyone realized they were sick.

> The business of the hour is the succor of the sick, the burial of the dead and the care of the needy living. The last words of those who are well, are at night farewells to the dead, and the first in the morning "Who lives, and who has died?" All day, and every hour of the day, this question is repeated, and the heart sickens at the reports, and the soul goes weary over the repetition. And yet there is no relief nor any release. Worse and worse the epidemic has grown, until to-day it has capped the climax, and the hearts of the brave men who have stood in the breach are blanched with fear, and with a dread that annihilation awaits us, and we are destined to be blotted from the earth . . . Hope have we none.[23]

Keating's editorial appeared on September 10, four days before the epidemic reached its peak and seven weeks before it ended. Twelve hundred people had died so far. Four thousand more would perish before frost. Three thousand were sick. Ten thousand had been left indigent. The next day and the day after and for days to come, Keating came to the office, wrote his copy, set into type long lists of the dead, ran his press. He continued to work for the CRC, now much diminished in size. Many organizing members had fled the city, and those who stayed went down with the fever. Of those members who stayed in the city, only seven survived; only three did not contract the fever. Keating was one of them. As people fell ill, died, or came back, pale and tired, to the relief effort, Keating became the CRC's institutional memory, its survivor. Afterward, another committee member said, "Had he fallen, it would have been like blowing out a light in a cavern."[24]

SIX

A Contagion of Kindness

HOW BAD WERE THINGS IN MEMPHIS? According to a physician just returned from the city, fever-stricken white women were being raped by their black male nurses, even as they lay dying.

In the second week of September, Dr. William T. Ramsey gave an interview to the *Washington Post* in which he described Memphis in the most lurid terms. According to Ramsey, you could smell the stench of Memphis from five miles out. "No words can describe the filth I saw, the rotten wood pavements, the dead animals, putrifying human bodies and the half-buried dead combining to make the atmosphere something dreadful." He described nurses, men and women, smoking cigars to mask the smell of their patients. The Peabody Hotel was a "perfect pesthouse," with two thirds of the rooms occupied by yellow fever victims and sulfur pans burning in the halls to keep down infection. Poor whites and blacks from 150 miles around had come to Memphis seeking food, Ramsey said. "Hundreds of them prowl around the streets with hardly any clothes on." He added, "They break into the vacant houses whenever they want." The city was in the hands of its black policemen, who behaved well.

But according to Ramsey, Memphis was so short of nurses "that the best a white woman can do is to have a male negro nurse; and strange as it may seem, I was authentically informed that these negro nurses will take advantage of their helpless white *victims*, even while they are in the agonies of death." This inflammatory statement appeared in the morning *Washington Post* on September 13. Before the day was over, John Keating had received a telegram from Washington begging him to deny the slander.

Keating immediately telegraphed the *Post* that the story was "untrue, every word of it." In the first place, he said, white women did not have to employ black male nurses. There were no rapes. Had any man, black or white, done such a thing, he would not have been "allowed to breathe" after the crime became known. The statement was a "gross libel" on Memphis blacks. Keating wrote, "All honor to them; they have done their duty. They have acted by us nobly as policemen and soldiers, as well as nurses. They have responded to every call made upon them in proportion to their numbers quite as promptly as the whites. The colored citizens of Memphis, as a body, deserve well of their white fellow-citizens. We appreciate and are proud of them."

Keating repeated his answer to the *Post* on the front page of the September 14 *Appeal*, adding, "Looking back across the gloomy vista of the past five weeks, and recalling all that we have passed through, how near to anarchy we have been several times, we are thankful that the negroes, forming as they do just now the great bulk of our population, have manifested a patience worthy of all praise." After the epidemic ended, he wrote about the rape accusation: "No charge ever made was so baseless, so wanton, so cruel, so unjust."[1]

Keating's attitude toward his black neighbors combined prejudice, condescension, paternalism, and human sympathy. He described the "cabins of the negro" as "comic settings of a deep and awful tragedy." Black people's houses were funny, but what had happened to the people within them, remarkably, was not. Tragedy demanded respect. So did courage and competence. In the pages of the *Appeal*, Keating printed stories about black Memphians that demonstrated both. What is startling about these stories is that they are written as if it were an ordinary thing for black policemen to apprehend a "desperado" after a gunfight on Main Street near Beale, or testify in court, "earnest in their efforts to show that their arrests were in the interest of law and order." In one such arrest, the accused was a man, apparently white, who was beating his horse with a club. A black woman had asked a black policeman to make him stop. When the policeman did so, the man brandished an ax. He was carried off to jail by a group of black policemen and fined twenty-five dollars for disorderly conduct. Although the *Appeal* story contains quotes from black policemen in minstrel-show dialect, the general tone is that of commendation.[2]

Keating was a man of his time and place, as casually racist as most other white Americans of the 1870s. He habitually wrote of blacks as inferior, uneducated, and primitive. He rarely used honorifics like Mr. or Mrs. when referring to them. He assumed white superiority and supported white supremacy, but he was also a self-made gentleman. A gentleman does not ignore a good deed, even when done by someone he thinks inferior. A gentleman says thank you. He thought the black nurses, police, and soldiers had been respectful and loyal. He considered black nurses intellectually inferior to whites, but also kinder and more reliable. In his eyes, these were attributes that deserved recognition.[3]

Keating's reaction to the rape libel also suggests that he and the other white relief community leaders were aware that the fragile order they had created was not sustainable without the help of African Americans. He may have personally believed black Memphians praiseworthy, but he may also have thought it was a good idea to publicly praise the men upon whose goodwill the city's survival depended. However, black cooperation with whites during the epidemic did not necessarily imply any need for approval by the white leaders of the CRC or of whites in general. Many men and women in the city's black community had reasons to support the CRC, the black relief committee, and the black militia as they tried to keep the peace, save lives, and protect property. An encore performance of the 1866 riots, this time with white Memphians cast as victims, would not have been in the interests of black people with aspirations to middle-class status and political power.

Black Memphis, like white Memphis, had churches and fraternal organizations, politics and political divisions, and, by mid-September, many yellow fever cases. As it turned out, those of African descent did not have immunity against infection by the disease, although the number of cases among blacks remained much lower than among whites. (About 80 percent of the blacks who stayed in the city contracted the fever and 10 percent died, whereas 98 percent of the whites in the city took the fever and 70 percent died.) During the epidemic the African American community fell back on established institutions and leaders. Ed Shaw, former wharfmaster and acknowledged leader of one political faction, presided over the meeting that established the African American relief committee. Black churches took the lead in organizing relief. The Colored Sisters of Zion, who met at Zion Methodist Episcopal Church on Gayoso Street, offered their aid to the black relief committee. On September 3 black ministers formed the Colored Preachers' Aid Society and sent out a call for help "To the Colored People of the United States,

Especially of the North." They pleaded, "For heaven's sake, relieve us all you can by sending us means! We are not able to bury our dead, or to nurse and feed the sick and destitute."[4]

It is misleading to talk about "the black community," as if all the people of color in the town went to the same churches, belonged to the same lodges, voted the same way, or even knew one another. After the great stampede, about seventeen thousand black people remained in the city. Within that group, there were communities, in the plural. The men who guarded the Court Square commissary were not necessarily acquainted with the people waiting there with food baskets. Some black people in Memphis owned property; some were day laborers. There were people who had been born and raised in Memphis; others were newcomers, and still others had moved into the city when the epidemic began. There were people whose families had been free before the war and people who had been born into slavery.

There were people like Robert Church. By the summer of 1878 Church was single again. He and Louisa had split up, and she had moved to New York. Mollie and Thomas, who had been sent to schools in the North, joined their mother for the summer. Church was running a saloon at the corner of Second Street and Gayoso. His friend John Overton owned the property, but Church was purchasing it, making payments of hundreds of dollars at frequent intervals. Although adamantly determined to maintain his rights as a freeman, Church was more interested in money than in politics. Memphis was about to offer real bargains to an ambitious man with cash to spend.[5]

Bob Church was about forty in 1878. As far as can be determined, he did not serve in either of the militia units, nor in the CRC's ward committee, nor on the African American relief committee. He did contribute twenty-five dollars to the McClellan Guards. In later years, his family said that he had worked with his white friend John Gaston, owner of Gaston's Hotel, to help victims of the fever, but there is no evidence to confirm that story. It is impossible to tell whether or not Church even stayed in Memphis during the epidemic, but it is not likely that he would have left his saloon and his stock unprotected.[6]

A "CONTAGION OF KINDNESS," Keating called the world's response to the city's plea for help. In September, shipments of food and other supplies began to roll into Memphis, transported free of charge by the rail companies. Keating singled out the Southern Express Company for special praise: "Its superintendent [Major W. A. Willis] and many of his subordinates sickened and died, and yet its work was continued as if it were merely part of the general machinery by which the city was governed and the sick and needy were provided for." People in neighboring southern states wired money to Memphis, but large donations also came from New York and Chicago, citadels of the former enemy, and from Europe, South America, India, and Australia. Eventually the world contributed almost $400,000 to the Howard Association of Memphis, a sum equivalent to about $8 million today. In addition to cash, people sent the Howards pounds of tea and cases of champagne, barrels of flour and whiskey, smoked hams, and coops of live chickens. The CRC raised approximately $200,000 in contributions. The Masons received $21,196 from lodges around the nation and with it hired doctors and nurses, bought supplies, supplied welfare for indigent brothers, and buried the dead. Other fraternal orders followed the same course.[7]

According to historian Edward Blum, the epidemic helped renew a sense of national unity. Northerners praised brave southern volunteers like the Howards. They also gave generously. According to Blum, northern contributions to yellow fever relief throughout the South totaled about $4.5 million at a time when a national political campaign did well to raise more than $300,000. Blum quotes John Greenleaf Whittier, a poet famous for his prewar abolitionist advocacy: "The great sorrow effaces all sectional and party lines and sweeps away all [sectional] prejudice and jealousy," he wrote. "Under its solemn shadow we are one people, fellow countrymen and brothers united in a common prayer." Blum argues that the epidemic "served as an occasion for a wide variety of southerners to assert new memories of northerners, to participate in reunion, and to claim a new national solidarity without feeling any compulsion to reject their allegiance to the South or the Lost Cause." They could "surrender" to the love sent south without loss of honor. Southern businessmen used regional gratitude for northern charity as a rationale for the sectional reconciliation they deemed necessary to the birth of a New South of industry and economic development. One man who suffered through the Mississippi Valley epidemic said that he never wanted to hear the disparaging word "Yankee" again: "Were the people of the North our own flesh and blood they could not be more our brothers."[8]

In addition to the supplies donated and purchased, the Howards received daily shipments of beef, courtesy of Tennessee governor James D. Porter. According to Robert Mitchell, slabs of fresh beef were impractical: "The continued hot weather soon made it necessary to procure live stock instead, and then a great difficulty followed in finding a butcher." Once one had been located, the cattle were slaughtered as needed. Cut into two-pound portions, the beef was sent out to the Howards' neighborhood depots and then to the houses of the sick, where "it furnished material to make broth for the sick, and also answered as food for the nurses."[9]

With food rolling in from their former enemies, plus supplies from the state government, the CRC seems to have relaxed its rules on rations for the indigent. In mid-September a citizens' meeting—not clearly labeled a CRC event, but dominated by its members—passed a resolution that "hereafter," rations would not be furnished to well people unless they applied at one of the refugee camp commissaries. This implies that the CRC *had* been feeding the poor at its Court Square commissary. Despite the resolution, they kept on doing so. On September 17 Kezia DePelchin described to her sister the work of the "committees" whose function was to "supply the wants of the destitute. They issue rations every day, mostly to colored people, because they cannot leave the town now, and of course must be fed."[10]

J. M. Keating's attitude toward the CRC's "free lunchroom" changed drastically in mid-September. From the start of the epidemic he had opposed extending charity to people who were not sick, just unemployed. When blacks began to come in from the countryside for rations, the *Appeal* suggested that the roads into town might be blocked. Keating chaired the September 13 meeting that voted to stop rations to the idle poor. He reconsidered when he understood better the situation outside the city.[11]

White people in the relief community thought that the blacks who drew rations in Memphis should go out and work in the cotton fields. That was not possible. The last thing people in the Delta wanted to see was a work crew from pestilential Memphis. When another Memphis paper ran an editorial arguing that rations should be denied to healthy people who ought to be out picking cotton, Keating publically demurred. He explained that the country roads around Memphis were guarded by

men "with double-barreled shotguns in their hands to forbid the presence of labor from Memphis or any of the yellow-fever cities and towns.
Along the river, for instance, as far as Vicksburg, the whole country is
picketed." Despite the shotgun quarantine, several cotton planters had
come to Memphis to hire gangs of workers for the harvest. When the
planters tried to bring the workers to their plantations, however, they
"were driven back on board the boats that had carried them to their plantations by armed men crazed with the dread of the epidemic." The black
workers had to stay in Memphis; they had nowhere else to go.

In addition, Keating said circumspectly, he had been "compelled to
admit the force of arguments, many of them having for their basis the
peace of the community and the safety of life and property." Lest anyone
miss his reference to the near riot at the commissary, he added, "We will
not soon forget those critical days, burdened as they were with other terrors than those of the fever. We have passed them by in safety; let it be
our care not to encourage their recurrence." Although it was painfully
humiliating to see Memphis's "able-bodied labor fed by the charitable
hands of the whole country," Keating counseled patience. The problem
was "one that will solve itself only when we have a series of severe frosts."
In early October, the CRC was still dispensing rations at the rate of eighteen thousand per day.[12]

Guarded by black soldiers, the Howard Association and the CRC
created an urban village in and around Court Square. The Howards
employed 111 doctors and 2,995 nurses, 529 of them volunteers from
outside the city. (Of the "foreign" nurses, 362 were male, 167 female.) Not
all the relief workers were present at any one time. The numbers given
above are the totals for the summer, including the people who served a
few days or weeks, then died. Just the same, there were enough medical
relief workers to populate a small town.

Kezia DePelchin never had to join the crowds waiting for food on
Court Square, but she told her sister, "If I had not joined the Howards I
expect I should." Official Howard nurses received meal tickets ("and
how I do laugh at myself when I go for a meal ticket, just like a section
railroad hand," she wrote). At the Howard canteen, nurses presented
their tickets and were fed at long tables. DePelchin's friend Kate Heckle,
also a Houston nurse, was offended: "Negroes and whites male and female ate at the same table and the negroes were the first to set down."

(Mrs. Heckle took her plate and found a place to sit alone.) They gossiped and complained about each other—a sure sign of community life—but they also laughed and told stories, and not all of them were sad.[13]

Dr. W. F. Besancny of Jonestown, Mississippi, had just finished his screening interview with Dr. Mitchell when a messenger rushed into the office to ask for help for a young woman who had just been attacked by the fever. Mitchell turned to Besancny and asked him if he would like to go on duty immediately. The young doctor followed the messenger back to a residence on Adams Street, where he found Miss D. P. Rutter down with a bad case of the fever. He took care of her until she recovered. Shortly thereafter the doctor himself took the fever. Miss Rutter nursed him until he recovered. Keating wrote, "Nothing more was known or thought about the matter by the few intimate friends of the young lady until yesterday afternoon, when the doctor, accompanied by Esquire Quigley and a few friends, drove up to the residence, and in less time than it takes us to write this paragraph, the two were joined together in the holy bonds of wedlock. Such a union, consummated under such circumstances, can not fail to abound with happiness."[14]

UNACCLIMATED VOLUNTEER PHYSICIANS swelled the ranks of Dr. Mitchell's Howard medical corps. Mitchell urged them to leave, but if they insisted on staying—and most did—he warned each to take care of himself, "to put himself in the best possible condition for recovery if attacked; to accomplish all the work he could between the hours of sunrise and nightfall; to get eight hours uninterrupted rest." Mitchell thought that "to be stricken down when exhausted mentally and physically was to ensure death."[15]

DePelchin had been appalled to see unacclimated nurses from Little Rock on the train to Memphis. Her anxiety for those not immune surfaced again when she ran into an acquaintance from Houston at the Howard infirmary. Although he had never had the fever, he told her that he had come to Memphis for the same reason she had, " 'to help my fellowmen.' " The two Texans had a pleasant visit, joking together about the news from home. When they parted, DePelchin wondered if they would ever meet again. It was a question "that now arises every time I bid goodbye to anyone here much more to one unacclimated. Why is it that these young men will come, when it is almost certain death?" Men took similar risks when they marched off to battle, she thought, but in Memphis, recruits had "no gilded trappings, no martial music to stir the blood." Their human sympathy had brought them to a different battle-field, one where the enemy's "ensign is the black flag, and he gives no quarter."[16]

The virulence of the fever shocked Dr. W. L. Coleman, a Houston vol-unteer. From long experience he knew well the odor of yellow fever, but the smell was so strong in the lower floors of the Peabody Hotel that he could not stand it. Coleman slept in the homes of patients in the suburbs. He was, he wrote, "also astonished to see the number of inexperienced officers in this terrible battle." The Howard volunteer corps included many young doctors from the Midwest "who had never seen the disease and were totally ignorant of its nature." Howard records show that it was not just the midwestern doctors who were unacclimated. Many of the physicians from Memphis had never had the disease.[17]

Coleman saw an opportunity to further the interests of science. He decided to keep statistics on the fates of the unacclimated doctors. "I therefore made it a point to obtain the name, address, and time of ar-rival in Memphis of everyone I saw wearing a Howard Medical badge," he wrote. "One evening after supper quite a number of them gathered around me while I was entering data obtained that day, and were very curious to know why I was thus getting their names and addresses." Coleman told the young men that he was "deeply interested in the study of yellow fever of which I know nothing, though I have been seeing it at intervals for twenty-five years. I am also much pained to see you mani-fest such careless indifference to the great danger into which you have unwittingly rushed, for let me tell you that in the fiercest battle of the late war the danger to the number of officers was never half as great as that to which you are all exposed."

The unacclimated doctors laughed at him. Coleman recalled them saying, "Why, it is only a malignant form of bilious fever, totally non-contagious, and we are going to cure it with calomel and quinine, and keep it off with quinine." He retorted, "If one in twenty of you escape an attack, I will be much surprised." He showed them his book, in which their names were listed adjacent to columns headed "date of arrival, date of attack, period of incubation, result, recovery, died." He said, "I very much fear that many of your names will appear in the last column."[18]

Coleman's apprehension proved prophetic. Of the 111 physicians in

the Howard medical corps, 54 were unacclimated. All but one contracted the fever, and 33 died. Doctors J. C. Meade of Hopefield, Arkansas, and R. B. Williams of Woodburn, Kentucky, came to Memphis on
August 30, went down with the fever two days later, and died on September 7. Others struggled through bouts of fever only to relapse and
die weeks later. Finally Dr. Mitchell asked the Associated Press to inform the country that he would in the future refuse to put unacclimated
doctors on duty. It did no good. "They still continued to report to me,"
he wrote later.[19]

Some of the volunteer physicians believed themselves acclimated,
only to find out that they were not. In a region beset by malaria, it was
easy to mistake one kind of fever for another. Such was the case for Dr.
M. L. Keating (no relation to the editor) of New York, a man who suffered from a chronic intermittent fever, probably malaria. Dr. Keating
distinguished this malady from the fever attack he had suffered in Mobile twenty years previously. He identified the latter as yellow fever and
believed himself immune.

One night Dr. Coleman was called to the New York physician's bedside. "I found him sitting on the side of the bed and clad in his under-
clothes," Coleman recalled. "I greeted him pleasantly with 'Well, Doctor,
are you having another one of those annoying paroxysms of malarial
fevers?'" Yes, the doctor said, but "a very anomalous one, for it postponed a week, and I was feeling better than usual, when to my surprise
at three o'clock yesterday morning I had a very severe chill followed by a
fever lasting till noon today." The doctor dosed himself that night with
three compound cathartic pills (designed to empty his digestive system),
followed by forty grains of quinine in ten-grain doses through the day,
and he expected a quick recovery. Despite the medications, he still felt
strange.

While the doctor outlined his symptoms and self-prescribed treatment, Coleman took his pulse and observed his face. To Coleman's
"intense surprise," he felt the "characteristic yellow fever pulse." The
visiting physician's face already had the look of oncoming death. Making an excuse, Coleman hurried down to Howard headquarters to fetch
Dr. Mitchell. When Mitchell entered the room and saw Dr. Keating, his
eyes opened wide. "He asked abruptly, 'Dr. K, when did your kidneys act?
How much urine have you passed today?'" Dr. Keating well knew the
portent of these questions and insisted that he did not have yellow fever,

although he could not remember passing any urine since the previous afternoon. Application of a catheter produced only a small amount of urine. Mitchell prescribed a diuretic and sent a nurse to stay with Keating despite the physician's protest that he did not need one.

On their way down the stairs Mitchell said to Coleman, "How sad! Is it our duty to inform the doomed man that he is dying?" The Houston doctor advised against it. Dr. Keating died in the morning, forty-eight hours after his bout with the disease began.[20]

The first black doctor to practice in Memphis was one of the unacclimated. Dr. R. H. Tate came from Cincinnati with seven white physicians. Admitted to the Howard medical corps, Tate stayed in the home of T. R. Morgan, the Beale Street dentist who headed the African American relief committee. "Dr. Tate was a friend of the suffering sick of his own race—a true and noble man," said another Ohio physician. "Without hesitancy, he worked, without rest, day and night. His own race caused him the greatest distress. Home physicians, with but very few exceptions, cared little for the colored race. I have seen how colored men have placed their hands on Dr. Tate's coat collar, carrying him "per force' (the doctor) to their wretched habitations. If a man had been cast of iron, he must, under such trying circumstances, have succumbed." Tate took the fever, but after four days thought himself well enough to go back to work. He had a relapse and died three weeks after coming to Memphis.[21]

Kezia DePelchin understood that the unacclimated volunteer's reward for good works was "a lowly, oft an unmarked grave." Perhaps, she thought, their fate was a sign of God's mercy. By taking the young men "just when the noblest attributes of their natures were called forth," God "called them at a time when they were best fitted to enter into the promised rest." She concluded, "God is more merciful than man."[22]

DR. JOHN ERSKINE HAD OPPOSED Dr. Mitchell's quarantine proposal in July. When the fever began to move upstream, he changed his mind and helped devise and run the Memphis quarantine stations. In mid-August he directed the health board's frantic efforts to clean the city. When Kate Bionda died, he supervised the cleanup of her snack shop and house. As the fever spread, he spent his days on horseback going from outbreak to outbreak. He ordered barricades set up around infected areas and put crews to work sprinkling carbolic acid in the streets. But while he carried out his duties as health officer, he also cared for ever-increasing numbers of patients. Born to play the hero, Erskine was an imposing presence. A quarter century later a colleague called him the "chivalric Hotspur" of the Memphis medical profession. Yet Erskine had a sensitive, gentle heart. He reproached himself for his inability to do more for his patients and constantly questioned his own ideas about remedies for the disease. His friends thought it a foregone conclusion that the epidemic would kill him. Erskine died of the fever on September 17. Keating wrote that he had "literally given his life in the service of those who had trusted him as health officer."[23]

If you could not cure the sick, you might at least hope to learn something from this epidemic that might save yellow fever victims in the future. The young Nashville physician T. O. Summers came to Memphis specifically to study yellow fever. He took notes on 482 cases and performed autopsies in the city hospital's dissecting room. In 1879 Summers published a detailed scientific analysis of the symptoms and effects of the disease. He described patients with fevers reaching as high as 110 degrees, with pulse rates approaching 130 before falling, a sign of impending death. He concluded that no treatment cured the fever: "Opposite therapeutic lines have been followed with like failure, and with the same apparent success."

Summers's observations confirmed what yellow fever specialists had been saying for years; nonetheless, doing research was better than doing nothing. Researchers could hope that their work might supply a bit of insight some future scientist could use to find a cure. In that spirit, Howard doctors met nightly to discuss cases and exchange observations. "With every energy strained," Keating said, "they did not forget the cause of science." In the midst of mass death, he thought that these meetings were "the light and life of each day."[24]

Camaraderie sustained relief efforts in the midst of desolation, but it carried its own risks. As the summer lingered into fall and their friends died, the survivors grieved and worked without surcease. Few had time for mourning rituals designed to dignify death.

MRS. CALHOUN, AGE TWENTY-TWO, and her husband were parents of one child, Arthur. Husband and wife both fell sick on Friday, September 13. The husband was sent to the hospital, where he died on the following Thursday. DePelchin took charge of Mrs. Calhoun on September 14; she died the next night. All the adults in the Calhoun family had either died or fled Memphis. DePelchin had not intended to take any money for nursing, but in this situation she went to the Howard office, drew her pay, bought coal and wood, and gave the remaining cash to the neighbor woman who had agreed to care for Arthur.

On the night of Mrs. Calhoun's death DePelchin dressed the body in clean clothing. She informed the police of the death and then, with the help of a neighbor, spent the day trying to keep Arthur amused. At ten that night she heard the death wagon rumbling its way to the tenement door. She went down with a light. Three black men carried a rough coffin up the three flights of stairs to the Calhoun apartment. As they picked up the body, they asked if the corpse was male or female. "A woman," she replied. "Lay her in gently." She placed a white coverlet over the body and gave the burial crew some camphor to mask the smell. With DePelchin holding a lamp to light the way, the men maneuvered the coffin down the stairs. All was done with as much decorum as possible, but it bothered her that Mrs. Calhoun was being buried by people who did not know her. She wrote, "The moon is shining brightly down upon the stricken city, where so many such scenes are being enacted."[25]

Victorians of all classes put great stock in funerary rituals. Fashionable women wore black for a year after the death of a family member and "half-mourning" clothing in dark hues of gray and purple for a year thereafter. People who lacked aspiration to fashion (or the wherewithal to maintain separate mourning wardrobes) made do with black crepe. This ubiquitous fabric festooned the front doors of houses in mourning and, attached to dress skirts and bodices, swathed women in dull, lusterless "widow's weeds." Men wore black suits or, if their business circumstances did not permit, black crepe armbands. Both sexes were supposed to abstain from social events while in full mourning, and woe to the widow who remarried while still in black. By exhibiting their grief publicly, the upper classes also differentiated themselves from working-class Americans, most of whom could spare neither the money nor the time for elaborate mourning.

However, even the poorest attempted to bury their dead in style—to send them off proper, as they might have said. People spent considerable time, effort, and money to plan and pay for first-class funerals. Working-class Americans learned about insurance by purchasing burial policies. They paid minuscule premiums weekly to an agency's collector, who went door-to-door in poor neighborhoods. Fraternal organizations were so popular in part because they acted as funerary societies for their members. Even a poor man could imagine with pleasure his trip to the graveyard: a hearse, black as night but ornamented with silver fittings, drawn by a fine horse in black harness with black plumes, his coffin resting inside, visible to all through the glass windows on the sides and back as the procession made its way to the cemetery. The day might conclude with quiet conversations among the bereaved, or with an emotional, whiskey-fueled wake. The average man could not expect the kind of funeral parade Memphis threw for Nathan Bedford Forrest in 1875; ordinary people were not escorted to their graves by gray-clad militia units with thousands of citizens following behind. But even the most obscure could look forward to a day when he would be the center of attention, the star of the show.

Forrest was buried in Elmwood, a new-style graveyard Keating called the "loveliest of the cities of the dead," and the most famous of the city's six cemeteries. Elmwood's paths wind along through trees and flowers; graves do not stretch in regimented rows, but are clustered in garden-like spaces and ornamented with decorative stones and statuary. As the designers intended, the cemetery's beauty pays honor to the dead and comforts the living. At the opposite end of the scale of social status, the traditional Potters Field provided burial space for the indigent interred at public expense.[26]

The epidemic stripped away consoling rituals. There would be no careful preparation of the body, no lying in state, no tolling of church bells, no processions—and in many cases no individual graves.

People who bought plots in Elmwood purchased the implicit promise of a properly ritualized burial. In normal times, the staff at Elmwood rang a bell when a coffin passed through the gates, and they recorded in a ledger the name, cause of death, age, and burial plot for each interment. As "yellow fever" replaced diseases like meningitis and consumption in the cause-of-death column, Elmwood's serenity disappeared. Keating described dozens of coffins lying around the cemetery "daily waiting interment, which had to be postponed for days, sometimes, owing to the scarcity of gravediggers, the terrible death-rate, and the sickness of those in charge of the cemetery." Deep trenches gaped like open wounds in Elmwood's lawn, and the CRC's burial teams stacked coffins in, two by two. Some families managed to bury their own dead in numbered plots, but the Elmwood staff recorded many names with no mention of location. In the rush to get corpses away from the living and into the sod, cemetery workers sometimes paid little respect to persons or to the feelings of the bereaved; there was no time for what Keating called "the luxuries of woe."[27]

One evening at about five fifteen a hearse rolled through the gates of Elmwood carrying the body of Mrs. Ben K. Pullen. Her aged husband and their children followed in a carriage. As the black gravediggers began work on Mrs. Pullen's grave, their white boss berated them. He said that if they worked past the six P.M. closing time, they would not be paid. Keating wrote, "The negroes, more humane than he, and indignant at such an exhibition of brutality before the husband and children, standing beside all that remained to them of a good wife and mother, replied that sometimes they worked for friendship." They dug Mrs. Pullen's grave, lowered her coffin, and had almost finished filling in the grave when their white supervisor reappeared. In the presence of the grieving family the boss again told the workers that they would receive no pay for working late. He added that no more work would be done after six o'clock, "no matter how many d—d carcasses are brought here."[28]

As the death toll mounted, ugly scenes alternated with surprising moments of grace. Reverend Landrum later mused, "As in war, so in times of pestilence, there are remarkable revealments of character. Where you have counted on firmness, patience, and self-sacrifice, you have been surprised by weakness, fear and meanness. Where you have had little hope of noble deeds, you have found magnanimity, kindness, tenderness, love." The *Chicago Tribune* sent a special correspondent down to Memphis during the epidemic. He wrote, "Gamblers, outcasts, and outlaws among the males, with those among the females who were marked by the scarlet letter, felt as keen sympathies, labored as heroically, nursed as tenderly, and died as bravely" as upper-class heroes clad in "purple and fine linen." The people who read of the plague summer in the daily papers were as fascinated by the vagaries of character as the firsthand observers in Memphis. It is almost comical how surprised they were—how surprised we all are—when the same things happened in Thucydides's Athens, Boccaccio's Florence, Defoe's London, and in every major epidemic, over and over again.[29]

IN THE MANSION HOUSE parlor, the piano stood silent. The velvet sofas and fine carpets had been removed, and army cots lined the bare floors. Annie Cook, the brothel's madam, moved from patient to patient, sponging the sick, cleaning away the black vomit, coaxing them to take spoonfuls of tea, until in early September she joined the roll of the sick. She took the fever bad, and soon it became known that she was dying. In her last days she received a message from Louisville, her former home. A group of women, moved by the prostitute's sacrifice, wrote to her: "God speed you, dear madam, and when the time comes, may the light of a better world guide you to a home beyond."[30]

Keating wrote of her death:

Annie Cook, the woman who, after a long life of shame, ventured all she had of life and property for the sick, died Sept. 11 of yellow fever, which she contracted while nursing her patients. If there was virtue in the faith of the woman who but touched the hem of the garment of the Divine Redeemer, surely the sins of this woman must have been forgiven her. Her faith has made her whole—made her one with the living Christ, whose example she followed in giving her life that others might live.[31]

She was buried in the Elmwood plot reserved for the Howards. Someone—we don't know who—brought flowers to her grave. When her estate was settled and all the bills paid, her son inherited a gold watch and chain, a set of sleeve buttons, and two diamond rings. The estate inventory listed another significant piece of jewelry, sold during the process of settlement: a diamond cross.[32]

IF THE MEMPHIS epidemic reiterated the classic lesson that humans cannot effectively predict how other humans will behave in a crisis, it also pointed toward the future by demonstrating the importance of people trained in new technologies. In the new world created by railroads and telegraph wires, keeping the lines of transportation and communication open required expertise as well as courage, skill as well as self-sacrifice. The railroad men and the telegraphers did the work they had hired on for, but they paid a very high price for what we today would call professionalism.

The Louisville and Nashville Railroad (L&N) was the principal line into the fever districts. The L&N brought in 1,500,000 pounds of relief supplies for free, running special relief trains to rural areas. With very few exceptions, the railroad men and women stayed on the job. Seventy-one died, most of them on the stretch of lines from Memphis to Paris, Tennessee. The fever touched every sector of employment on the line: engineers, brakemen, firemen; station agents and section men; the couple who ran the railroad hotel at Paris; and the woman who did the laundry.[33]

The Western Union wires were the city's primary means of communication with the outside world. Through them, relief leaders broadcast pleas for help and received assurances that the city would not be forgotten, and individuals exchanged messages with family and friends. By transmitting information and linking individuals, the telegraph served the same functions that telephones, computers, radio, and television do today. Sending messages by wire required skilled operators. Without much fanfare, the Western Union men stayed at their posts. As clerks and operators fell to the fever, volunteers replaced them and were in turn replaced.

At one point Memphis's telegraphic communications depended on one man, George Putnam. Keating described "the solitary occupant of the operating-room, the click of the instruments, as they told the story of the busy world abroad, being the only accompaniments [Putnam] had to feelings that must have been sad indeed." Of the twenty-five men who served in the Memphis telegraph office during the epidemic, twenty had the fever. Eleven died. Their quiet heroism did not rivet public attention the way that dastardly husbands or golden-hearted prostitutes did, but afterward Keating did write of them: "Undismayed by the intelligence which every hour was flashed to and from us of the growing strength of the epidemic, and the increase of its victims, the telegraphers continued to interpret sad and joyful messages; to be the medium of death and life;

the harbingers of hope or the messengers of despair. They stood to their posts like men, and did their duty like heroes indeed."[34]

BACK IN AUGUST, Father William Walsh's superiors had been dubious about the assistant priest's plan to create a refugee camp for the members of the Father Mathew Society, an Irish temperance organization. The young priest had proceeded on his own responsibility. Funded by $29,000 in donations from Irish temperance societies, Camp Father Mathew turned out to be a conspicuous success. As Father Walsh recalled afterward, the Father Mathew Society soon had "any number of applicants for admission." They issued occupation permits to people of good character who would follow the society's strict prohibition against drinking, and required them to stay in quarantine for fifteen days before admission. Father Walsh said Mass each morning at a tiny wheeled church (his "Ark") dedicated to the Sacred Heart. He went into the city to work each day but returned in the evening to recite the Rosary and, he said, "give the benediction of the most blessed sacrament."[35]

As the bodies piled up in Memphis, Camp Father Mathew proved to be a safe haven. Five babies were born there, and two marriages celebrated. As the epidemic extended into the autumn, the society rented a building nearby and opened a school staffed by the Sisters of St. Joseph. Of the four hundred people sheltered in Camp Father Mathew, only ten died of the fever. Father Walsh believed that "in each case the fever was *contracted* in the city." He added, "We had not one certain case, of a fatal or unfavorable result, contracted in our camp. Providence must have assisted us." Perhaps Providence helped those who helped themselves. The camp's location near a spring meant that people did not have to store water in buckets or barrels near their tents. No water containers meant no habitat for *Ae. aegypti*.[36]

A MIDDLE-AGED WOMAN with long experience of epidemics, sickness, and grief, Kezia DePelchin could sleep all night on a patient's floor, breakfast on crackers and coffee, and still have the energy to observe and comment (often humorously) on the scene around her. Her early letters leave the impression of a woman secure in her ability to meet events with equanimity and provide good care for her patients. An educated woman, the sort of person John Keating called "refined," she was an acceptable foreign nurse for the Memphis upper class. In mid-September a veteran member of the Howards requested that DePelchin serve as nurse for his wife.

John G. Lonsdale Sr. was a founding member of the Memphis Howard Association and had served during the 1867 and 1873 epidemics. As Howard treasurer, he was charged with helping to keep track of money received and expended, thereby assuring the public that the contributions they made were put to honest use. His son John Jr. held a similar position in the Citizens Relief Committee until he died from the fever. DePelchin was waiting for an assignment at the Howard offices when Lonsdale asked for a private word with her. Like her, Lonsdale had been born a subject of the queen. The Englishman wept as he described the death of his son the previous week. His wife had gone down with the fever that morning, and he needed DePelchin's help. She went with him to his home on Bellevue Avenue, three miles out of town, in mid-September.[37]

Mrs. Lonsdale lay in a heavily curtained bedroom, trembling and suffering from a severe headache. DePelchin knelt on the floor next to her bed as the elderly woman talked of her children. "I resolved to wait on her as I would have had anyone wait on my own precious mother," she wrote. With Dr. Mitchell himself as her physician, Mrs. Lonsdale had all the "attention that love or money could obtain." Although Mr. Lonsdale brought another nurse to relieve her, DePelchin stayed at Mrs. Lonsdale's bedside through the night, catching a nap of two hours the next morning. The next night, "we all sat up. By morning the silent, unwelcome visitor was there . . . he mocks at science, puts love aside, wealth could not bribe him." DePelchin dressed the corpse in white. Two of the Howards and a neighbor lady accompanied Mr. Lonsdale to the cemetery. After it was over, Mr. Lonsdale went back to work in the Howard office.[38]

A TELEGRAM SENT from Memphis to New York to be read at Booth's Theater on September 21:

DEATHS TO DATE, 2,250; NUMBER SICK NOW, ABOUT 3,000; AVERAGE DEATHS, SIXTY PER CENT OF THE SICK. WE ARE FEEDING SOME 10,000

PEOPLE, SICK AND DESTITUTE, IN CAMPS AND IN THE CITY. OUR CITY IS
A HOSPITAL. FIFTEEN VOLUNTEER PHYSICIANS HAVE DIED; TWENTY
OTHERS ARE SICK. A GREAT MANY NURSES HAVE DIED—MANY THAT
HAD THE FEVER BEFORE, AND THOUGHT THEMSELVES PROOF. FEVER
ABATING SOME TODAY, FOR WANT OF MATERIAL, PERHAPS, AND THINGS
LOOK MORE HOPEFUL. WE ARE PRAYING FOR FROST—IT IS OUR ONLY
HOPE. A THOUSAND THANKS TO THE GENEROUS PEOPLE OF NEW YORK.[39]

Through August and early September, Reverend Sylvanus Landrum
did volunteer work for the Citizens' Relief Committee. He visited the sick
of his congregation and others. People outside the city sent him money to
pay for burials and to help widows and orphans. He sought out chances to
do "*gospel* work" in the refugee camps, "open every day with six or seven
hundred people to the herald of the cross." He felt that he was doing good
and useful work; he was walking in the path of Jesus. But he also knew
that his family had stayed in Memphis because he had chosen to stay.

In the second week of September, Herbert Landrum went down with
a violent case of the fever. Reverend Landrum sat by his son's bedside
for three days and nights and watched the young man pay for his father's sense of duty. The pastor talked to his son about his faith. They
discussed Herbert's business affairs. Herbert made suggestions as to
how he might be buried. Then Reverend Landrum broached the matter
of his personal culpability. "I called attention to the fact that he might
have gone away, and that he was *dying for me*. He replied, 'I would do the
same again under similar circumstances.'" Herbert had but one regret:
"'I leave my life so unfinished.'"

The Landrums' cook, Eliza, had been with them for years, and they
loved her. She had the fever too. Reverend Landrum left his son's side to
read and pray with her until she died. The next morning, Mrs. Landrum took the fever. Reverend Landrum was "seized with the fever"
that night. He wrote, "It is a bitter thought that, for the last six hours,
Herbert was left in the hands of a strange nurse; neither parent being
able to see him or to say a last word of farewell." Herbert Landrum died
on September 12. He was twenty-two years old.

Reverend Landrum had persuaded his youngest son, nineteen-year-
old George, to take a friend's children to safety in Chattanooga. Having
received word of his parents' illness, George returned to Memphis. When
George walked into the sickroom, Reverend Landrum screamed at his

Elmwood cemetery registry, with yellow fever deaths recorded in ditto marks. Herbert Landrum's name is midway down the page.

son. "'You are a dead man! Is not one son enough to sacrifice to this plague! Fly from this place!" George told him to be quiet, adding, "We are not afraid to die." George took charge of the household, obtained better nurses, and ensured that his parents had the best care. But three days later he took the fever. He had gone out into the suburbs to visit the father of the children he had escorted to safety, and he fell sick there. When it became clear that George was dying, Reverend Landrum risked his own recovery to go to him. He was able to stay with his son until he passed. "Now we had 'sorrow upon sorrow,'" Landrum wrote. Early the next morning Mr. and Mrs. Landrum went to bury their dead. "We were both very feeble, and there was no church member, no neighbor, no citizen, to go with us. The two nurses, one Italian and one negro, were our only attendants to and from the grave."[40]

Many times Reverend Landrum had preached sermons on the necessity of submitting to God's power, of saying "Thy will be done." In a post-epidemic sermon to the Memphis survivors, Landrum said that the "words are brief and simple—so easy to say, but how hard to pray it, to utter it from the heart, when that prayer alone is left to you. I have repeated it a thousand times without feeling it. When called to speak it from the heart, I found it no easy thing."[41]

In early October, Kezia DePelchin began to wonder if the God she praised as merciful and loving had turned against her. DePelchin's days of despair began when John Johnston came to ask for her nursing services. Johnston; his wife, Annie; her mother, Julia Morrow; and Annie's siblings had all moved to a house far out on Manassas Street to get away from the fever. But Annie Johnston had died within forty-eight hours of the move and was quickly followed by one of her sisters. DePelchin wrote, "The mother was bowed down with grief. She took the fever, and before I reached there in the afternoon another daughter, about 16, was also down." The Morrow sons had less serious cases of fever. "The family was much attached to each other; when I staid [sic] with Mrs. Morrow a few hours, she begged me to go to Jennie, her daughter, then if I did anything for Jennie, she would say, you wait on me so nicely, now I'll lie still if you will go and wait on mother"—a level of selflessness DePelchin found very unusual. A Creole nurse named Almira was obtained, and she and DePelchin shared the nursing duties.[42]

Of Jennie and Julia Morrow, DePelchin wrote, "I loved them both as soon as I saw them and waited on them accordingly." On the third day, Jennie reported that the headache that signified the start of the disease had stopped, but DePelchin noted with fear that the girl's temperature had not lowered. Soon the black vomit appeared. "O what is this hidden fatal chemistry, that works inwardly, turning everything to death, that silently gnaws the vitals and writes the Death warrant, not in red like the laws of Draco, but with just as sure destruction its warrant is written in black, black as midnight, the pure ice water is turned to ink color in a few seconds." DePelchin was taking a nap on a rug in an adjacent room when Mr. Johnston called her to Jennie's side. "The bed was as if several bottles of ink had been thrown around. I threw my arms around her, exclaiming my darling, has it come to this." She had prayed so for Jennie. "Was it aught that I had done that God would not hear me?" she wrote.

The beautiful young girl's fair skin had turned the color of brass. She was almost unrecognizable. In a room across a narrow hall, her mother was also dying. "By morning both began that hard breathing and screaming, the sure forerunner of Death." The Creole nurse said that both women were panting like racehorses; DePelchin thought it was a race to see which would cross into Heaven first. Jennie died first, Julia soon followed. Almira and Kezia laid them out, Julia Morrow in black, Jennie in white. Their bodies were carried to Elmwood Cemetery in two hearses, one black and one white. DePelchin and Johnston walked over. "The graves were close together, and there were the two new-made graves of the other children. Thus in life they were beautiful, and in death they were not separated." As they turned away from the graves, Johnston repeated the words "I am the resurrection and the life." They walked back to the house by the light of the new-risen moon.[43]

"Would to God I could feel I was doing some good; do I not pray aright?" DePelchin wrote. She felt sick, body and soul, and broken down by sorrow. She started another assignment but soon returned to the Chambers House and took to her bed. Although she was sure that she just had a cold, the Howards worried about her. They dispatched a nurse with instructions not to let her die. (The nurse told Kezia about it, adding that she could see that DePelchin was "some account" and she planned to make her reputation as a nurse by taking good care of her.) Kate Heckle, another Texas nurse, stopped by briefly; it was so good to see someone from home, even if Mrs. Heckle did make her take castor oil for her cold. But most of the time, alone in her upstairs room, she thought about the epidemic and the will of God.[44]

Sitting with Jennie Morrow late one night, DePelchin had not been able to get the Church Home out of her mind. She knelt by the bed of her patient to pray for Sister Frances and the little ones. The next morning, she was shocked to see Sister Frances listed among the dead. Sister Frances had been ill earlier in the summer, and everyone assumed she had the fever. When she recovered, people assumed she now had acquired immunity. Apparently both assumptions were erroneous.

Kezia DePelchin thought her luck had turned bad after her stay at the Church Home. Prior to that, most of her patients had done well.

Afterward, she lost one patient after the other. She had been unable to help Mrs. Lonsdale. Although Mr. Lonsdale had gone back to work after his wife's death, he did not last long and soon joined his wife and son in Elmwood. DePelchin had buried Mrs. Calhoun. Her prayers and best efforts had not saved Jennie Morrow. Her acquaintances in Memphis were being decimated by the disease. Most of the unacclimated nurses from Little Rock had died, just as she predicted, but being right brought her no joy. The ranks of the Howards had been radically thinned out by death and continued illness. The news in the paper distressed her, "but everything is sad, only some things are sadder than others."

"I am willing to do anything," she wrote. "I will humble myself before God if He will only hear my prayer for the recovery of those I nurse." Like Job, DePelchin wanted to know what she had done to earn God's wrath. Yet she clung to the concept of God's mercy. Surely, she believed, the people she nursed had repented their sins and reconciled with Jesus at the point of their death. Her prayers for their bodies had not availed, but surely God had heard her prayers for their souls. As for herself, "My Heavenly Father who put it into my heart to come here will care for me in this world, and when my work is done, take me home."[45]

DR. WILLIAM ARMSTRONG wrote a long letter to Lula on September 11. "I am feeling splendidly today," he said. "The cool breeze has braced me up. I wish we could have an inch of frost tonight." He sent news of friends and neighbors and closed with a blessing: "God grant you health & a full share of His Grace." After that Lula received a series of telegrams from her husband's doctor stating that he was doing fine. It must have been a relief to get Dr. Mitchell's telegram stating, "Dr. Armstrong very sick but doing well today. Says must not come here under any circumstances." Finally a card came from Armstrong himself. He scrawled in pencil the following message: "My dear wife—I have passed through the fever stages and have only to get the stomach right. Hope I can do this and see you soon. Husband." It was postmarked September 16. He died four days later.[46]

A woman friend wrote to Lula, "He did not want you to come to him, knowing that you would take the fever as sure as you came—and for your eight children's sake, you must not now think of coming. Memphis is like a wave of poison, if you come within its bounds you or anyone

*Lula Armstrong and four of her eight children. (The Letters of
William J. Armstrong, Health Sciences Historical Collections, Health Sciences
Library and Biocommunications Center, the University of Tennessee Health
Science Center, Memphis)*

else is drowned." She assured the widow that the doctor had been well cared for, with two nurses and his neighbor Benjamin Fithian to watch over him. "If Dr. Armstrong had had any other disease, he would liked to have had you with him," but under the circumstances Lula's presence would only have made matters worse for the doctor, "for he would have been troubled on your account. Do not reproach yourself for not coming, for wives have been taken from a loving husband's care as well as husbands from the clinging arms of devoted wives."[47]

Armstrong had entrusted his available cash to Fithian, who wrote Lula to assure her that he and Dr. Mitchell had laid out the dead man "nicely" and that he had seen personally to the burial in the doctors' plot in Elmwood. Fithian said that he had $210 in cash for her, with $110 still due from the Howards. He added that Mary the cook had let him know that she was still owed her wages.[48]

SEVEN

Lost Graves

WHEN THE SUMMER BEGAN, MEMPHIS had a thriving Jewish community of three thousand. On September 27, eighteen people gathered in the Congregation Children of Israel (Reform) synagogue for Rosh Hashanah, the New Year and the beginning of the High Holy Days leading to Yom Kippur. According to J. M. Keating, "Of the eighteen nine were fever convalescents, three were nurses from distant cities, the remaining six being those who alone escaped of all who remained to brave the disease." The gathering brought together the survivors of the city's two synagogues, with the secretary of Beth El Emeth (Orthodox) reading the service. Keating said that no one who was there would ever forget it: "There was not a dry eye among all those present, as they recalled the festival as it was observed in other and happier years, and remembered the brave and noble Menken, and many others who had passed away . . ."[1]

A month later, on October 29, the Memphis Board of Health declared the epidemic over. Since mid-August, the people in Memphis had witnessed terrible things. DePelchin wrote, "When I look back over these past few weeks, I exclaim in my heart, 'Oh days of horror! never to be erased from my memory.'" Keating described a corpse decomposed into liquid and bones, carried out on a rug; people so distraught and afraid that they threw a family member's dead body into a hog pen; a woman's body found in an outbuilding behind the *Appeal* office half eaten by rats. There is no medicine to heal the sight, no ritual sufficient to wipe such memories from the mind. What does it do to you, to have lived through something like that?[2]

The service at Children of Israel was one of the first of a series of ceremonies enacted in Memphis as the autumn advanced. Some were religious in nature, others emphatically, even rollickingly secular, but they all marked transition: from the old Memphis to the new, from the epidemic to the return of normal life, from grief to celebration. Through sermons and parties, parades and speeches and awards, the people of Memphis began to turn the horrors of the summer into a series of stories that would become legends, in the process deciding collectively who was a hero and who was not. The ceremonies bound together those who had stayed and those who had fled, drawing a line under the summer's experience and marking a new start.

Individuals reconciled what they had seen and done in ways suited to their own character and needs. Some sought liquid oblivion. The *Appeal* noted, "A great many quiet drunks are indulged in by the heroes, convalescents and refugees, now that *the war* is nearly over."[3] Others got back to business as soon as possible, whether that business was cotton or politics. Reverend Landrum and Kezia DePelchin continued to ponder the will of God. J. M. Keating worked out his reaction to the epidemic in public, in the columns of the *Appeal*, and in doing so, he helped to transform his city.

THE MEN AND WOMEN of the relief community saw themselves as fighting a war against yellow fever. Nathan Menken spent his days making sure that people had food to eat and medical care, but he spoke of himself as a soldier on the front lines. One of the Catholic priests who died in Memphis told Father Quinn that he looked forward to a "tussle with *Yellow Jack*." (Quinn commented, "Like a gallant son of Tipperary, he fought till he fell.") Luke Wright was the "General" in charge of Memphis's black troops. William Armstrong said that Memphis would be so broken up that when " 'this cruel war is over,' " society would have to start anew. Dr. Mitchell mourned the physicians who "fell by our sides in the darkest moments of our dreadful and deadly strife." Even Kezia DePelchin and J. M. Keating, neither particularly warlike persons, drew metaphors from the field of battle. DePelchin compared unacclimated young men to volunteer soldiers. "A true heart-felt sympathy has brought them; to contend on the battlefield; for is it not a battle, the enemy is silent but strong, and subtle." Keating wrote that relief workers who died had fallen with their faces to the foe.[4]

The world outside Memphis agreed with the relief community that the epidemic was equivalent to a war. The *New York Herald* said that "a noble army of men and women" had fought the fever, each of them leading "a forlorn hope." The *Herald* noted that veterans of the Civil War had died trying to save their former enemies: "In the presence of such heroism the bravest soldier and sailor stands abased in honorable humility." And in a perfervid editorial, the *London Standard* praised white southerners by saying that other branches of the Aryan family could have furnished troops like those who followed Robert E. Lee, but few could have sent their children to face the fever in order to save the lives of others.[5] Military language came naturally to men who had spent four years in uniform, who still called each other by titles indicating army rank, but this was a war that the valiant soldiers of Memphis could never win. They had no weapon that could kill the enemy, no stratagem with which to force the fever to withdraw. The epidemic would never surrender, never strike the Yellow Jack flag and sail away. Frost was their only ally, survival the only possible victory.

The death toll per day reached its climax on September 14. The official count said 127, but Keating insisted that it was more than two hundred. On that day, Keating remembered, even the most optimistic despaired. Only later could it be seen that the epidemic had peaked and that the number of dead per day was tending downward. The cooler days also encouraged people to believe that summer would end, frost would come, and life would continue. On September 20 Keating wrote, "We draw a freer breath, as if suddenly transported to a different atmosphere, and like the weary traveler ascending a lofty mountain, who finds unexpectedly a pleasant resting place on his perilous march, we pause, and rest our wearied minds and hearts, and take fresh courage to meet what remains of disease and death."[6]

As the epidemic grew to its close, many of the people who had done the most to fight it fell like soldiers killed in the last moments before Armistice: Sister Constance on September 9, Herbert Landrum on September 12, John Lonsdale Jr. and Major Willis of the Southern Express Company on September 15, Father Riordan of St. Patrick's and Dr. John Erskine on September 17, the A.P. stringer Robert Catron on September 24, Citizens' Relief Committee chairman Charles Fisher on September 26, and John Lonsdale Sr., having buried his wife and son, on October 1.

Keating considered them martyrs, people who had worked so hard to help others that they had worn themselves out and were unable to rally when the disease hit them.

While the old guard fell, Keating said, the convalescents moved up to the front to replace them. Howard Association president A. D. Langstaff had the fever, but recovered. So did Luke Wright of the CRC. On September 19 Rev. George Harris came in to dine at the Peabody. Reverend Landrum and his Presbyterian colleague Rev. W. E. Boggs were among the convalescents, as was police chief Pat Athy. Mayor Flippin survived. On September 22 the *Appeal* staff began returning to their posts. Fred Brennan, city editor, was still out. (Brennan may have had the longest-lasting case in the city. He was sick for ten weeks, had three separate bouts of black vomit, and at one point hiccuped for twenty-four hours, but he recovered and lived to practice journalism in Memphis for years to come.)[7]

The disease did strange things to survivors. Some came out of the fever demented. On the other hand, there was the case of the twelve-year-old girl who three years before had been attacked by some unspecified disease that left her deaf, mute, paralyzed on one side, and afflicted with a tremor on the other. Yellow fever cured all the child's ailments, Keating said, leaving her "mistress of all her powers of mind and body, as fresh and vigorous as if they had never been impaired." Others weathered the toxic stage of the fever but remained physically weak for days after. Much more commonly, however, people felt very well indeed, so well that they overextended themselves. After two weeks of convalescence Francis Schley left his home one afternoon to pick up some groceries. A passing doctor found him lying dead on Market Street with a basket of potatoes at his side.[8]

ON THE MORNING of October 7 the "National Relief Boat" reached Memphis. The *Appeal* called it the "first incident in river circles being worthy of note that has transpired within the last sixty days." Organized by businessmen and supported by charitable donations from towns and cities throughout the North, the *John Chambers* was on a mission to bring aid to river towns. Two army lieutenants commanded the expedition. Memphis did not need supplies. However, ten tons of mail had accumulated in the city during the epidemic, and the expedition was asked to deliver it to points south. The expedition report noted that the mail "was carefully fumigated with sulphur every night in the Memphis office, but when it came on board we had it disinfected with turpentine." The *John Chambers* left that afternoon. At Vicksburg, one of the army officers died of yellow fever and the War Department ordered the boat home to St. Louis.[9]

FARTHER NORTH, autumn had arrived. The Memphis evacuees wanted to come home, to open shop, to get back to business. In the last week of September cotton bales began to appear on Front Row, a sign of returning commerce, but on October 6 the *Appeal* warned the absentees to stay away and urged merchants to stay closed: "There is no trade. There is no likelihood of trade." The paper pointed out that planters were fighting the fever like everyone else, the cotton harvest had been postponed, and railroad travel was still limited. The trains that did come to Memphis devoted their cargo space to food and medicine. "From Cairo, Illinois, to New Orleans, a distance of eleven hundred miles, and from the river eastward for one hundred miles the yellow-fever holds sovereign sway," the *Appeal* said. On that day Memphis had 105 new fever cases. The midday temperatures still reached into the eighties. Neither the summer nor the fever was yet through with Memphis.[10]

On October 19 Memphis finally got its frost. *Ae. aegypti's* feeding time probably shrank to a relatively short period in the middle of the day, but that was enough to keep the epidemic going for another fortnight. Before the weather turned cold, it seemed that everyone who could have the fever did. Most of the fourteen thousand blacks left in Memphis had fallen sick, to the shock of people who assumed that African Americans were immune. Almost all the six thousand whites had contracted the disease. Keating estimated that there were only about two hundred white people in all of Memphis who did not get the fever, probably because they had acquired immunity from previous encounters with the disease. When there were no more new people left to infect, the epidemic wound down.[11]

DESPITE WARNINGS that Yellow Jack was still there, the absentees started to drift back into town in October. Some found that the houses

they had deserted two months before had been stripped of all valu-
ables, including the marble mantelpieces. Others discovered the decayed
corpses of housebreakers who had used the family's beds, foods, and liquor until the fever struck them down. As predicted, some of the people
who came back before cold weather took the fever and died. Among
these latter was W.J.D. Lonsdale, son of John Lonsdale Sr., who returned
to town late in October to take up the family insurance business. He
died on November 2.[12]

Recovering convalescents and newly returned refugees tried to rein-
stitute the rituals of mourning by placing flowers on the graves of their
departed friends and relatives. When mourners arrived at Elmwood
Cemetery, they were shocked to discover that many of their loved ones
did not have individual graves. Herbert Landrum had described the
undertaker's "wholesale burial business" in early September. In order to
get the bodies under the sod as quickly as possible, the undertaker and
the CRC had resorted to using gangs of laborers to dig trench graves.
Bodies, encased in coffins, were placed in the graves side by side, one
after another in lines, like fallen dominoes. Most of the original Elmwood staff had died or fled the city. The new staffers could not tell the
grieving where their lost ones lay. To have the person you loved buried
like a pauper in a common grave offended the sensibilities; to have that
happen when you had paid for a private plot was doubly outrageous.
People wept as they wandered through Elmwood with bouquets of
flowers.[13]

In August, Memphis had begged the nation for charity. By the end of
September the Howards had a storehouse full of stuff: potatoes, flour,
coffee, and other essentials, plus delicacies like jellies (most of which
the physicians forbade their patients) and all manner of peculiar sun-
dries. Among the latter, the *Avalanche* listed "double-lined buckskin
gloves, that would be useful in Alaska" and a dozen beautifully embroi-
dered secondhand chemises, leading the reporter to surmise that some
good woman had stripped herself of her underwear for the poor of
Memphis. He wrote, "So much of this stuff is so utterly useless that we
must laugh at the donors' lack of knowledge of our wants, but when we
think of the generous spirit that has prompted these liberal donations,
we feel more like crying." Although Dr. Mitchell continued to pressure
the state government for beef on the hoof, Memphis had enough food to
see the population through.[14]

So the Howards rallied Memphis's resources and organized relief efforts for the surrounding countryside. The fever had followed the railroad lines with devastating impact, and physicians in the stricken small towns telegraphed Dr. Mitchell and A. D. Langstaff for help. When Langstaff took the train out to Brownsville, Tennessee, about fifty miles east of Memphis, he found that most of the country doctors had remained at their posts during the epidemic, but many had died. "Persons were dying—had died, and had remained unburied—to whom, in some instances, no assistance had been rendered," Langstaff said. "Then it was I saw the necessity of establishing relief trains, which might leave Memphis each morning with physicians, nurses, medicines, etc., which trains would stop at each depot long enough to enable the physicians to visit the afflicted and leave them with nurses and supplies." Langstaff telegraphed James Montgomery, superintendent of the Louisville and Memphis Railroad, asking if the line could supply a locomotive and baggage car for this project. Montgomery promised an engine, coach, and express car, plus any help the company could provide, and suggested extending the service even farther along the line. The Howards received similar responses from the Memphis and Charleston and the Mississippi and Tennessee railroads, and in early October they began running relief trains to nearby and far-distant towns, including Bowling Green, Kentucky, almost three hundred miles to the northeast.[15]

The Howards sent DePelchin's friend Kate Heckle to Decatur, Alabama, a train trip of more than 150 miles. On the day of the trip, Heckle went to the Howard office early. She "found it crowded with people of all shades, from the jetty hue of Africa to the delicate blonde of northern Europe," waiting for assignments or nurses or coffins. After a ride to the terminal in an ambulance packed with nurses, Heckle embarked on an eastbound supply train accompanied by A. D. Langstaff. Heckle marveled at his "powers of ubiquity, for you could see him here, there, and everywhere, and treated all with kindness alike." The supply train was moving slowly, so Langstaff had the nurses transferred to the regular line and sent them off with loaves of bread for their breakfast.

As it turned out, the bread was all they had to eat that day. No one had thought about feeding the nurses, and they were unable to buy food at the stations along the way. Finally Heckle decided to improvise. She had brought some coffee and sugar. They got a tin bucket, scoured it with sand, wiped it out with a towel, and boiled up some very strong coffee on the stove in the railroad car. They served it in Heckle's tin traveling cup, a chipped china mug supplied by a "colored lady," and some mustard tins from Heckle's satchel. (Many treatments for fever victims included mustard baths, so these were probably medicinal rather than culinary supplies.) Heckle wrote to DePelchin, "Some of the passengers were too dignified to drink coffee made in an old tin pail, with only bread to eat, but I tell you it was far better than nothing." The next morning at Decatur they were fed breakfast, much to Heckle's relief, and she set to work.

When she returned to Memphis later in the month, the Howards were winding down their relief operation. The nurses from South Carolina, Georgia, and Mobile had gone home; their quarantine had been lifted. In downtown Memphis, businesses were open and wagons rumbled down the formerly empty streets. It looked very cheerful except for all the people dressed in black. DePelchin was missing, rumored to be dead. Without further nursing work in Memphis, Heckle decided to go and stay with friends in New Orleans. Waiting at the depot on an icy cold morning, she heard someone say DePelchin's name. Upon inquiry, the speaker, a black nurse named Sarah Jackson, told Heckle that De-Pelchin had been sent to help nurse yellow fever patients in a little town in Mississippi.[16]

AFTER MRS. HECKLE HAD LEFT for Decatur, DePelchin nursed her cold and rested. When she felt better, she began to make excursions around Memphis. It was the second week of October, and as she rode the street-cars, she watched the houses being opened up and aired. Wearing a clean linen dress instead of her nursing wrapper, she went to hear Dr. Dalzell preach on Sunday to a small congregation that included two Episcopal nuns and the children from the Church Home. She checked on her patients. She found that Mrs. Calhoun's little boy had been sent to the Leath Orphan Asylum, and Julia Morrow's sons were recovering from the fever. When DePelchin went to visit her first patients at the brothel, the youngest threw her arms around her and cried. She said, "I did not mean you to find me here again." Once again, Linda and Myra both promised that they would leave the life. They told DePelchin that they could go to family members or to the women's refuge there in Memphis. Privately, DePelchin was dubious. "Poor creatures, now they are in the meshes of sin, it is hard to do better. Society, ever ready to help a man back into the right way, scorns a woman's efforts to do better." She was willing to help them if she could, but she told them that they had to show willingness to reform: "You must leave this house." She left them "with a very sad heart."[17]

Recuperated, DePelchin went back to work for the Howards. They sent her to Senatobia, Mississippi. Most of the population there had fled to camps in the surrounding countryside, leaving behind a small cadre of "Andersons" (named after Butler Anderson, the deceased Memphis Howard Association president) to care for the sick. With only five families left in Senatobia, the Andersons consolidated their operations in the center of town, setting up a dining hall in the jail and sleeping quarters in the courthouse. "Just think of it," DePelchin wrote. "Eating in the jail, sleeping in the Court-house, a nice state of affairs to write home to Houston." The work was slower paced than it had been in Memphis, although equally emotionally draining. Rather than moving rapidly from case to case, DePelchin settled in with one family, the Dickeys. She watched one after another die until only Mrs. Dickey was left.[18]

A CORRESPONDENT from the Louisville Courier-Journal risked a trip to Memphis. He interviewed Dr. Mitchell and went out to Elmwood with Langstaff and other Howard leaders. During the four-mile trip they told him stories. "There lived Mr.——, who became delirious, jumped out of that second-story window, and killed himself" and "Nine persons were taken to the potters' field, all in one load, from that dwelling across the way." Kezia DePelchin heard similar conversations on the streetcars as people pointed out the windows at this locus of death, that house where everyone died. For those who had lived through the epidemic, old landmarks had been replaced with new ones denoting the summer's agony. Their mental Memphis would always be different from the Memphis in the minds of the people who fled.[19]

"Of those who die we can only know they have gone to their reward, and the gratitude of those they have served keep their memory green," wrote Kezia DePelchin.[20] His memory will be cherished, we will always remember their sacrifices, his name will live among us: similar phrases abound in newspaper stories and letters from the epidemic summer.

Over and over again, those who lived through the epidemic made the promise of remembrance. Although an *Avalanche* writer concluded that the men who died fighting the epidemic would "have no other reward than the assurance of good deeds well performed," this existential assurance was not enough for most people. They wanted their graves marked, their works remembered. Therefore, as the days grew shorter and the nights colder, members of the relief community held ceremonies to commemorate what they had been through and honor the comrades they had lost.

At the Peabody Hotel, the volunteer doctors packed their bags in the third week of October. They sat at the tall windows in the hotel lobby and watched the black-clad people at their business in the street below. They shared a last cup of coffee in the restaurant. All that remained was to say good-bye. For that purpose, the Howards hurriedly commissioned an "impromptu banquet." A. D. Langstaff was there, as were Keating, Major Walthall, and other leaders of the relief effort, but it was the doctors' night. Dr. Robert W. Mitchell addressed his corps: "I will speak no further of what you have seen, and done, and suffered. My heart is too full, and my words are too barren to convey what I feel. What you have seen can never be described; what you have done and endured will need no language to be perpetuated in the hearts of this people." He read the names of the thirty-four dead physicians, beginning with William Armstrong.[21]

Throughout the autumn the survivors ritualized their gratitude to one another and to the world at large by presenting gifts to the illustrious. There was a brief fad for fancy canes. The Howards gave one to W. S. Brooks, *Appeal* subeditor, who had suffered the loss of his entire family during the epidemic. The surviving *Appeal* staff gave an gold-headed ebony cane to Keating, accompanied by a letter praising his courage, dedication to the public welfare, and "your uniform kindness to all your employees under all circumstances." A few weeks later, members of Memphis's elite—large landowners, wealthy merchants, and "the very spirit of the Young America of Memphis"—gave Keating a fine gold watch. At a formal banquet honoring Dr. Mitchell, the assembled men of the relief community presented him with a silver tea set, including separate pots for chocolate, coffee, and tea, in a rosewood case lined in white satin.[22]

The farewell banquets featured numerous toasts. Today most Americans encounter formal toasts at wedding receptions, if at all, but in the 1870s toasting was a way of honoring, thanking, or otherwise expressing appreciation for individuals or groups. At Mitchell's banquet a toast honored the clergy, highlighting the heroism of the Church of Rome but with proper respect for the few Protestant ministers who stayed. There was a toast to "the noble little band of Hebrews of Memphis, whose faith was alone reposed in the Great Jehovah." The journalists present praised one another, the printers, and especially Keating. Reverend Dalzell commended Keating for a recent editorial in which he had said, "The steadiness and tenacity, the bravery and determination of the north, and the élan, dash, courage and endurance of the south, are the common heritage of every citizen of the Union." When Keating himself offered a toast to "the Women Nurses," the men rose to their feet and drank in silence, signifying the highest respect and honor.[23]

There were no women present. If there were any black men present, they were carrying trays to and from the tables. A few weeks earlier the men around the table had sheltered behind black soldiers; they had noted with disgust the cowardice of men and contrasted it to the courage of women. Now that the crisis was over, it was time to honor heroes, but the very process of commemoration wrote into the city's collective memory a story that featured white men as the heroes of the epidemic, cast women in supporting roles, and, when possible, elided blacks entirely.

The survivors also had to deal with their resentment of the returning refugees. The people who had fled Memphis in August had done exactly what the board of health suggested. Had those 20,000 people stayed, most of them would have gone down with the fever, and somewhere between 10,000 and 15,000 would have died. Just the same, it would be surprising if the people who stayed—the heroes of Memphis, as they were being called—did not resent the evacuees. In early September the *Avalanche* had bluntly stated what was surely known to all of the relief community. "Memphis has many rich men who own palatial stores along Main Street. There is not one of those rich men here to-day in the hour of our greatest calamity. These rich men are neither represented in person nor by their surplus dollars," said the unnamed writer. "The majority of the men who are standing in the deadly breach, fighting the most gigantic plague that ever cursed American soil, are men who do not own one dollar in real estate in Memphis." Where are John Overton Jr. and the others? he asked. "Have we seen the light of their countenances or the color of their money?" In another equally bitter editorial, the writer predicted that the evacuees would "return well and happy and the laborers here will be forgotten."[24] Having passed through a season in hell, having lived in a charnel house, having risked one's life to save the lives and property of others, a person might well emerge in the autumn exhausted, heartsick, and inclined to sneer at people who had not been to the wars.

THE TEMPERATURE had been slowly dropping for days, but on the last Saturday night of October a front came through, cold rain fell, and Sunday morning dawned clear and frigid. It was the sort of abrupt change that sends contemporary southerners rummaging through trunks and searching the backs of closets for the heavy clothes put away in the early spring. In 1878 people probably looked for that shawl not seen since March and wondered where their long winter underwear was. They would need warm clothes if they planned to go to Central Baptist, where Rev. Sylvanis Landrum would preach for the first time in ten weeks.[25]

The only white Baptist preacher who stayed had become one of the most beloved ministers in the city. During the epidemic, CRC head Charles Fisher wrote to his sister of Dr. Landrum, "He is the best man I ever saw." Keating described Landrum's constant work during the epidemic, saying that he was sometimes a nurse, sometimes an adviser, but always a man of God, bearing with him the consolation of the Gospel. The *Appeal* kept the public apprised of his recovery from the fever and said, "God bless the dear old man, who has never wearied in his good works."[26]

Inside Central Baptist, the pews filled with people clad in the dark clothes of mourning. They knew that the man in the pulpit was grieving too. Landrum's decision to live up to his own concept of pastoral duty had cost the lives of his two youngest sons, making him Memphis's apostle to the bereaved. On the previous day, he had been called to see a widow who was not one of his congregation. She told him, "I wanted to talk to one who had suffered; I, therefore, sent for you." When Landrum asked God to help them understand His word and obey His will, the people assembled knew what he meant.

Landrum pointed out that this epidemic had passed all previous expectations for morbidity and geographic extent. Never before had the fever "extended its baneful, blighting influence over so vast an area, and with a malignity as fatal in the country as in the city." It also hit the young harder than any previous epidemic, sweeping them away "by scores and by hundreds." He said to the congregation, "Look around you and see how many parents have been left, with the children all, or nearly all, gone. Many Rachels are weeping because her children are not; many Davids, in agony, cry out, 'Oh my son Absalom! My son, my son Absalom! Would God I had died for thee, oh Absalom my son, my son!'"

What had been learned? The pastor listed three lessons. First, the practical: the city should pay attention to drainage and sewage. "It is wiser to pay taxes in money than in the lives of your citizens, and the tears and suffering of the widow and the orphan. These will not pave your streets, nor restore a dishonored credit, nor rebuild broken fortunes." Second, you cannot tell in advance who will be the hero, who the coward, in a crisis like the epidemic. People who were expected to behave well had been cowardly, and meanwhile, those from whom nothing good was expected had proved to be heroes. Third, you cannot judge whether or not someone is behaving as a Christian should. You do not know your brother's circumstances or motives. "Judge yourself, not another. Leave him to himself and to God." Landrum said that he had seen true religion, the power of God, manifested during the summer's ordeal. Unexpected, "it has shown forth as a light in the darkness, a glorious reality." The dying proclaimed their faith and, with their eyes toward heaven, submitted themselves to the will of God, although the pastor confessed that he personally found such submission very difficult.

What was there to do? Be grateful to those who sent help. "The United States are a nation, a grand national brotherhood with one heart." Be repentant. Turn from wickedness to God. Help the poor and needy. Finally, Landrum said, have faith. "Heaven is not a world of strangers. We shall sit down at our Elder Brother's table with the loved ones who have gone on before—gone only for a short while before. They wait our coming." In proper Baptist fashion, he concluded with Scripture: "Fear not; believe only." The congregation sang, soprano voices soaring out and bass answering, "In the sweet by-and-by we shall meet on that heavenly shore."[27]

ON OCTOBER TWENTY-NINE, with a heavy frost on the ground, the board of health declared the epidemic over. Wagons full of cotton were rolling into town. The CRC had stopped giving out rations three days earlier, and the local newspapers urged blacks to get themselves out to the cotton fields, where they would now be welcome. Businesses reopened, and the Memphis, Clarksville, and Louisville Railroad ran extra trains to bring home the refugees.[28]

When the refugee camps outside of town closed on October 30, the two militia units assigned to guard duty there returned to the city on the same train. Brown's Zouaves met the white Bluff City Grays and the black McClellan Guards at the train station. They formed a battalion headed by the Bluff City cornet band ("one of the best colored musical organizations in the country," according to the *Appeal*), and they all marched up Main Street. The *Appeal* said that the Grays and the Guards made a "striking appearance," bringing tears to the eyes of the old Confederates. (The Grays wore uniforms reminiscent of the Confederate army, while the McClellan Guards were attired in federal blue.) At the Grays' armory, Colonel John Cameron gave a farewell address to men he addressed as "citizen-soldiers." When called to service, you regarded it as a compliment, he said. "For have you not long paraded these streets, clad in the habiliments of war, seeking servage? And did you not point out a field of duty? And you have well discharged it." The colonel told them that their reward lay in the approval of their fellow citizens and "the gracious smiles of fair women, which every manly fellow yearns to merit." He said that they could have the satisfaction of knowing that they had done their duty to the community. Seven of the Grays and six of the Guards had died during their service at the camps.

The *Appeal* noted that the Bluff City Grays were "composed, rank and file, of some of our most promising young men, and the McClellan Guards, of the same class of our colored citizens . . ." The last sentence casually advances two radical propositions: that young black men could be "promising" in exactly the same way as young white men, and that Memphis had colored *citizens*. A later *Appeal* saluted Brown's Zouave Guards: "Too much praise cannot be accorded both officers and privates for the excellent and trusty manner in which they performed their duty, coming to the rescue, as it were, at a time when threats were made to raid the citizens' relief commissary." He listed the names of black officers and men, noting that two privates and a lieutenant had died (presumably of the fever) during the epidemic.[29]

These positive stories about black soldiers may have reflected political reality in Memphis. There was no way of knowing how much the epidemic was going to change the city, but simply looking at the complexion of the people on the streets would have been enough to convince the politically astute that reviving the city would require African American support. The Democrats had already accepted black citizenship and were actively courting black voters before the epidemic sent whites scurrying for safer cities.

All true, but Keating's public praise reflects more than political expediency. At the age of eighteen he had joined a rebellion to gain rights for Irish Catholic peasants, although he was neither Catholic nor a peasant; as a young man in New York, he had fought against a political party that sought to deny rights to people on the basis of their nativity and religion. He valued black Memphians' patience and kindness. He respected the way that black policemen and black soldiers had conducted themselves during the crisis. He did not think that blacks and whites were equal—he still thought that blacks were in the primary school of civilization—but when the McClellan Guards marched down Main Street, Keating saw citizens, not savages. After 1878 he would denigrate blacks who aspired to "social equality"—defined as equal treatment in public accommodations—but he maintained a strong commitment to political equality and economic opportunity for black men. He thought that blacks could and should be able to vote and go to school and advance in the world, all on their side of the color line. In years to come, he would maintain those ideals at considerable personal cost.

ON ALL HALLOWS' DAY, Father William Walsh celebrated a Thanksgiving Mass for his abstemious Irish and a throng of well-wishers. It was a grand scene, Walsh said, and worth commemoration. He had a photographer present to make pictures. The people struck camp and in solemn procession marched back into Memphis, to St. Bridget's, where the Benediction of the Sacrament was followed by the chanting of the Te Deum.[30]

IN OCTOBER a Mississippi writer weighed in on what Keating called the "runaway clergymen." In a letter to the Appeal, D. W. Allen of Coldwater protested that public opinion had forced ministers to "sacrifice themselves uselessly" ever since the epidemic began. Devoting time and services to congregations and friends was proper under normal

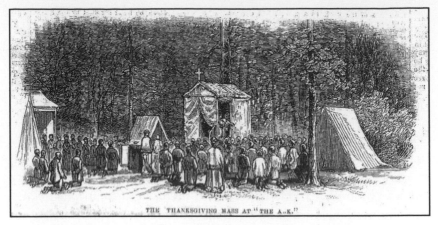

*The Thanksgiving Mass at Camp Father Mathew, celebrated from
Father Walsh's altar on wheels. Illustration from* Frank Leslie's Illustrated,
January 11, 1879.

circumstances, he said, but doing so now was suicidal. Why, he asked, should ministers risk their lives when it would do so little good? In the first place, the fever came on so fast that patients had little time for spiritual counseling, and patients in their final delirium were "incapable of profiting by any spiritual advice that may be offered them." A man who had lived a Christian life was always prepared to die, and if a "man has lived in outbreaking sin and open rebellion against his maker, there is but little confidence to be placed in any profession of religion he may make on a dying bed." Allen argued that it was cruel to expect a "good man" to expose himself to danger in such circumstances.

But who was a good man? People in Memphis had learned some un-comfortable truths about goodness. Back in September, when the news of Annie Cook's death made the papers throughout the nation, an Arkansas journalist had written that when the fever came, "men and women fled for their lives; the most sacred ties were broken; brothers fled from sisters, husbands left their wives and children, and children deserted their parents." The madam turned her house into a hospital and nursed the sick until she herself contracted the fever and died. "Now tell me," the journalist asked, "ye world of prim morality and cold, prudential modesty—is there one chance of heaven for this poor, betrayed woman! Will those pearly gates be closed upon this repentant Magdalen, and yet open to those selfish, hollow-hearted creatures who left their kith and kin to perish in poverty and disease?"[31]

Keating told of a Memphis woman who had written to a friend in the North, "I believe this plague has made a Universalist of me. I have seen men in a moment rise from the depths of degradation and wickedness to Christ-like sublimity in devotion and sacrifice, and the most polluted of my own sex suddenly changed into angels of love and mercy. Thus God teaches us to scorn none of his creatures."

Keating himself believed that all Christians had the same aspirations, hopes, and fears. He argued that the role of a Protestant minister was much the same as that of a Catholic priest: "Confronting the inevitable, doctrine and dogma almost wholly disappear. The terms of forgiveness and restoration to the Father's love are the same with all." The ministers who stayed in Memphis visited the sick, prayed with the dying, and comforted the bereaved. Their wives shared their faith and sustained their ministry. As for the preachers who left, Keating wrote that "it was said" they had set an example of faithlessness. "They could not even faintly imitate the compassion of Christ. They falsified their own teachings and inflicted an injury on the church that the work of their braver brethren could only in part repair."[32]

DePelchin wrote that people who criticized the absent ministers should ask themselves if the minister could count on his church to care for his family should he die, "or must he know that gaunt poverty will be the life of the preacher's widow." Nonetheless, she thought that the "shepherds who ran" had done poorly. "It is no use mincing the matter, we do look for those who at camp meetings, and in the assembly, sing 'I am a Soldier of the Cross' to be one."[33]

As the weather slowly turned autumnal, DePelchin stayed on in Senatobia. While Mrs. Dickey recovered, DePelchin did the laundry, cooked, cleaned, fumigated the house, buried the vomit-stained mattresses in the garden, and took care of livestock. She and Alec Tate, a black man who was one of the "Andersons," cleaned the fever room in the Dickey house, Kezia using a brush to scrub the walls as high as she could reach and Alec scouring the floor with lye water.[34]

Sometimes the work made her so tired she trembled; at one point she fell to the kitchen floor in a faint. But the Senatobia people she worked with, black and white, were brave and kind. She became fond of Alec Tate and quoted his wisdom when she wrote to her sister. When she could get another nurse to sit with Mrs. Dickey, she went for long walks through Senatobia, one of the prettiest towns she had ever seen. Most of all, she had time to reflect on her experiences in Memphis. She wrote, "I often wondered if I had sinned that my patients did not recover. I have prayed more than in all my life put together. I sometimes when out in the yard, look up and think will God not hear me? The stars look down upon me with their diamond eyes are they smiling on me or are they mocking me in my despair?" She was grateful when a doctor reminded her that no one in the Mississippi Valley had been able to cure patients of this fever.[35]

The temperatures at night dipped below freezing, although the days were still warm. In Memphis, the epidemic was declared officially over on October 29. The Howards began to pay off nurses and hand out passes for rail travel home. DePelchin felt that she could not abandon Mrs. Dickey, but she knew that she had better pick up her pass from the Howards while she could. So she made a quick trip to Memphis, where she found that she had been reported dead. "But no one had administered on my estate," she wrote. She found her trunk, battered and broken, a "dilapidated umbrella, a water proof cloak, and sundry other articles of equal beauty, and value," and with railroad pass in hand, she returned to Senatobia.[36]

AT SOME POINT in the late autumn, J. M. Keating left Memphis for New York and an extended vacation. During his months off he would author a book on yellow fever. *A History of the Yellow Fever: The Yellow Fever Epidemic of 1878, in Memphis, Tenn.*, was published in 1879, with all proceeds going to the Howard Association, and is still the standard source on the topic. Always the self-taught scholar, Keating compiled information on history, medical science, and theories, meteorology, sanitation, contagion and anti-contagion, and treatments. He wrote a short history of the Memphis epidemic, supplemented by a chapter called "Incidents of the Epidemic" in which he created a day-by-day narrative by quoting the *Appeal*, the *Avalanche*, and other Memphis papers. He included reports from the relief organizations. He listed all the dead of Memphis in alphabetical order by day.

But before he settled down with pen, paper, newspaper clippings, and stacks of research materials, he traveled to Washington, where he and Representative Casey Young were feted as representatives of the heroes of Memphis. Later in December he accepted the accolades of his peers at a New York Press Club reception. Keating's solitary stand at the *Appeal* office had gripped the imagination of the national press. "When the precincts of labor became as silent as the tomb, when desertion, death and disease visited the office, Colonel Keating, like the Roman sentry whose erect form was found amid the ruins of buried Herculaneum, never forsook his post," said the *Chicago Tribune*'s Memphis correspondent. Noting that Keating was Irish, the writer called him "frank, generous, chivalric, and brave," and "withal a genuine type of his nationality."[37]

DEPELCHIN REMAINED ISOLATED in Senatobia. Knowing that she was a fever nurse, people in town shunned her. She felt "as lonely as Robinson Crusoe, minus the being monarch of all I survey!" Mrs. Dickey wrote to her sister in Colliersville, Tennessee, but got no reply. Finally, in mid-November the sister's husband (Mr. Dill) showed up, dusty from travel. Apparently Mrs. Dickey's letters had not made it through to Colliersville until the previous day. After learning of her situation, Dill had come to Senatobia to ask Mrs. Dickey to come live with her sister and him. ("A brother-in-law worth having," DePelchin noted.) They agreed that she and DePelchin would go to Memphis, where they could board an eastbound train to Colliersville. After leaving Mrs. Dickey there, DePelchin would go to stay with friends at Sewanee. Alex Tate and his wife agreed to move into the house and take care of things until the fever scare ended, and Mrs. Dickey and DePelchin left for Memphis.

On arrival, DePelchin drew her last pay from the Howards, took Mrs. Dickey to a ladies' restaurant for lunch, then set off to find Myra and Linda. She had written to say that she would be in town, but had received no reply. DePelchin happened to meet a member of the Women's Christian Association, the group that ran the city's mission for prostitutes, and together they went out to the brothel, only to find a red auction flag on the door. A servant in the house told her where she could find Linda—in a new brothel. "I went with fear and trembling," DePelchin wrote. "The woman of the house was polite, said Linda had received my letter, could say no more. She was then out." DePelchin could not find Myra at all. "It only shows me how powerless we are. Even with good motives we cannot turn the heart, that is for God alone. How I hope and pray they may yet be saved."[38]

DePelchin had joined the Howards for support and security, not for pay. She took her last wages because she knew that there were people in Memphis who would need them. She left $50 for Sallie Blew, the one surviving child of the editor of the *Western Methodist* magazine, $27 to the mission for reformed prostitutes, and $10 for Arthur Calhoun, son of the young mother whose moonlight burial had so distressed her. Had she been able to find the orphaned boy, she would have given him all the money, but inquiring letters had produced no information as to his whereabouts.[39]

She and Mrs. Dickey walked down to the river, now stirring with traffic. The long-delayed cotton harvest was on its way to Memphis's Front Street factors, and the working class of Memphis had jobs again. In the evening they waited at the Memphis and Charleston Railroad depot for the midnight train to Colliersville. Once aboard, they found an acquaintance who offered to escort Mrs. Dickey to her sister's house. DePelchin's last patient sat with her until the conductor called the Colliersville whistle-stop. "She left and I looked in vain out into the darkness to see her on the platform, but I know that she too looked after the train that took me from her," DePelchin wrote. After two days of traveling and waiting for trains, she caught a night coal train up a steep grade to the village of Sewanee, home of the University of the South, an Episcopalian college located far from any city, deep in the forests of the Cumberland Plateau. On a cold night, her former teacher welcomed her to a cozy house with a warm fire, a kitten purring by the hearth, and a tasty supper. She wrote, "As I look around and find myself waited on, and petted I can hardly realize it is I or that I am in the same world I have been in the last few weeks."[40]

THE YEAR 1878 saw a subdued Christmas in Memphis; although the re-opening of the cotton market had revived the city's economy, most of the people on the streets wore black. On Christmas Day the *Appeal* printed a poem called "Christmas Reverie." In it, a woman remembers her husband and son.

Though in Elmwood they're sleeping,
 I cannot find the spot,
That marks their place of resting,
Long I searched but found it not.
I wandered through its silent shades,
 I prayed to find my dead,
None but kind angels e'er may know
 The lonely tears I shed.[41]

Kezia DePelchin stayed in Sewanee well into December. The University of the South, founded in the 1850s by southern Episcopalians, maintained high standards in academics and demeanor. DePelchin thought the views on the mountain were "enchanting," the company refined, but she felt so bad that she did not get out much. Her letters do not explain what ailed her, but given that her host's doctor prescribed rest and regular meals, it may have been simple exhaustion. The doctor also told her to drink less coffee. "You may have observed that I often speak of coffee," she wrote to her sister. "I have drank a great deal." Defensively, she wrote that in Memphis she needed some kind of stimulant, and coffee was certainly safer than whiskey.[42]

After several weeks of rest, she felt well enough to commence the long journey home: down the mountain and west by train to Nashville and then to Memphis, where she had time to visit her colleagues' graves in Elmwood. On the last leg of the trip she journeyed with emigrants heading west, whole families looking for a new and better future on the frontier. As the train turned south, they left behind winter's cold and people threw open the windows to the warm air. At Christmastide the train pulled into Houston, where the flowers bloomed, oranges ripened in the trees, and Cordelia Buckner Morris's children waited for their Aunt Kizzie. She wrote, "It is almost worth the trouble of going, to have everyone so glad to see me back."[43]

EIGHT

After the Fever

"FOUR THOUSAND LIVES, AND FIVE MILLIONS of dollars, not to speak of the humiliations of our position as suppliants for the world's charity, are an awful price to pay for our negligence in sanitary affairs, and for the recklessness which disregarded the lessons of 1873," Keating wrote. For years he had been interested in municipal sanitation. In late October he took up the theme again in an editorial titled "The Future of Memphis." He said that the city had to be cleaned up: "Take up the Nicholson pavement, sewer the bayou, pave the streets with stone or asphalt, or macadamize them, and give us a board of health with power to enforce its degrees, and intelligent enough to know that its duties are something more than compiling a list of the sick and dead, and the epidemic will not have been in vain. Unless this is done, it will be useless, and Memphis has no future."[1]

None of the reforms Keating envisioned could be accomplished until the first, most basic one was accomplished: getting the city's finances straightened out. The people who had bought Memphis bonds wanted their money, just as they had before the epidemic, and as before, the city had no money with which to pay. In 1875 elite Memphians had campaigned to get out from under the debt by repealing the city charter, in effect committing municipal suicide. This plan failed owing to popular opposition. But in the wake of the fever, the majority of the city's voters came to accept that abolishing the city was the only way to save it.

As was the pattern in Memphis, the process began with a mass meeting that authorized the creation of a committee. Headed by D. T. Porter, wholesale grocer, head of the Planters' Insurance Company, and one of the surviving leaders of the Citizens' Relief Committee, this group of businessmen steered Memphis through dissolution. In January, at the behest of the entire Shelby County delegation, the state legislature passed legislation rescinding charters of all cities in the state with more than thirty-five thousand in population, Memphis being the only one to fit that description. Further legislation replaced the mayor and the thirty-member city council with a commission government. This new government could collect the taxes authorized by the state legislature but could not issue bonds nor incur debts. Keating considered the law dissolving the city charter essential, arguing that it "protected the people against their creditors, and gave them time in this respect to put their house in order before resuming their obligations to pay their debts." The governor appointed the first set of commissioners, not one of them a professional politician, and named Porter as president of the district. On the last day of January 1879 Memphis ceased to exist. Until 1893, the Bluff City was officially named the Taxing District of Shelby County.[2]

The city's creditors promptly sued and over the next three months pursued their case all the way to the Tennessee Supreme Court. With its legal status still unsettled, the new government found it difficult to collect taxes. When the court upheld the Taxing District in May, people in Memphis celebrated with cannons and bonfires. According to D. T. Porter, "The object in creating the Taxing District was not to repudiate the debt of the old city of Memphis, but to have a cheap and efficient system of government so as to put the municipality in a good sanitary condition, pave the streets, and enable us to pay that debt upon terms that may be agreed upon by the commissioners that may be appointed, and the creditors." Over the next twelve years the Taxing District actually managed to take in revenues and pay employees on time, a feat that had eluded previous governments. But the new government did not take power in time to stave off another yellow fever epidemic.[3]

Spring arrived, and nothing had been done to clean up the city. In places the garbage was so high that wagons could not pass through. Once again, a public meeting was held, this time to work out some way to better sanitary conditions before the fever season returned. J. M. Keating, back from New York, spoke on the economic advantages of sanitation. Funded by voluntary contributions from the public, the Auxiliary Sanitary Commission set crews to cleaning. Their efforts had no impact on the *Ae. aegypti,* which as usual began to fly, mate, feed, and lay eggs in the cisterns as the weather grew warmer. In July, fever cases began to appear in Memphis. What followed provokes a sense of déjà vu: panicked refugees, pleas for help, camps opened in the countryside, and deaths, 587 of them.[4]

Exasperation undercut public sympathy for Memphis's plight. It was hard to feel sorry for people who did not have the good sense to clean up. For that matter, it was hard to feel sorry for people whose solution to debt was to dissolve their government and refuse payment; as the *New York Times* said in February 1879, a community like that was "insensible to shame." In October the *Times* suggested that Memphis's "bitter lesson" had been repeated "because it needed the severe instruction, and it is to be hoped that it will profit by it. If it does not, the chances are that another season of correction will reduce it from a mere 'taxing district,' that has no debts to pay, to an abode of desolation and a haunt for the owls and the bats, that never incur debts." The *Indianapolis News* suggested that the germ of fever could be incinerated, noting that "it was the great fire of London that ended the great plague." Rather than let the city become a perpetual source for pestilence, the paper argued, the federal government should buy out property owners and burn the city to the ground. The Cairo, Illinois, *Bulletin* said that Memphis was "the leper among American cities, shunned and avoided by its own people, held as a thing of horror, not to be seen or touched, a dreaded spot."[5]

AS THE FEVER once again made its way through the city, a group of upper-class refugees in St. Louis devised a campaign to build sewers in the Taxing District as quickly as possible. This required convincing the governor of Tennessee to call a special session of the legislature so that a special tax could be authorized. Meanwhile, a survey of actual conditions in Memphis proceeded under the direction of a National Board of Health officer, Dr. Frank W. Reilly, and seven physicians. In his 1888 history of Memphis, Keating described the report as "one of the most valuable contributions ever made to sanitary history." It was packed with the kind of data that Keating loved.

Dr. Reilly and his team inspected more than 12,000 structures, 6,000 of them dwellings. They counted 1,515 cellars/basements and assessed them by depth, ventilation, degree of moisture, and cleanliness. They found 5,914 privies and 4,744 cisterns and wells, 3,000 of them within 50 feet of the privy. They counted the water closets (flush toilets) and

reported on their level of cleanliness (273 clean, 125 foul). They enumer-
ated the pools of stagnant water. Keating thought Reilly's final report "a
sickening summing up of filth that appalled the citizens and reconciled
a majority of them to any possible measures of quick relief."[6]

The Taxing District, having received legislative approval, began work
on a new sewage system in 1880. By mid-decade, forty miles of sewer
lines had been constructed in the central city. The system was extended
to neighborhoods to the north and south (Chelsea and South Memphis)
in the 1890s. The original sewer lines had design flaws and required
modifications as the years passed. Not everyone with access installed
indoor toilets and connected to the new lines, although ordinances required that they do so. The lines reached predominantly black neighborhoods on the outskirts of town five to ten years later than the white
neighborhoods nearer the center of the city. But no one could deny that
the city's sanitation was much better. In addition, the Taxing District
instituted and enforced sanitary laws and replaced the Nicholson pavement with gravel, granite, and, in some upper-class neighborhoods, brick.
Much of the unskilled work was done by convict labor, prisoners from
the city jail marched out each day in a chain gang. By 1890 downtown
Memphis was no longer embarrassingly dirty and ill kept.[7]

Memphians then and many historians since assumed that cleaning
up the town got rid of the fever. When Memphis hosted the American
Public Health Association in 1887, according to historian John Ellis, "its
business and social leaders basked in the effusive compliments bestowed
by the visiting sanitarians." The new sewers saved lives by reducing the
amount of contamination seeping into wells and cisterns, but they had
no impact, positive or negative, on *Ae. aegypti*. Memphis could have
had another epidemic at any point in the 1880s. That it did not is probably due to the Louisiana Board of Health's new, stronger quarantine
system, the fact that so many people in the Mississippi Valley were now
immune, and pure dumb luck.[8]

Ae. aegypti lived in the cisterns, not in the sewers, and continued to
flourish each summer until the cisterns were replaced by piped-in water. As of 1885 the city still lacked a municipal water system. The Memphis Water Company offered a limited amount of nasty water from the
polluted Wolf River, but most people did not bother to connect their
houses to the lines. Instead, they flushed their new toilets with water
carried in buckets from wells and cisterns. Since city contracts gave the

water company a monopoly, attempts to build a modern water infra-structure had to go through, or around, Memphis Water. Years of con-troversy, lawsuits, campaigns, and committees ensued.[9]

Meanwhile, the Bohlen-Huse Machine and Lake Ice Company began to drill for water. In antebellum America, tons of natural lake ice were "harvested" in the North, shipped to southern ice companies, and car-ried in blocks to residential and commercial iceboxes. By the 1880s, how-ever, companies were manufacturing ice. Machine ice required clean water—no one wishes to purchase brown ice—so Richard C. Graves, the Massachusetts-born ice plant superintendent, sank well after well for years. In 1887 the ice company hit an aquifer at a depth of 354 feet. Water bubbled up to the surface, and so many people showed up with buckets that the police had to be called to manage the crowd. A contemporary study determined the water to be "sparking, refreshing to the taste . . . and, as it comes from the wells, has a temperature of 62° Fahrenheit, constant the year round." A new water company was formed, a buyout for the old company effected, and by 1890 thirty-two artesian wells supplied the city with clean, pure water.[10]

In 1890 the *New York Times* commented, "A few years ago sanitarians could justly point at Memphis as 'a horrible example.' With respect to sewerage and water supply, its condition was almost medieval . . . There has been a great change in Memphis since those days." The change seems to have had an impact on all sectors of the Memphis population. Although the black mortality rate continued to be higher than the white, both declined. A recent study shows that the mortality rate (deaths per 100,000 persons) dropped 50 percent for whites and for blacks between 1884 and 1895. Under the auspices of the Taxing District, Memphis be-came a modern American city.[11]

On an autumn morning in 1902 Luke Wright went down to the rail-road station to welcome a distinguished friend to Memphis. President Theodore Roosevelt had come to town to honor Wright, who had just returned from serving as vice-governor of the Philippines, and also to mend some political fences. General Wright's ginger hair was fading into gray, but after a long career as a lawyer and politician in Memphis, he retained the public affection he had earned in 1878. He was a popu-lar man in Memphis, but TR was not. Roosevelt had offended southern whites' racial sensibilities earlier in the year by inviting Booker T. Washington to dinner at the White House. Southern Democrats seized the occasion to label the president a race traitor. The Memphis *Evening Scimitar* protested the idea that the city would honor President Roosevelt with a banquet. To sit down at dinner with Roosevelt was to accept him as a social equal, and that meant "recognition of his widely announced doctrine of social equality with the negro." A parade organized to escort TR from the station to a breakfast at the Gayoso Hotel became problematic after the Confederate veterans, the Governor's Guard, and other militia units announced that they would not participate.[12]

Under these circumstances, Wright insisted on meeting Roosevelt at the station and personally escorting him to the hotel. Although he didn't say so publicly, the implication was clear: the president was under his protection and sponsorship. The parade went well, though the New York *Sun* reported that the sidewalks were not crowded with people. (Press reports discounted rumors that people had hissed at TR.) At the hotel, however, "there was a big crowd which, black and white, cheered the President, vociferously." Inside, Memphis ladies had arranged a breakfast, demonstrating that they did not think "that the Booker T. Washington incident at the White House had made it impossible to sit at the same table as the President."[13]

In 1878, black and white relief workers ate at the same tables at the Howard canteen, black policemen patrolled the streets, and black militia guarded the CRC commissary. But by the early twentieth century Memphis was such a Jim Crow town that some whites refused to honor a president who had committed the crime of sitting down to a meal with a black man. Racial attitudes in early-twentieth-century Memphis reflected changed conditions in the city and the nation.

During Reconstruction, constitutional amendments had clarified the status of African Americans. The Fourteenth Amendment declared that all born in the United States are citizens, thus transforming former slaves into citizens, and the Fifteenth Amendment gave black men the right to vote. In the postwar period blacks voted and held political office throughout the South, backed up by federal troops. After the Union pulled out the last occupation forces in 1877, state governments began to attack black political power. Slowly, cautiously at first, then with greater speed and force, states moved to disfranchise black men. Outright violation of the Constitution seemed ill-advised, so legislatures did not simply

write laws saying "Negroes cannot vote." Instead, lawmakers used various legislative mechanisms such as the poll tax (which disfranchised
poor whites as well as blacks); the literacy test (which could be graded
according to the complexion of the would-be voter); the grandfather
clause (which assured the vote to men whose grandfathers had voted at a
particular date, while denying it to men whose grandfathers had not, being enslaved at the time); and a plethora of restrictions, delays, and tech-
nicalities that could be used to restrict voting to men approved by the
local authorities. Stripped of political rights, blacks were denied equal
access to public space. Segregation was de jure (accomplished by Jim
Crow laws) and de facto, enforced by local custom and violence.

Therefore, when President Roosevelt wanted to speak to the city's
biggest block of Republicans—its black citizens—he went to an auditorium in a black-owned private park.[14] The president, his entourage, supporters, and the press rode in carriages to the park, escorted by the chief
of police and twenty-five men on horseback. Inside the auditorium, African American ministers gave the invocation and benediction, an orchestra played, and a choir sang "America" and "God Be with You Till
We Meet Again." Guests, including the mayor of Memphis, the gover-
nors of Tennessee and Mississippi, John Overton, and a contingent of
journalists, heard the crowd cheer speeches by Luke Wright and the
president.[15]

In the auditorium, the stage's fireproof drop curtain featured a paint-
ing of a burning steamboat, *Bulletin No. 2*, upon which a young man
named Robert Church had once served as steward. In the years since the
yellow fever epidemic Bob Church had become the richest black man in
town. He owned the auditorium where the meeting was held and the
park in which it stood, the only park in Memphis open to blacks.[16]

In 1878 no one in Memphis would have foreseen a future in which
blacks would be systematically blocked from exercising the rights of
citizenship guaranteed to them under the Fourteenth and Fifteenth
Amendments, and where the federal government would acquiesce while
this was done. No one would have predicted that black men would be
pushed out of the police force or that the black militias would be disbanded. No one would have expected that resurgent white supremacists
would claim public space in Memphis for whites only, that the Independence Day parades would disappear, that black families would not be

allowed to picnic in the parks. But of all the transformations Memphis witnessed in the last two decades of the century, none were more startling than the emergence of Bob Church—saloonkeeper, gambler, hard man with a violent temper—as Robert Church, real estate entrepreneur and cultural impresario.

The yellow fever epidemic, more than any other event, made Memphis the city that it is today. In 1878 Memphis's municipal character had yet to be determined: Was it to be the northernmost city on the southern Mississippi, an inland New Orleans, or the southernmost midwestern city, a hotter, more humid Cincinnati or St. Louis? The epidemic set Memphis's course in an entirely new direction. By the end of the century the Bluff City had become a less cosmopolitan place, with an economy that serviced the cotton trade and a population drawn increasingly from poor white and black southerners. While white Memphians set about systematically taking away the rights blacks had attained during Reconstruction, Bob Church rose to wealth and power, in the process creating an oasis in which black cultural and economic dreams could flower. Bob Church's Memphis became the home of the blues and the cradle of rock 'n' roll.

IN 1879 A TENNESSEE NEWSPAPER had scoffed at the idea that Memphis was doomed: "An earthquake will have to sink all the rich cotton lands for 200 miles around for Memphis to be ruined." The epidemic years did slow the city's growth. The population declined from 40,226 in 1870 to 33,592 in 1880. The cotton lands did not disappear, the crops had to be sold and the plantations serviced, and in the 1880s the Taxing District's economy began to recover. Although promoters touted Memphis as a gateway to markets throughout the region, local business remained focused on cotton. By the end of the decade, one of the largest cotton press and warehousing firms in town turned out six thousand bales of compressed cotton per day, each bale weighing about five hundred pounds. Cottonseeds, once considered simply a nuisance in the way of processing the fiber, became a major resource in the late nineteenth century. The oil pressed out of the seeds was used in soaps, foods, and ointments. When lumbermen from the Midwest began to harvest the Mississippi Delta's stands of oak, cherry, and other hardwoods, Memphis became a center for wood processing. These and other developing industries drew workers to the city. By 1890 the population had more than doubled, to 64,495; ten years later, to 102,320.[17]

However, the nature of that population had changed drastically. In 1870 the foreign-born comprised 17 percent of the Memphis population; in 1890, just over 8 percent, and in 1900, it was 5 percent. Those foreign-born survivors of the epidemic years who remained in Memphis were swamped by native-born newcomers. Whether immigrants stopped coming to Memphis because the economy was weak, or because transportation patterns changed, or because they were afraid of yellow fever, the results were the same. The new Memphis working class was poor, southern, and in need of places to live. Robert Church rented them houses.[18]

IF THIS WERE A BOOK of fiction rather than history, Bob Church would not appear in the first chapter, then disappear, except for brief vignettes, until the last chapter. You may wonder what he was doing during the epidemic. Did he play a role in the black community's relief efforts? Did he nurse the sick or help the needy? We cannot know the answers to those questions. History depends on evidence—newspapers, letters, documents—and nineteenth-century white southerners did not usually archive materials about even the most respectable black people, let alone the rounders and sporting men of the demimonde. When the 1880s began, Church was a saloonkeeper and a gambler. As the decade progressed and Church transitioned into businessman and real estate magnate, he was probably featured in the pages of Memphis's black newspapers, of which there were several. No one bothered to keep those papers, so we will never know. We see him through legal documents, court records, the occasional mention in a white newspaper, his daughter Mollie's memoirs, a hagiographic biography written by family members, and some photos and letters they saved. Just the same, it would be wrong to leave Church out of the story, since he played a major role in the transformation of Memphis after the yellow fever.

By the early twentieth century Robert Church was reckoned to be the richest black man in Memphis. His climb to respectability accelerated under the relatively benign government of the Taxing District oligarchy. His father, the late C. B. Church, a prominent Mason and a founding director of Union and Planters' Bank, had been a member of the city's business elite.[19] John Overton Jr., the second Taxing District president, had known Bob Church for years and considered him a personal friend. When his father's old friends and business acquaintances took over the city, Bob was already well-to-do. However, he was not a typical member of the rising black middle class. In 1878 he had donated money to the black relief effort but had not served on the CRC or the African American relief committee. He was not a member of any church. He did not teach at a black academy like Howe Institute or LeMoyne, run a freight-hauling business, own a barbershop, or work for white people in a hotel or for the federal government at the post office. Nonetheless, he made sure that people knew who he was.

He advertised Church's Billiard Hall as "The Finest Billiards, Pool and Saloon owned and controlled by ANY ONE COLORED MAN IN THE UNITED STATES." He opened Church's Hotel, advertised it as "The Only First Class Colored Hotel in the City," and promised that the hotel agent would meet you at the depot. As the years passed, stories accrued to his name. One recounts how in 1886 he was targeted by some white men who wanted to take over on Beale Street. He was warned that they planned to attack him, so he got a white friend to bear witness as he walked down to the corner where the men waited. He faced them and told them to shoot if they dared. They backed off. Over a decade later, when Church was sixty-four, two white men picked a fight with him in his own Beale neighborhood. He sustained a head injury and some cuts, but the two men finished the day in jail "with their heads broken."[20]

Church profited from his various businesses, but rent made him rich. People said that he bought land and never sold it. Enemies of the Church family later alleged that Church's properties were in the red-light district and that he owned brothels, but when he began buying property, Memphis had no distinct red-light district. Brothels were sometimes located in respectable neighborhoods, as Kezia DePelchin could have testified. Given the ubiquity of the trade in Memphis, it would be surprising if Church did not rent to prostitutes; whether they were the majority of his tenants cannot be determined, but it seems unlikely. He accumulated dozens of rental properties, and he rented to all kinds of people. Before the end of the 1880s he was said to be worth $125,000, the equivalent today of about two million dollars.[21]

In 1885 Church married one of the most esteemed women in Memphis's black community. Anna Wright was the sort of person J. M. Keating would have called cultivated and refined, the daughter of a free black woman and a white man. Born in 1856, Anna had every advantage, socially and culturally, that her mother could obtain for her. She graduated from Antioch College in Ohio and studied piano and singing at Oberlin Conservatory. She taught in Memphis schools and eventually became principal of one. She had been confirmed by Bishop Quintard at Calvary Episcopal; and George White, the aged rector, performed the ceremony when she married Robert Church on January 1, 1885. He took her home to a three-story, fourteen-room Queen Anne house on South Lauderdale Street. Some of their neighbors were white; others were members of the city's black elite. By all accounts it was a good marriage. With Anna, Robert Church had two children, Robert Junior and Annette.[22]

The house on South Lauderdale blazed with light from every window on the October night in 1891 when Mollie Church married Robert Terrell in her father's parlor, the dean of St. Mary's Episcopal officiating. Mollie's father had sent her to Oberlin, and then funded further education in Europe. While studying German in Berlin she had refused a marriage proposal from a baron on the grounds that her father would never approve. So the baron wrote Robert Church in Memphis to ask for the hand of his daughter, and the son of an enslaved woman and a white father wrote back that he did not believe in mixed marriages. Terrell, Harvard graduate, educator, lawyer, and scion of a prominent black Washington family, was precisely the kind of husband Church would have wanted for his daughter. The African American *Washington Bee* called the wedding "The Most Notable Event That Has Ever Taken Place in the South" and described the guests as the "elite of colored society." The Memphis papers covered the wedding respectfully, giving it the society page treatment usually reserved for white brides: "As they discussed the elaborate menu and drank the excellent champagne of the host, the guests were regaled with the sensuous strains of Joe Hall's orchestra, which, hidden in an alcove, made the air sweet with its beautiful music."[23]

THE 1880S HAD BEEN GOOD to Robert Church, but the 1890s saw a decline in freedom for all black people in Memphis. White Memphis politicians succeeded in disfranchising most black male voters in 1889.

Whites demonstrated their dominance through violence, including lynching, and also denied blacks the implements of community self-protection they had had since the 1870s. The last black militia unit disbanded in 1892. The last black police officer retired in 1896. Blacks did regain the vote in the early twentieth century, but whites maintained control of city government.[24]

As the city's population grew, reaching 131,105 in 1910, and Memphis became more and more a city of strangers, whites drew the color line with great seriousness and care, ensuring that public space throughout most of the town belonged to them. There would be no social equality for the 52,411 African Americans in Memphis. As a young man, Robert Church had raced his horse against a white friend's, won his bet and his dinner at a good restaurant, and sat down to enjoy it with his white friend and little Mollie by his side. In those days he sat where he pleased on streetcars and bought first-class tickets on trains. None of those options would be available to young men coming of age in the 1890s. Those who had grown up in Memphis, who could remember (for example) black Independence Day parades, may have felt a sense of loss, whereas for blacks who came from plantations and segregated small towns, Memphis could seem a place of great opportunity and vitality.[25]

In segregated Memphis, Church emerged as the undisputed boss of Beale Street. People said he was the city's first black millionaire; people said he was the richest black man in the state, or in the entire South. People said that when Memphis emerged from the Taxing District, no one would buy the new Memphis bonds until John Overton asked Bob Church to step up, and after he bought the first bond, Caucasian investors followed. They said that when Memphis cops came to his saloon and arrested all his patrons as vagrants, he asked them how much the fines would be, pulled out the cash, and paid on the spot. He was rumored to be a powerhouse in the local Republican Party. It is hard to say how many of these stories are true, if any. This much is: He owned commercial property and scores of houses on and around Beale and made a great deal of money from rents. He donated generously to charities. He gave his two younger children the best education possible, employing private tutors before sending them to Oberlin. He was a delegate to the 1900 Republican Party Convention. His properties became the nucleus of a neighborhood that offered black Memphians public space and relative freedom.[26]

Beale Street—Avenue, it was then—is as encrusted with mythology as Church himself. Like Bourbon Street in New Orleans, it had a raffish reputation for booze and bars and women, perhaps exaggerated in the interests of commerce. Beale had its share of vice and violence, but in Robert Church's day it was the black business district of an increasingly segregated Memphis. A historian of Memphis described it as "a polyglot street featuring dry goods and clothing stores, pawn shops, real estate and banking offices, saloons, gambling dens, theaters and houses of prostitution," most of the latter on side streets. Black professionals had offices there; blacks and whites (many Jewish) ran stores and restaurants. The neighborhood had churches, the most striking being Beale Street Baptist, its twin towers ornate and handsome in brick and stone. In 1906 Church founded the Solvent Savings Bank and Trust on Beale, and in 1908, when the Beale Street congregation could not meet its debts and faced foreclosure, the Solvent Bank bought the notes and gave the congregation an extension that allowed them to save the building.[27]

In the 1870s Memphis had no black or white parks, just parks, but by 1899 there were only white parks. In that year Robert Church bought seven acres of land and opened a park fronting on Beale Street. Much later the story was told that "Mr. R. R. Church learning of the condition that robbed the race in the city of its picnic pleasures rolled up his sleeves, slipped his white handkerchief in his right hand pocket" and told his crew of workmen "to tear down remove grade and build" Church Park. The same author remembered that Church kept his own order in the park, "as no officer of the law was allowed to come in." For a small fee, you could stroll through landscaped grounds, take your children to the playground, or go into the auditorium to the bar or the soda shop.[28]

Shortly after the park opened, Church made a gesture that insured him years of goodwill from Memphis whites. When the United Confederate Veterans Reunion was held in Memphis in 1901, Church contributed $1,000 toward the building of Confederate Hall, an eighteen-thousand-seat auditorium. Black and white newspapers lauded him as a credit to his race, and his friend John Overton wrote him a personal thank-you note. After that, it would indeed have been embarrassing for Memphis had anything untoward—a lynching, for example—happened at Church Park. None did; the park remained a safe space for years to come, while Memphis cemented its standing as the murder capital of the United States.[29]

Robert Church in old age. (Papers of the Robert R. Church Family
of Memphis, Special Collections, University of Memphis Libraries)

The park and auditorium became centers of black life in Memphis. Schools held recitals and graduations there. The Church of God in Christ, a black holiness sect, had its first convocation there. Touring companies played the auditorium, musicians gave concerts, opera singers performed, vaudeville troupes made people laugh. Church hired the classically trained musician W. C. Handy to play for dances and rented him an office above the Solvent Bank; Handy's musical partner and co-publisher was a Solvent Bank cashier. Under the wing of the boss of Beale Street, Handy wrote the compositions that earned him the title Father of the Blues. Handy told Church's daughter Annette, "When I was quite a youngster I used to ride excursions to Memphis and in those days it was the name of Bob Church that drew people to Memphis from all over the South."[30]

By the 1920s Memphis was one of the capitals of black music, sending out blues and jazz performers to the nation; by the 1950s the sound had evolved into rhythm and blues, but the city continued to draw talented newcomers to perform at its clubs and radio shows. Elvis Presley, a skinny white boy whose rural parents' emigration to Memphis in search of work recapitulated the experience of thousands of black and white southerners, listened to blues on the radio and aspired to dress like the black performers who bought their clothes at Lansky's on Beale. The Memphis that the world knows is not the marketing center of the cotton lands, the home of General Nathan Bedford Forrest, nor even the city ravaged by yellow fever in 1878. It is the Memphis of the blues, of B.B. King and Elvis, of Beale Street, and that Memphis grew in a space created and nurtured by Robert Church.[31]

Epilogue: Memory

IT IS HARD TO AVOID THE CLICHÉ: for the survivors, life went on.

Dr. Robert Mitchell continued to practice medicine in Memphis. In the 1880s he and his partner, Dr. R. B. Maury, opened an infirmary for the diseases of women. They specialized in surgery. Mitchell and Maury also established the Memphis Training School for Nurses, which graduated its first class (of four) in 1889. He was a member of the county and state medical societies, the American Medical Association, and the National Board of Health. He died in 1903 at the age of seventy-one.[1]

Lula Armstrong returned to her home on Alabama Avenue in Memphis. She raised her children there, drawing support from funds raised by her husband's friends and colleagues. She died in 1924 at the age of seventy-seven and was buried in Elmwood Cemetery.[2]

Rev. George Harris left St. Mary's in the early 1880s. He served as archdeacon of the Diocese of Mississippi and, briefly, as minister at Trinity Church in St. Louis. His wife had inherited property in Mississippi, and in 1890 the Harrises moved to the Delta. He founded the Chapel of the Cross in nearby Rolling Fork and served as rector there for many years. He died in 1911.[3]

Luke Wright was governor-general of the Philippines from 1904 to 1906, U.S. ambassador to Japan in 1907, and Theodore Roosevelt's secretary of war from 1908 to 1909. The irony of a Democrat and Confederate veteran in that position was noted. Wright died in Memphis in 1922.

Rev. Sylvanus Landrum and his wife moved back to Savannah, Georgia, in 1879. Landrum returned to the pastorate at Savannah First Baptist Church, a position he had held before coming to Memphis. After two years he resigned to take a position as "traveling agent" for Mercer University, and then he accepted a call from the Coliseum Place Baptist Church of New Orleans, where he served until his death, in 1886.[4]

Although the surviving Menken brothers kept the store in Memphis—and even expanded into a modern building in the 1880s—the family did not establish itself there. One of Nathan's children died young, but by the 1890s the surviving sons and daughters were busily assimilating into society in the Northeast. His oldest son, Solomon Stanwood, obtained a law degree from Columbia, converted to Christianity, married a New York socialite, pushed for the creation of the Hall of Records Association in New York City, and founded the National Security League, an organization that campaigned for military preparedness prior to U.S. entry into the Great War. His son Arthur became a newsreel cameraman for Paramount and *The March of Time* and covered the Spanish Civil War, the Japanese conquest of Nanking, and the Battle of Britain.[5]

Robert Church died in 1912 and was buried in the family mausoleum in Elmwood Cemetery. Robert Junior was more interested in politics than business and divested his interest in the Solvent Bank. After a brutal lynching in 1917, Church Jr. helped found Memphis's NAACP chapter. By organizing black voters in Memphis, he became a force to be reckoned with in national politics. In 1940 the city government decided to destroy that force. At the end of their campaign, Church had been driven out of town and Robert Senior's house on Lauderdale Street had been burned down as a "training exercise" for the city fire department. Bob Church's granddaughter Roberta lived to see times change again. In 1984 the Memphis Chamber of Commerce installed a Memphis Hall of Fame at the city's airport; Robert Senior was one of seven men honored as a pioneer in Memphis business.[6]

Mollie Church is better known today as Mary Church Terrell. She was a charter member of the NAACP and the first president of the National Association of Colored Women's Clubs. In 1940 she published her autobiography, *A Colored Woman in a White World*. An activist all her life, she marched for civil rights in Washington, D.C., in the 1950s, although by that point she had to use a cane. She died in 1954 at the age of ninety.

IN THE 1880s J. M. Keating and Matt Galloway presided over the city's largest paper. In his spare time, Keating wrote a history of Memphis. He also built a national reputation as a sanitarian. His carefully researched papers on the economic value of sanitation and the use of fire to destroy waste were published in the American Public Health Association's journal. He was president of the Memphis chapter of the Red Cross and a supporter of the Memphis Medical College, and he gave the first graduation address at Dr. Mitchell's new Training School for Nurses.[7]

In the years after the epidemic, Keating began to study race relations with the same fervor he had applied to sanitary reform. In the 1880s there was much debate over the "Negro question"—or, more bluntly, the "Negro problem"—and one of the solutions suggested was the deportation of all blacks to Africa. In 1885 *Popular Science* published "Twenty Years of Negro Education," in which Keating said, "The negro is no longer a problem. He is a part of the body politic and the body social of the republic. He is firmly rooted and cannot be moved. He is here to stay, and any attempt to disturb him, or to excite his fears as to his right to life, liberty and the pursuit of happiness, is nothing less than a crime." Surveying the history of education for blacks since 1860, Keating optimistically saw the glass as half full: emerging from slavery illiterate, freedpeople and their children had made steady gains in education thanks to schools funded by northern philanthropists and, increasingly, by southern state governments. Keating wrote, "Illuminate him with the intelligence of the ages and the light of reason, and the negro will see his way and walk without help. He will become a stronger, a more self-reliant man, and by that strength and self-reliance he will beat down all the barriers and shake off all the make-weights that impede his progress and stand in his way."[8]

Keating became a strong supporter of education for blacks. "Col. Keating, a personal friend of Jeff. Davis . . . is our public friend and advocate in his paper," wrote a teacher at LeMoyne Normal Institute in a report to the American Missionary Association (AMA) in 1886. "He is to make the address at the formal opening of our shop; and he will do it. Ten years ago he would not have dared to mention the matter, let alone come near it." Like the AMA, the John F. Slater Fund promoted black education in the South. When Slater Fund agent Atticus Haygood came to Memphis, Keating asked him to come to his office, talked with him for an hour, and then told him to use the *Appeal* as needed.[9]

In mid-decade Keating made another bid to get out of the newspaper business. After long years of service to the Democratic Party in general and the interests of Tennessee's senior senator Isham Harris in particular, he asked for a patronage job. He wanted to be printer of the United States, or postmaster of Memphis. When Harris failed to come through with either position, Keating turned against him. At odds with his partner, Matt Galloway sold his share of the paper to a group of investors and retired in 1887. Meanwhile, Memphis's tumultuous local politics erupted again, pitting the city's long-term mayor David "Pappy" Hadden against a coalition of anti-Hadden politicos. Keating, Luke Wright, and John Overton supported Hadden, but Keating's new partners joined the anti-Hadden coalition. Keating and his partners quarreled. At some point during the summer of 1889 Keating lost his battle to maintain control of the *Appeal*. Unable to raise the funds necessary to buy out his partners, he accepted an offer of $50,000 for his stock in the paper. Very quickly Hadden supporters set Keating up with a new paper, the *Commercial*.[10]

Although the Hadden faction lost the next election, Keating stayed on as editor and continued to make his opinions known. In October he sent an essay on "The Southern Question" to the Chicago meeting of the American Missionary Association and so impressed the group that they voted to have it printed and circulated in the South. Keating took a paternalistic stand, supporting education and "Christianization" for blacks, but he also emphasized, in italics, *"The right of the Negro to vote is necessary to the maintenance of his freedom."* Give the Negro his rights, Keating said, and leave him alone. A northern newspaper said that Keating's paper placed him in the company of the best-known southern white advocates for black education "among the leaders of thought in creating the true New South."[11]

Labor solidarity led to Keating's final departure from Memphis journalism. In 1892 the *Commercial* management, embroiled in a conflict with the printers' union, resorted to a lockout. As a young man, Keating had been a member of Typographical Union No. 6, organized in New York by Horace Greeley, and he was an honorary member of the Memphis Typographical Union. He refused to side with management or to write anything criticizing the union. When his employers inserted anti-union material in the paper without his knowledge, Keating denounced their action as "mendacious and cowardly." He quit the paper, and he left Memphis. By 1893 he had moved to Washington, D.C., where he lived for about fourteen years. He died of nephritis in August 1906 while visiting Carrie's summer home in Gloucester, Massachusetts. His body was cremated.[12]

By the time of Keating's death, the premier newspaper in Memphis was the *Commercial Appeal,* formed in 1894 from the two papers Keating had edited. Stating that the city owned a great debt to Keating, the paper eulogized him as a journalist and a civic leader, credited him as being instrumental in the formation of the Taxing District, and praised him for his pro-sanitation crusade. The journalist who wrote the piece saw Keating as a transitional figure between the old and new journalism. Unlike many of his contemporaries, Keating was "remarkably free of the passion and heat of the older journalism, and believed in clean and honorable methods. There is indeed no more honorable name in Memphis—or indeed Southern—journalism than that of J. M. Keating."[13]

KEZIA DEPELCHIN CONTINUED to work as a teacher and nurse in Houston. In later years she traveled to visit friends and relatives in Europe and got to spend some time with her sister in Madeira. Her niece came to live with her in Texas. In 1888 she became the first matron of the Bayland Orphans' Home for Boys. She came home one day in 1892 to find several small children abandoned on her doorstep. They were too young to take to Bayland, impossible to turn away. She asked a friend to open a room in her house to care for the children. Soon there were more. DePelchin called her small orphanage "Faith Home" because she had faith that God and the people of Houston would supply funds to keep it going. She used her own small salary to support the home, walking from home to work to save the nickel streetcar fare.[14]

She died on January 13, 1893, at the age of sixty-four, and was buried at public expense. On January 30 a group of Houston women founded the Kezia DePelchin Faith Home in her honor. Today the DePelchin Children's Center serves more than thirty thousand children annually. The center offers adoptions, foster care, counseling, school programs, services for teen parents, and many other programs. When hundreds of refugee children wound up in Houston schools after Hurricanes Katrina and Rita, the DePelchin Center was instrumental in providing help, counseling, and relief.[15]

In her reflections on the Memphis epidemic, DePelchin explained that her religious beliefs, while still strong, had become less orthodox.

"I believe that many a one in the last agonies looked to the cross and was saved." She owned that this might not be "safe doctrine," but added, "standing face to face with death, as I did for weeks, I learned more of God's mercy and dealings with men, and we never get worse by contemplating his mercy."[16]

Epidemics follow predictable patterns, writes the historian Charles Rosenberg. He compared them to drama. The curtain opens with apprehension, followed by denial, then recognition. Once the epidemic is acknowledged, Rosenberg said, societies react in ways that are peculiar to their own nature and their own time. In time, the epidemic subsides. Afterward comes a stage Rosenberg called retrospective contemplation, as people try to make sense out of what happened to them. The Memphis experience of 1878 follows Rosenberg's scenario: debate over quarantine, insistence that the fever would never reach Memphis, recognition of the first deaths, panicked flight, and a strong, determined, organized resistance against the disease followed by subsidence and reinstitution of the social order. The behavior of humans in the aggregate is roughly predictable. But Reverend Landrum was right too. Compassion and courage are wild cards.

This lesson is taught in every epidemic, every war, flood, earthquake, catastrophe. Taught, and forgotten just as quickly. Epidemics strip away social pretensions and show us for what we are, Shakespeare's poor forked animals, naked before the force of nature. Nor can we count on one another. The people we trust may not be trustworthy, and the people we scorn may rise to heroism. Reverend Landrum and other religious survivors could comfort themselves with a hope of the sweet by-and-by and an acceptance of God's will. But even for those who lived in expectation of the Resurrection, as the reverend testified, saying amen was no easy thing.

At the end of every catastrophe, survivors must reconstruct, burying the dead bodies and the unbearable memories. In places like Memphis, where the material damage was minimal but the human loss enormous, reconstruction requires creating a public memory that comforts the survivors, puts back in place the social structures damaged by the catastrophe, and encourages the essential process of forgetting how powerless we are.

In Memphis this process required the reinstitution of boundaries and hierarchies. We can see this reconstruction beginning in the October banquets, to which women, blacks, and working-class Irish were not invited. Officially, the heroes of Memphis were all white and all male. Keating knew better—said so publicly, repeatedly—but he did not turn down his gold-headed cane. The very fact that white Memphians (and white Memphis) would not have survived without the aid of blacks was something that whites had to deny and hide, rather like the existence of African American brothers and sisters.

When Robert Church donated a thousand dollars to the Confederate reunion, it made headlines. The newspaper stories usually gave a short biography of Church that mentioned his training as a steward while a steamboat captain's slave. White papers did not mention that he was Captain C. B. Church's son. The relationship was hardly a secret in Memphis. When the old captain died, he made sure that the money he had left to Bob did not get finangled away, and he made Colonel Josiah Patterson guardian of his estate. Judging from the papers they left and the things they wrote, Robert Church's children and grandchildren never had any doubts as to his parentage. White southerners chose not to know.[17]

Although people who lived through the epidemic knew that black militias and black policemen had been crucial to the city's survival, the next generation of white Memphians preferred to overlook that part of the city's history. Keating's history of the epidemic, written in 1878–79, focuses on the people and events closest to his own experience, but he made clear the role of the black militia, gave the names of the men and officers, discussed the role of black policemen, and included black victims in the list of the dead. By contrast, in Judge John Preston Young's history of Memphis, published in 1912, black troops ("loyal negro militia") popped up to save the CRC's commissary and then disappeared. The judge did not mention by name the McClellan Guards or Brown's Zouaves. A student reading Memphis history in 1912 would have to pay very close attention to discern that black militias existed at all. There was no mention of black policemen. Ed Shaw's name appeared in a list of aldermen; his race was not noted. Young's history was a paradigm of segregation: he praises black educators and philanthropists for their efforts in the black community, but the history of Memphis itself was white. Prominent black families remembered the role of black Memphians in the Gilded Age city, but whites did their best to forget.

The other unpleasant truth exposed by the epidemic—that fathers, whether literally the heads of families or spiritually the heads of religious congregations, could not always be trusted to sacrifice their own lives for their dependents—also had to be woven into the constructed memory of the epidemic. This was done in a most peculiar fashion. The big news in the summer of 1878 was about John Donovan, whose refusal to come to the aid of his pregnant wife and his children made the national news, and about the Protestant ministers who fled. Public memory of the epidemic has little to say about these miscreants and the women they deserted, focusing instead on the virgins of St. Mary's Episcopal and the prostitute of Gayoso Street.

In November 1878 Sister Constance's mother superior, Mother Harriet, wrote to Dr. Harris, "You know what we have lost in our precious sister. No one can fully enter into all that I have lost in that precious lily of St. Mary's community. I loved the others very, very dearly, but Sister Constance was the darling of my heart . . . I can only try not to think—when I do think, my heart just breaks, breaks, breaks . . ." Today the Sisters of St. Mary are commemorated on September 9 in the Anglican calendar. The prayer for that day reads, "We give thee thanks and praise, O God of compassion, for the Heroic witness of Constance and her companions, who, in a time of plague and pestilence, were steadfast in their care for the sick and the dying, and loved not their own lives, even unto death. Inspire in us a like love and commitment to those in need, following the example of our Savior Jesus Christ . . ."[18] The church in which they worked and worshipped was replaced by a larger, more elaborate building. The names of the sister martyrs of Memphis are inlaid in the steps of the high altar, which is ornamented with Constance's last words, "Alleluia Osanna," picked out in gold.

Even in 1878 Annie Cook's sacrifice attracted public attention. She was buried in the Howard plot at Elmwood, surrounded by the honored dead. However, her resting place remained without a marker until the 1970s, when a Memphis couple erected a stone with her name and the epitaph "A Nineteenth Century Mary Magdalene who gave her life trying to save the lives of others." Her estate probate papers are among the most requested public documents at the Shelby County Archives.[19]

Although members of the relief community in Memphis swore that they would hold in honor the remembrance of the epidemic heroes, an *Avalanche* editorial predicted that the people who fled would return, healthy and happy, and those who stayed, suffered, and died would be forgotten.[20] *Avalanche* editor Herbert Landrum probably wrote that editorial. He wrote beautifully, and excerpts from his essays on the epidemic appear in every book on the fever. No one remembers the young man who was, Keating said, "quick, witty and bright," nor his friends

Martyrs Park. The inscription below the Memorial reads: "In grateful memory of the sacrifice of the heroes and heroines of Memphis, in the 1870s, who gave their lives serving the victims of yellow fever . . . The acts of love and courage, far beyond the call of duty, merited the gratitude and admiration of the citizens of Memphis, and of the world, as history revealed the story. 'Greater love than this no one has, that one lay down his life for his friends.' John 15:13."

who stayed at their posts in Memphis and died, nor his mother and his brother, nor his father, Reverend Landrum, whose grief enabled him to speak to, and for, the mourning survivors of Memphis.

Societies choose what they want to remember about the past. Enshrined in statues, monuments, and institutions, official remembrance of the past serves the political purposes of the present. Although relatively young as cities go, Memphis has a lot of past to pick from in constructing public memory. Moreover, that past is highly contested and racially divisive. Memphis has parks named for Nathan Bedford Forrest, Jefferson Davis, and the Confederacy, and parks named for Martin Luther King Jr., Frederick Douglass, and W. C. Handy. In the 1960s the Memphis City Council created a memorial and park to commemorate the yellow fever heroes. The civil rights movement was remaking race relations in Memphis and throughout the South. At the groundbreaking ceremony in 1969, less than a year after Martin Luther King's death in Memphis, the memorial association's secretary commented, "If people could once come together in tragedy, why can we not solve our differences today without tragedy?"[21]

The memorial itself shows figures of people stripped of race and gender and abstracted into common humanity, confined in a small space but silhouetted against the sky. The plaque below the memorial briefly describes the yellow fever epidemics and says, "The acts of love and courage, far beyond the call of duty, merited the gratitude and admiration of the citizens of Memphis and of the world, as history revealed the story." It concludes with a biblical quote: "Greater love than this no one has, that one lay down his life for his friends." The park stretches along the Mississippi south of downtown. Visit in late afternoon and watch the sun go down over the river.

Acknowledgments

Thanks to the following people and institutions: John Dougan, former archivist at the Shelby County Archives, and Vincent Clark, current archivist; Ed Frank at the University of Memphis, Special Collections; Patricia LaPointe McFarland, who shared some of her deep knowledge of the history of Memphis; Richard Nollan, at the Health Sciences Historical Collection, Health Sciences Library, University of Tennessee Health Science Center, Memphis; Margie Kerstine, archivist at Temple Israel, Memphis; Tanya Elder, archivist at the American Jewish Historical Society; Susan Gordon and Darla Brock, at the Tennessee State Library and Archives; Mike Birdwell, Tennessee Tech; and the helpful people at Rice University's Fondren Library; Howard University's Moorland-Spingarn Research Center; Memphis and Shelby County Room, Benjamin Hooks Central Library; Elmwood Cemetery and the Episcopal Cathedral of St. Mary's (thanks to Bette Callow for the tour.)

Connie Lester, Wayne Dowdy, Vincent Clark, and Stephen Ash read sections of the manuscript and provided useful critiques. Steve also shared his research and patiently answered queries on Reconstruction. Jerrold Harris, director of Research and Sponsored Programs at Bloomsburg University, allowed me to draw upon his expertise as an entomologist. Karl Henry, assistant professor in the Department of Biological and Allied Health Sciences at Bloomsburg, helped with my research at various points and took time out of a busy schedule to read and correct some of the medical sections. Professor William Hudon helped me understand some of the elements of Catholicism present in 1878 Memphis. Susan Stemont's careful reading of the finished manuscript was invaluable; her friendship, even more so. All mistakes are, of course, down to me and not to these kind people.

I am grateful to Bloomsburg University for supporting this project with a travel grant and, one semester, a reduction in my teaching load.

Thanks to Mike Hickey, Safa Sarcoglu, Luke Springman, Lydia Kegler, Scott Lowe, Russell and Martha Brown, Gary and Jenna Keith, Joyce Bielen, Ryan and Sue Denning, and my husband, Tony Allen, for help with this project. The friends and family whose help and support sustain me day to day are too numerous to list here; much gratitude to all of you.

I am especially grateful to David Miller at Garamond Agency; at Bloomsbury Press, Peter Ginna, for his interest in the book, Pete Beatty for his acute reading, his clarity, and his patience; Nate Knaebel, for helpful, clear direction; and Maxine Bartow, for superb copyediting.

My sister, Martha Keith Brown, loved Memphis. This book is dedicated to her.

Notes

On Sources

Technology is transforming the historian's craft. In years past, researchers often had to journey to far-distant archives and attempt to ferret out information as best they could from crumbling books and paper documents. We still do that, and most of us love it. However, the difficulty of accessing information made it unlikely that the average reader could ever check the sources cited to see if the historian was using them fairly and accurately. These days, you can find online many of the sources used in this book.

J. M. Keating's *A History of the Yellow Fever: The Yellow Fever Epidemic of 1878, in Memphis, Tenn.* (Memphis: Printed for the Howard Association by Wrightson and Company of Cincinnati, 1879), cited below as Keating, can be read in its entirety at Google Books and at Internet Archive (http://www.archive.org/). Since its publication in the year following the epidemic, it has been accepted as an authoritative source. Keating compiled a history of yellow fever in the Americas, tables of meteorological data, and information on quarantine and sanitation, but the book's value lies in his personal history of the epidemic; the day-by-day chronology he constructed from the *Memphis Daily Appeal*, the *Memphis Daily Avalanche*, and other Memphis papers (all carefully attributed to the appropriate source); a list of the dead by day, alphabetized; and reports from the Howards and other relief agencies. Keating also wrote the first volume of *History of the City of Memphis and Shelby County, Tennessee* (Syracuse, N.Y.: D. Mason & Co., 1889); to avoid confusion, that work will be cited as *History of Memphis*. Other sources include Dr. J. P. Dromgoole, *Dr. Dromgoole's Yellow Fever: Heroes, Honors and Horrors of 1878* (Louisville: John Morton and Company, 1879), cited as Dromgoole; and Father D. A. Quinn's *Heroes and Heroines of Memphis* (Providence, R.I.: E. L. Freeman and Sons, 1879), cited as Quinn. Dromgoole's book includes material reprinted from the *Avalanche* and the *Appeal*, sans attribution, but it also contains statements from the medical profession of the time concerning the etiology and treatment of yellow fever. Quinn's book, available online at Open Library, http://openlibrary.org/, supplies useful details about the Catholic religious orders in Memphis.

Memphis city directories and birth, marriage, death, and property records are available at the website of the Memphis and Shelby County Archives, http://register.shelby.tn.us/, as are *The West Tennessee Historical Society Papers* (up to 2005).

Rice University has made Kezia DePelchin's letters available in its Digital Scholarship Archive, http://scholarship.rice.edu/; they are cited below as DePelchin, by month and day. Unless otherwise noted, the letters cited here were written in 1878.

Dr. William J. Armstrong's letters are archived at the Health Sciences Historical Collection, Health Sciences Library, University of Tennessee Health Science Center, Memphis. They are cited as Armstrong, by month and date. All the Armstrong letters cited here were written in 1878.

Information on Sister Constance and her companions can be found in *The Sisters of St. Mary at Memphis: With the Acts and Sufferings of the Priests and Others Who Were There with Them During the Yellow Fever Season of 1878* (New York: Printed, but not Published, 1879), transcribed by Elizabeth Boggs 2000–2001; cited here as *The Sisters of St. Mary.* On the order itself, see Sister Mary Hilary, CSM, *Ten Decades of Praise: The Story of the Community of St. Mary During Its First Century.* Both can be read at *Project Canterbury*, http://anglicanhistory.org/.

I also used collections of letters, family papers, and clippings at the Memphis and Shelby County Room, Benjamin Hooks Central Library, Memphis; the University of Memphis Special Collections, also known as the Mississippi Valley Collection; and the Tennessee State Library and Archives (TSLA). These collections are cited by name, followed by locale: Memphis/Shelby Room, University of Memphis, and TSLA.

The Memphis newspapers provided much information about the city and the epidemic. The *Memphis Daily Appeal* is cited below as *Appeal*; the *Memphis Daily Avalanche* is cited as *Avalanche*. The *Appeal* has been digitalized and is becoming available at the Library of Congress's *Chronicling America* site, http://chroniclingamerica.loc.gov/. As of this publication, the run of papers is from 1856 through 1876.

Although I have tried to use sources from the time period whenever possible, I have also drawn extensively from the work of other historians, cited in full below. The reader will find repeated references to the following: Khaled Bloom, *The Mississippi Valley's Great Yellow Fever Epidemic of 1878* (Baton Rouge: Louisiana State University Press, 1993), cited as Bloom; John H. Ellis, *Yellow*

Fever and Public Health in the New South (Lexington: University Press of Kentucky, 1992), cited as Ellis. On the general history of Memphis, I have drawn from Lynette Boney Wrenn, *Crisis and Commission Government in Memphis: Elite Rule in a Gilded Age City* (Knoxville: University of Tennessee Press, 1998), and Robert A. Sigafoos, *Cotton Row to Beale Street: A Business History of Memphis* (Memphis: Memphis State University Press, 1979).

In general, the first citation of a book or article is given in full. Further citations are given as the last name of the author and a shortened form of the book title.

Introduction

1. *Avalanche*, August 20, 1878; DePelchin, September 23; William J. Armstrong letter, September 10; John McLeod Keating, *A History of the Yellow Fever: The Yellow Fever Epidemic of 1878, in Memphis, Tenn.*, 110; Dr. Charles T. Davis, quoted in April 7, 1932, *Memphis Press-Scimitar*; newspaper clipping collection, Memphis-Yellow Fever, Memphis and Shelby County Room, Benjamin L. Hooks Central Library, Memphis; population in 1870, Campbell Gibson, "POPULATION OF THE 100 LARGEST CITIES AND OTHER URBAN PLACES IN THE UNITED STATES: 1790 TO 1990," Table 10. Population of the 100 Largest Urban Places: 1870, U.S. Bureau of the Census, June 15, 1998.

2. For estimates concerning the number of Memphis refugees and remaining people in the city, see Keating, 108; Bloom, 162; Ellis, 47. A 2006 FEMA document rates the 1878 epidemic as the fifth-worst disaster, in terms of lives lost, in the history of the United States. Interestingly, the top four are also biological: influenza epidemics in 1918, 1957, and 1968, and the long-running smallpox epidemic of 1775–82. The death rates in these epidemics were higher, but also nationwide. Wayne Blanchard, Ph.D., CEM, Federal Emergency Management Higher Education Project, "Worst Disasters—Lives Lost," http://training.fema.gov/EMIweb/edu/docs /hazdem/Appendix-WORST%20DISASTERS%20lives%20lost.doc., accessed July 2, 2009.

3. The paragraphs concerning the etiology and symptoms of yellow fever draw from: *Control of Yellow Fever Field Guide*, Pan American Health Organization, Regional Office of the World Health Association, Scientific and Technical Publication No. 603 (2005): 1–5, accessed February 15, 2012; Catherine Zettel and Philip Kaufman, "Yellow Fever Mosquito *Aedes aegypti* (Linnaeus) Insecta: Diptera: Culicidae," on University of Florida IFAS Extension website, http://edis.ifas.ufl.edu/IN792, accessed June 20, 2009; Dorothy Crawford, *Deadly Companions: How Microbes Shaped Our History* (Oxford: Oxford University Press, 2007), 120–21; Bloom, 4–7,

25–26; Michael B. A. Oldstone, *Viruses, Plagues, and History*, paperback edition (New York: Oxford University Press, 2000), 49; Dr. Michael Womack, "The Yellow Fever Mosquito, Aedes Aegypti," *Wing Beats*, vol. 5 (4): 4; accessed at http://www.rci.rutgers.edu/~insects/sp5.htm, February 15, 2012; see also the National Institutes of Health, World Health Organization, and Centers for Disease Control and Prevention sites referenced in Note 4, below.

4. Although these three institutions have varying information on the fever and suggestions for patient care, all three use exactly the same phrase quoted above. "Yellow Fever," MedLine Plus Medical Encyclopedia, National Library of Medicine, National Institutes of Health, http://www.nlm.nih.gov/medlineplus/ency/article/001365.htm#Expectations%20(prognosis), accessed June 29, 2009; "Yellow Fever," World Health Organization, http://www.who.int/mediacentre/factsheets/fs100/en/, accessed June 29, 2009; "Yellow Fever Fact Sheet," Centers for Disease Control and Prevention, http://www.cdc.gov/yellowfever/, accessed February 15, 2012.

5. In the nineteenth century, whites and blacks in the American South accepted as fact that blacks either did not contract the fever or that, if they did, they had milder cases. The 1878 Memphis epidemic proved that many African Americans had no immunity to contracting the disease—about 11,000 of the 14,000 African Americans in Memphis did indeed take the fever. On the other hand, the death rate for whites was much higher, about 70 percent of those who fell ill, while the death rate for blacks in Memphis was about 9 percent. [Ellis, 57] Even if deaths among the black population were underreported, it is obvious that in Memphis the disease was much more deadly for whites than for blacks. For insight into how data like that can be construed, and the political implications hereof, see the exchange between Kenneth Kiple and Sheldon Watts in the *Journal of Social History* 34, no. 4 (Summer 2001). Oldstone, *Viruses, Plagues and History*, 2010 revised and updated edition, 103; on the disease in children, Bloom, 11.

6. Crawford, *Deadly Companions*, 120–21.

7. Oldstone, *Viruses, Plagues and History* (2000), 46; Crawford, *Deadly Companions*, 121.

8. The classic study of Philadelphia during the fever is J. H. Powell's *Bring Out Your Dead: The Great Plague of Yellow Fever in Philadelphia in 1793* (Philadelphia: University of Pennsylvania Press, 1949); other sources are listed at Harvard University's *Contagion: Historical Views of Diseases and Epidemics*, "The Yellow Fever Epidemic in Philadelphia, 1793," http://ocp.hul.harvard.edu/contagion/yellowfever.html, accessed July 3, 2011. For the best scholarly books on yellow fever and the American South, see Bloom,

Ellis, and Margaret Humphreys, *Yellow Fever and the South*, paperback edition (Baltimore: Johns Hopkins University Press, 1999).

9. On the complexity of identity in Louisiana, see Carl A. Brasseaux, *French, Cajun, Creole, Houma: A Primer on Francophone Louisiana* (Baton Rouge: Louisiana State University Press, 2005).

10. "Yellow Fever Epidemics," *The Tennessee Encyclopedia of History and Culture*, http://tennesseeencyclopedia.net/imagegallery.php?EntryID=Y002, accessed June 30, 2009.

11. Humphreys, *Yellow Fever and the South*, 17; see also Ellis, whose entire book is about the impact of yellow fever on public health in the South; Bloom, 13–33, 233–35.

12. Oldstone describes the United States Army Yellow Fever Commission's experiments in *Viruses, Plagues and History*. For a short, well-written narrative on the same topic, see Molly Caldwell Crosby, *The American Plague: The Untold Story of Yellow Fever, the Epidemic That Shaped Our History* (New York: Berkeley Publishing, 2006). The Phillip S. Hench Walter Reed Yellow Fever Collection at the University of Virginia has an outstanding website that includes biographies, bibliographies, photos, and many digitalized documents. http://yellowfever.lib.virginia.edu/reed/.

13. Jeffery K. Taubenberger and David M. Morens, "1918 Influenza: The Mother of All Pandemics," *Emerging Infectious Diseases* 12 (January 2006), at Centers for Disease Control and Prevention, http://www.cdc.gov/ncidod/EID/vol12no01/05-0979.htm#cit; on the 1918 epidemic, see Albert Crosby, *America's Forgotten Pandemic: the Influenza of 1918* (New York: Cambridge University Press; 2nd edition, 2003); John Barry, *The Great Influenza* (New York: Penguin Books, Revised edition, 2005); and for a brief summary of the dangers of H5N1, see Nathan Wolfe, *The Viral Storm: The Dawn of a New Pandemic Age* (New York: Times Books, 2011), 9–16. See also "The Great Pandemic: The United States in 1918–1919," United States Department of Health and Human Services, http://1918.pandemicflu.gov/the_pandemic/index.htm.

14. G. Wayne Dowdy, *A Brief History of Memphis* (Charleston, S.C.: History Press, 2011), 32.

15. Paul H. Bergeron, Stephen Ash, and Jeanette Keith, *Tennesseans and Their History* (Knoxville: University of Tennessee Press, 1999), 166–72.

Chapter 1: Bluff City Panorama

1. *Appeal*, September 4 and 7.

2. "Panoramic Maps 1847–1920," *American Memory*, Library of Congress website, http://lcweb2.loc.gov/ammem/pmhtml/, accessed February 16,

2012. Site contains biography of Ruger and a digital image of "Birds eye view of the city of Memphis, Tennessee, 1870."

3. Biographical details concerning Keating are from the following: Thomas Harrison Baker, *The Memphis Commercial Appeal: The History of a Southern Newspaper* (Baton Rouge: Louisiana State University Press, 1971), 121–63; "Keating, J. M.," in John McLeod Keating and O. P. Vedder, *History of the City of Memphis and Shelby County, Tennessee*, Vol. II (Syracuse, N.Y.: D. Mason & Co., 1889), 195–205; Vol. II was written by Vedder and will in future be cited as Vedder. "Mr. John McLeod Keating," in William S. Speer, *Sketches of Prominent Tennesseans* (Nashville: Albert B. Tavel, 1888), 378–86, hereafter cited as Speer, *Prominent Tennesseans*. Speer's book was reprinted by Rev. S. Emmett Lucas Jr. and the Southern Historical Press, Easley, S.C., in 1978, but it is now available at openlibrary.org, accessible through *Internet Archive*, http://www.archive.org/.

4. Ellis, 38; Bloom, 61.

5. Keating, 105.

6. "R. W. Mitchell, M.D.," in Speer, *Prominent Tennesseans*, 556–58; *New Orleans Medical and Surgical Journal* 8 (1852): 3–5. The number of people killed in Memphis in 1873 is reported in Ellis as more than 2,000, in Bloom as at least 1,255. Ellis, 32; Bloom, 79. "In Memoriam. Robert Wood Mitchell, M.D." *Transactions of the Seventy-First Annual Session of the Tennessee State Medical Association*, 1904, 337.

7. Ellis, 38–40; Bloom, 86–90.

8. In a contribution to *Public Health*, Erskine said that the origins of the 1873 epidemic were "obscure," but added, "I think there is but little if any doubt that it was imported." However, Erskine argued, conditions in Memphis "were such as to have originated almost any disease, and certainly to have intensified one as naturally malignant as this one." John Erskine, "A Report on Yellow Fever as It Appeared in Memphis, Tenn., in 1873," *Public Health Papers and Reports* 1 (1873): 385–92.2., accessed http://www.ncbi.nlm.nih.gov/pmc/articles/PMC2272699/.

9. Ellis, 41; Crosby, *American Plague*, gives a strong description of the "doctors' war."

10. For discussion of the debates concerning yellow fever etiology, see Bloom, 1–33; Humphreys, *Yellow Fever and the South*, 17–44; Charles Rosenberg, *Explaining Epidemics and Other Essays in the History of Medicine* (Cambridge: Cambridge University Press, 1992), 296–97. For larger issues concerning the social construction of disease, Rosenberg's essay "Explaining Epidemics" (in this volume) is very useful.

11. Memphis and Little Rock, table 474, *Travelers' Official Guide of the Railway and Steam Navigation Lines of the United States and Canada* (1875),

437; accessed via Google Books; from New Orleans to Memphis on the *City of New Orleans* takes eight hours today by Amtrak.

12. Fomite: "an inanimate object (as a dish, toy, book, doorknob, or clothing) that may be contaminated with infectious organisms and serve in their transmission." Medical Dictionary, *MedlinePlus*, http://www.merriam-webster.com/medlineplus/fomite.

13. Bloom, 18. Italics in original quotation, which is found in Dromgoole, 17.

14. Erskine, "A Report on Yellow Fever as It Appeared in Memphis, Tennessee, in 1873."

15. *Appeal*, June 30.

16. *Appeal*, June 30; Ellis, 41. *The Sanitarian* started publication in 1873. See John Duffy, *The Sanitarians: A History of American Public Health* (Champaign: University of Illinois Press, 1992), 133.

17. Sigafoos, *Cotton Row to Beale Street*, 67, 347.

18. For a brief introduction to the historic cotton trade, see Merseyside Maritime Museum, "100% Cotton," http://www.liverpoolmuseums.org.uk/maritime/exhibitions/cotton/.

19. *Sholes Directory of the City of Memphis for 1878*, accessed through the online archives of the Shelby County Registrar of Deeds, http://register.shelby.tn.us/.

20. Thérèse Yelverton Longworth, *Teresina in America*, Vol. 2 (London: R. Bentley and Son, 1875); see chapter titled "Stuck in the Mud." For a description of Memphis as a walking city, see Lynette Boney Wrenn, *Crisis and Commission Government in Memphis: Elite Rule in a Gilded Age City* (Knoxville: University of Tennessee Press, 1998), 8–9.

21. Scott Faragher and Katherine Harrington, *The Peabody Hotel* (Charleston, S.C.: Arcadia Publishing, 2002), 16–23; Longworth, *Teresina in America*, 253.

22. Ellis, 112–13, based on 1879 survey; see also Keating, *History of Memphis*, 648–53.

23. Carl Abbot, "Plank Roads and Wood Block Pavements," *Journal of Forest History* 25 (October 1981): 216–18; Sigafoos, *Cotton Row to Beale Street*, 53–54; Lynette Boney Wrenn, "The Impact of Yellow Fever on Memphis: A Reappraisal," *West Tennessee Historical Society Papers* 41 (1987): 4–18.

24. Keating, *History of Memphis*, 652.

25. Description of the holiday from *Appeal*, July 4 and 5. "Molly McCarty," *Thoroughbred Heritage*, http://www.tbheritage.com/Portraits/MollieMcCarty.html.

26. *Appeal*, July 5, 1878; James C. Cobb, *Away Down South: A History of Southern Identity* (New York: Oxford University Press, 2005), 61.

27. Details of Keating's personal history from "Keating, J. M.," in Vedder,

195–205; "Mr. John McLeod Keating," in Speer, *Prominent Tennesseans*, 378–86.

28. Louis Dow Scisco, *Political Nativism in New York State*, Columbia University Studies in the Social Sciences, 1901 (reprint AMS Press, 1968), 84–131.

29. Specifically, in Brooklyn and Williamsburg. "Street Preaching in Brooklyn—Serious Riot—The Military Called Out—The 'Know-Nothings' and Irish Armed—Several Persons Dangerously Wounded," *New York Times*, June 5, 1854; "The City in 1854," *New York Times*, January 1, 1855. See also, on a riot in the Ninth Ward, *New York Times*, July 23, 1853.

30. "Keating, Mrs. Josephine E.," in Frances Elizabeth Willard and Mary Aston Rice Livermore, eds., *American Women: Fifteen Hundred Biographies with Over 1,400 Portraits: A Comprehensive Encyclopedia of the Lives and Achievements of American Women During the Nineteenth Century*, revised edition, vol. II (New York: Mast, Crowell and Kirkpatrick, 1897), 429–30; "Keating, J.M.," in Vedder; "Mr. John McLeod Keating," in Speer, *Prominent Tennesseans*, 378–86.

31. Quotation in Beverly G. Bond and Janann Sherman, *Memphis: In Black and White* (Charleston, S.C.: Arcadia Publishing, 2003), 49; Keating's political opinions are discussed in Speer, *Prominent Tennesseans*, 379–80; Memphis's conflicted views on secession in Dowdy, *A Brief History of Memphis*, 28–29.

32. Speer, *Prominent Tennesseans*, 378–79; Bond, *Memphis Black and White*, 50.

33. John Preston Young, *Standard History of Memphis, Tennessee* (Knoxville: H. W. Crew and Company, 1912), 338.

34. Speer, *Prominent Tennesseans*, 378–79.

35. Sigafoos, *Cotton Row to Beale Street*, 41–45; Dowdy, *Brief History of Memphis*, 29–38; Wrenn, *Crisis and Commission Government*.

36. *The Papers of Andrew Johnson, February-August 1867*, ed. Paul Bergeron (Knoxville: University of Tennessee Press, 1995), 222–23; sale of the Overton Hotel, the *Nashville Daily Union*, March 28, 1866; see also Barbara G. Ellis, *The Moving Appeal: Mr. McClanahan, Mrs. Dill, and the Civil War's Great Newspaper Run* (Macon, Ga.: Mercer University Press, 2003), 409. Sale in 1874, *Appeal*, April 16, 1874. Prices calculated using Inflation Calculator at www.westegg.com/inflation/, based on Consumer Price Index statistics from *Historical Statistics of the United States*, Gov. Printing Office, 1975.

37. Barbara Ellis, *The Moving Appeal*, xxvii, 6.

38. Speer, *Prominent Tennesseans*, 349; Baker, *Commercial Appeal*, 121–63.

39. "Col. Matthew C. Galloway," in Speer, *Prominent Tennesseans*, 346–50; Baker, *Commercial Appeal*, 117.

40. Speer, *Prominent Tennesseans*, 385; see also Keating obituary, *Commercial Appeal*, August 18, 1906.

41. Speer, *Prominent Tennesseans*, 385.

42. Baker, *Commercial Appeal*, 151.

43. Baker, *Commercial Appeal*, 130; number of staffers taken from Keating, 432–33; for a description of a contemporary morning paper, see James Grant, "Interior of a Morning Newspaper Establishment," in *The Newspaper Press—Its Origin—Progress—and Present Condition*, vol. 2 (Tinsley Brothers, 1871), 141–65, accessed through Google Books; descriptions of Keating's career and work in Speer, *Prominent Tennesseans*, and Vedder, vol. 2.

44. Caroline Keating went to New York in 1877; Josephine Keating served as New York correspondent for the *Appeal* for eight years; and Keating's biographic sketch in Speer, *Prominent Tennesseans*, 380, says that Mrs. Keating resided in New York for several years while Carrie and Neil studied music and art, respectively. "Reed, Mrs. Caroline Keating," and "Keating, Mrs. Josephine E.," in Willard and Livermore, *American Women*, 430, 601. The *Sholes* 1878 city directory lists Neil as a clerk for the Southern Express, resident at 41 Madison like his father.

45. Brian B. Page, "Stand by the Flag: Nationalism and African-American Celebrations of the Fourth of July in Memphis, 1866–1887," *Tennessee Historical Quarterly* 58 (Winter 1999): 284–301; William Fitzhugh Brundage, *The Southern Past: A Clash of Race and Memory* (Cambridge, Mass.: Harvard University Press, 2005), 61.

46. Page, "Stand by the Flag."

47. Statistics from Richard L. Saunders, "The Racial Demographics of West Tennessee: An Essay Based on U.S. Census Data, 1830–2000," *West Tennessee Historical Society* Papers LXI (2008): 122–53; and Dowdy, *Brief History of Memphis*, 38.

48. "Report of an investigation of the cause, origin, and results of the late riots in the city of Memphis made by Col. Charles F. Johnson, Inspector General States of Ky. and Tennessee, and Major T. W. Gilbreth, A. D. C. to Maj. Genl. Howard, Commissioner Bureau R. F. & A. Lands," in Report of Outrages, Riots and Murders, January 15, 1866–August 12, 1868, Records of the assistant commissioner for the State of Tennessee, Bureau of Refugees, Freedmen, and Abandoned Lands, 1865–1869, National Archives Microfilm Publication M999, roll 34, accessed Freedmen's Bureau OnLine, http://freedmensbureau.com/tennessee/outrages/memphisriot.htm.

49. Quote from Dowdy, *Brief History of Memphis*, 41; for an insightful analysis of the social origins of the riot, see Altina Waller, "Community, Class

and Race in the Memphis Riot of 1866," *Journal of Social History* 18, no. 2 (1984): 233–46; see also Hannah Rosen, *Terror in the Heart of Freedom: Citizenship, Sexual Violence, and the Meaning of Race in the Postemancipation South* (Chapel Hill: University of North Carolina Press, 2009), Part I, "A City of Refuge: Emancipation in Memphis, 1862–1866."

50. House of Representatives, 39th Congress, 1st Session, Report 101, "Memphis Riots and Massacres," July 25, 1866; Creighton quote 355, B.F.C. Brooks testimony blaming the *Avalanche,* 212–16, Galloway testimony 325–26, accessed via Google Books; "Memphis Race Riot of 1866," *Tennessee Encyclopedia of History and Culture,* http://tennesseeencyclopedia .net/; James Gilbert Ryan, "The Memphis Riots of 1866: Terror in a Black Community During Reconstruction," *Journal of Negro History* 62, no. 3 (July 1977): 243; Kevin R. Hardwick, " 'Your Old Father Abe Lincoln Is Dead and Damned': Black Soldiers and the Memphis Race Riot of 1866," *Journal of Social History* 27, no. 1 (Autumn 1993): 109–28.

51. Bergeron, Ash, and Keith, *Tennesseans and Their History,* 166–80; Kenneth W. Goings and Gerald L. Smith, " 'Duty of the Hour': African American Communities in Memphis, 1862–1923," in Carroll Van West, ed., *Tennessee History: The Land, the People and the Culture* (Knoxville: University of Tennessee Press, 1998), 224–42.

52. Here and below, material is from Bergeron, Ash, and Keith, *Tennesseans and Their History,* 158–80; Mark V. Wetherington, "Ku Klux Klan," *Tennessee Encyclopedia of History and Culture,* version 2.0, http://tennessee encyclopedia.net/. For a broader view of this time period, Eric Foner's *A Short History of Reconstruction, 1863–1877* (New York: Harper and Row, 1990) is the place to start; specifically for information on the suppression of the KKK, see 195–97.

53. Bergeron, Ash, and Keith, *Tennesseans and Their History,* 178–79; *Digest of the Charter and Ordinances of the City of Memphis,* 1873; Google Books, accessed January 3, 2011; Wrenn, *Crisis and Commission Government,* 24, notes that although two black men were elected to the council in 1878, one resigned to "become a market master"; David M. Tucker, "Black Politics in Memphis, 1865–1875," *West Tennessee Historical Society Papers* 72 (1972): 13–19. See also Sharon D. Wright, *Race, Power and Political Emergence in Memphis* (London: Garland, 2000), Chapter 2, for a view of Memphis race relations in the 1870s that differs from the view presented here.

54. Mary Church Terrell, *Colored Woman in a White World* (Washington, D.C.: Ransdell, Inc., 1940; reprint edition, New York: Arno Press, 1980), 7; House of Representatives, 39th Congress, 1st Session, Report 101, "Memphis Riots and Massacres," July 25, 1866, 226–27.

55. Material in this section comes from Terrell, *Colored Woman in a White World* (quote p. 2); Cookie Lommel, *Robert Church* (Los Angeles: Melrose Square Publishing Company, 1995). Although primarily concerned with Mary Church Terrell, Cherisse Jones-Branch's insightful article has also been useful; see "Mary Church Terrell (1863–1954): Revisiting the Politics of Race, Class and Gender," in Sarah Wilkerson Freeman and Beverly Greene Bond, eds., vol. 1, *Tennessee Women: Their Lives and Times* (Athens: University of Georgia Press, 2009).

56. In addition to the sources above, see Lommel, *Robert Church*, 53, for quotation.

57. Lommel, *Robert Church*, 49–60.

58. Letter, James Lewis to Robert Church, January 31, 1901, Box 1, Folder 2, the Robert R. Church Family Papers, Mississippi Valley Collection, Ned R. McWherter Library, University of Memphis, hereafter cited as the Church Family Papers, University of Memphis. The signature on the letter quoted is unclear. On Church's Louisiana marriage: "Napier v. Church et al.," Report of Cases Argued and Determined in the Supreme Court of Tennessee, Eastern Division, September Term, 1914, Middle Division, December Term, 1914, Western Division, April Term, 1915, vol. 5, 1915, 111–30, accessed through Google Books, January 4, 2012. The same information is available through Lexis-Nexis: 132 Tenn. 111; 177 S.W. 56; 1915 Tenn. LEXIS 5; 5 Thompson 111, accessed January 4, 2012.

59. Jonathan M. Atkins, "Politics and the Debate Over the Tennessee Free Negro Bill, 1859–1860," *The Journal of Southern History* 71, no. 2 (May 2005): 245–78.

60. Stephen Ash has helped me understand some of the complications of Emancipation in Memphis. Concerning the *Victoria*, see *Official Records of the Union and Confederate Navies in the War of the Rebellion*. Series I – volume 23: Naval Forces on Western Waters (April 12, 1862–December 31, 1862): 219, 253, 684; accessed as a Cornell University Library e-book produced for the Making of America Project; http://ebooks.library.cornell .edu/m/moawar//text/ofre0023.txt.

61. Thanks to Stephen Ash for this information, and these citations: *Avalanche*, April 15, April 17, 1866.

62. Terrell, *Colored Woman in a White World*, 1–2, 5–8; Annette E. Church and Roberta Church, *The Robert R. Churches of Memphis: A Father and Son Who Achieved in Spite of Race* (privately published, 1974), 40, describes the friendship between Overton and Church and quotes a letter (also in the family papers) in which Overton mentions "our life-long friendship."

63. Terrell, *Colored Woman in a White World*, 7–8, 15–17.

64. *Appeal*, July 4 and 5.
65. Quotation from Mimi White, "Memphis Ignored Repeated Warnings of Peril," *Commercial Appeal*, October 31.

Chapter 2: Yellow Jack

1. *Appeal*, July 16, 17; *Avalanche*, July 28.
2. *Appeal*, July 16, 17, 21; *Avalanche*, July 25; Keating, 109. See also "A Possible Connection Between the 1878 Yellow Fever Epidemic in the Southern United States and the 1877–78 El Niño Episode," Henry F. Diaz and Gregory J. McCabe, *Bulletin of the American Meteorological Society* 80, no. 1 (January 1999).
3. Bloom, 22–24; Captain Charles Smart, assistant surgeon, U.S.A., in *Annual Report of the National Board of Health*, 1880, 440–41. Google Books.
4. Bloom, 28.
5. Bloom, 20–33; *Appeal*, August 14, onion recipe.
6. See Harold Ellis, *A History of Surgery* (London: Cambridge University Press, 2001), 92–93; "Failure of Carbolic Acid as a General Disinfectant," *Journal of Materia Medica* XV, no. 1 (January 1876): 164. See also Wikipedia for discussion of phenol and its present-day uses in products from sunscreen to plastics. Older readers may remember carbolic soap; in the United States, the most common was Lifebuoy. Thanks to my colleague Dr. Toni Trumbo Bell, Bloomsburg University Department of Chemistry, for information on phenol. On New Orleans events, Samuel Choppin, M.D., "History of the Importation of Yellow Fever into the United States from 1693 to 1878," *Public Health Reports and Papers*, Vol. IV, presented at the meetings of the American Public Health Association in the years 1877–78 (Boston: Houghton, Osgood and Company, 1880), 197–205.
7. Choppin, "History of the Importation of Yellow Fever into the United States from 1693 to 1878."
8. Ellis, 40–41.
9. Just Touatre, *Yellow Fever: Clinical Notes*. Translated by Charles Chassaignac, M.D. *New Orleans Medical and Surgical Journal*, 1898, 109; Google Books.
10. Ellis, strangers' disease, 31–32, 40–41; Touatre, *Yellow Fever*.
11. Yellow Fever Epidemics, *Tennessee Encyclopedia of History and Culture*; S. R. Bruesch, M.D., "The Disasters and Epidemics of a River Town: Memphis, Tennessee, 1819–1879," *Bulletin of the Medical Library Association* 40, no. 3 (July 1952): 288–305, accessed through PubMed Central, National Institutes of Health, http://www.ncbi.nlm.nih.gov/pmc/articles /PMC195412/?pageindex=1, September 6, 2010; Keating, 103–5.
12. *Appeal*, July 26, 27; Keating, 114, 118; Ellis, 42.

13. See Bloom, 17–19, on fomites; on Memphis quarantine, Bloom, 153–55, Ellis, 42.

14. *New York Times*, July 29; *Daily Picayune*, August 2, 1878; *New Orleans Times*, August 9; Bloom, 154–55.

15. Bloom, 15–16.

16. *Appeal*, August 1 and 4; Bloom, 154.

17. On Howards, see Elizabeth Young Newsome, "Unto the Least of These: The Howard Association and Yellow Fever," *Southern Medical Journal* 85, no. 6 (June 1992): 632–37.

18. Ellis, 43.

19. *Appeal*, July 27; Keating, 154; Surgeon W. H. Long, "Yellow Fever at Gallipolis, 1878," 127–40. *Annual Report of the Supervising Surgeon-General of the Marine Hospital Service of the United States, for the Fiscal Years 1878 and 1879* (Washington, D.C.: Government Printing Office, 1879).

20. Historical Marker Database, hmdb.org, http://www.hmdb.org/marker.asp ?marker=30625; Long, "Yellow Fever at Gallipolis, 1878."

21. Keating, 146; *Appeal*, August 13.

22. DePelchin, August 28.

23. *Appeal*, July 27, August 11. On use of disinfectant see Humphries, *Yellow Fever and the South*.

24. R. B. Maury, M.D., "The Sanitary Necessities of Memphis and the Yellow Fever of 1878," in *First Report of the State Board of Health of the State of Tennessee, April, 1877 to October, 1880* (Nashville: Tavel and Howell, Printers to the State, 1880), 87–89; Keating, 107, 145.

25. *Sholes* city directory, 478; *New York Times*, July 6, 1862; Keating, 106–7; Maury, "Sanitary Necessities."

26. Bloom, 156; Keating, 146; Peter Murtough, *Condensed History of the Great Yellow Fever Epidemic of 1878* (Memphis: S. C., Toof & Co., 1879), 62; *Appeal*, August 14.

27. Keating, 146; *Appeal*, August 14; quote from *Avalanche* in Bloom, 156.

28. Keating, 107; *Appeal*, August 16.

29. *Chicago Tribune*, October 26. SAHO field guide; Erskine, "A Report on Yellow Fever as It Appeared in Memphis, Tenn., in 1873."

30. *Chicago Tribune*, October 26. The writer was the *Tribune*'s special correspondent in Memphis.

31. Keating; 20,000 from Bloom, 158; *Avalanche*, August 18, quoted in Bloom, 160.

32. Letter, quoted without attribution to individual writer, in *The Sisters of St. Mary at Memphis*; Keating, 108; J. H. Smith, secretary, Howard Report, in Keating, 334–36.

33. Keating, 107; *Appeal*, August 15; Vedder, 200.

34. Keating, 170, 405–10; *Appeal*, September 25.

35. Material on Nathan Menken and his family from the following: "Menken," *The Jewish Encyclopedia*, vol. VIII (New York: Funk and Wagnall's, c. 1905, 1909, 1912), 492–93; typed manuscript biography of Nathan Davis Menken, Menken Family Papers, Box 1 of 1, American Jewish Historical Society, New York, hereafter abbreviated as AJHS; "J. S. Menken," Goodspeed's *History of Tennessee* (1887), Shelby County Biographical Index, *Shelby County, Tennessee, Biography and History*, accessed through http://www.wdbj.net/shelby/goodspeed/history/, a part of the TNGen-Web project; "Personal Recollections of Nathan Davis Menken," *Jewish Spectator*, Thirtieth Anniversary Memorial Number, 1915, from the archives of Temple Israel, Memphis, courtesy of archivist Margie Kerstine; Patricia LaPointe McFarland, "Yellow Fever: The 'King of Terrors': The Memphis Jewish Community in the Epidemic of 1878," *Southern Jewish Heritage* 15, no. 1 (Spring 2002): 1–7.

36. The commander of Union occupying forces in Memphis, Major General Stephen Augustus Hurlbut, does not seem to have exiled any Jews, but he used his power to extort money from Jewish merchants. (Hurlbut was such a thorough scoundrel that it is hard to tell whether his actions reflected anti-Semitism or business as usual.) Selma S. Lewis, *A Biblical People in the Bible Belt: The Jewish Community of Memphis, Tennessee, 1840s–1960s* (Macon, Ga.: Mercer University Press, 1998), 31–54; Dowdy, *A Brief History*, 32; Jeffery Norman Lash, *A Politician Turned General: The Civil War Career of Stephen Augustus Hurlbut* (Kent, Ohio: Kent State University Press, 2003), 107–47; Frederic Cople Jaher, *A Scapegoat in the New Wilderness: The Origins and Rise of Anti-Semitism in America* (Cambridge, Mass.: Harvard University Press, 1996), 183–200. See also Jonathan D. Sarna, *When General Grant Expelled the Jews* (New York: Schocken Books, 2012).

37. Quote from Mimi White, "Memphis Ignored Repeated Warnings of Peril"; see also Menken letters in *Appeal*, November 3, 1878; "Report of the Hebrew Hospital Association," Keating, 417–78.

38. Armstrong information from the Letters of William J. Armstrong, Health Sciences Library and Biocommunications Center, University of Tennessee Medical Center, Memphis, and the biography accompanying those papers; Marshall Wingfield, "The Life and Letters of Dr. William J. Armstrong," West Tennessee Historical Society Papers 4 (1950), 97–114. Address of office, Armstrong's business card, in Armstrong papers.

39. Armstrong letters, August 17, 19, 20.

40. Keating, 153.

41. Sieck diary, Memphis and Shelby County Room, Benjamin L. Hooks Central Library, Memphis.

42. Little Rock's quarantine worked, thanks to enforcement by shotgun and community patrols along the rivers as well as the railroad lines. R. G. Jennings, M.D., "The Quarantine at Little Rock, Arkansas, During August, September and October, 1878, Against the Yellow Fever Epidemic in Memphis and the Mississippi Valley," *Public Health Papers and Reports*, American Public Health Association, vol. 4, 1877–1878 (Boston: Houghton, Osgood and Company, 1880).

43. Yellow Fever Clippings, folder 1 of 3, Memphis Central Library. Paper not given, date December 27, 1932; Keating, 108.

44. Bloom, 158–59, 186–87.

45. *Avalanche*, August 20.

46. *Appeal*, August 22; Keating, 149.

47. Keating, 108, 149, 322; Ellis, 57.

48. *Appeal*, August 15.

49. Keating, 382–86.

50. *Avalanche*, September 1; Speer, *Prominent Tennesseans*, 150–51; Keating, 140–41.

51. Ellis, 47; *Avalanche*, August 20.

52. *Avalanche*, August 23.

53. Keating, 162; *Appeal*, August 28, 30; Menken biography, AJHS.

54. August 28 *Appeal*. See Mitchell's report in Keating; *Chicago Tribune*, October 1.

Chapter 3: Siege

1. Keating, 109–10.

2. Keating, 133; *Appeal*, August 15, 18; Mimi White, "Memphis Ignored Repeated Warnings of Peril."

3. White, "Memphis Ignored Repeated Warnings of Peril"; *Appeal*, August 16, 17. During the epidemic year, the total receipts for cotton in the Memphis market declined from the previous year but exceeded receipts for 1876. Seven percent of the nation's cotton crop passed through Memphis in 1878, down one percentage point from the previous year. Sigafoos, *Cotton Row to Beale Street*, 147. Signatories to the call for meeting: C. G. Fisher, E. C. Mosby and S. Mosby, M.&C. Railroad; H. Furstenheim, cotton factor; E. B. Galbreath, cotton factor and vice president of Hernando Insurance Company; S. M. Gates, cotton buyer; J. M. Keating; W. H. Bates, and S. Toof, print/lithography shop; J. T. Pettit, cotton factor; R. A. Thompson; N. M. Jones and John M. Peters, coal dealers (Jones was also president of a steamboat company); J. S. Day, cotton factor; Orgil Brothers and Company, hardware and machinery; B. Babb, cotton broker; John S. Toof, secretary and superintendent of the Cotton Exchange, also secretary of

the chamber of commerce; A. Turner, agent for a freight line; Porter, Taylor and Company, cotton factors; C. P. Hunt, cotton factor; G. Falls and Company, cotton buyers; R. C. Nichols, newspaperman; W. P. Proudfit, cotton factor; Fader, Jacobs and Company, cotton factors; and J. R. Godwin, cotton factor. *Sholes* directory.

4. See *Appeal*, August 17 and 18.

5. Annual Reports of the Secretary of War, vol. 1, 1878, 409–11; the request for rations appears to have come from Representative Casey Young on August 19; *Avalanche*, August 20.

6. *Appeal*, August 18.

7. *Avalanche*, August 20. Quotation from *Frank Leslie's Illustrated*, in Edward J. Blum, *Reforging the White Republic: Race, Religion and American Nationalism* (Baton Rouge: Louisiana State University Press, 2005), 170. Blum charges that the choice of location for the camp indicated gross disregard for the health of the black farmers thereabouts. However, he also writes that the camp was a hospital to which yellow fever patients would be transported. The camps were intended to be refuges for the healthy, not hospitals for the sick. The whole point was to keep the people in the camps from getting the fever. The CRC thought that yellow fever would not spread to the camp, situated as it was out of town on higher ground. They did not think they were endangering the neighbors, although in fact they did. When they let people go back and forth from the camp to the town on a daily basis, some people contracted the fever and brought it to the countryside. It seems to me that the CRC's ignorance of the fever's etiology, rather than gross disregard, is most to blame for the fever cases near the camp.

8. *Avalanche*, August 20.

9. *Avalanche*, August 20; *Appeal*, August 27; corpses in house, Keating. On the black policemen, see Dennis C. Rousey, "Yellow Fever and Black Policemen in Memphis: A Post-Reconstruction Anomaly," *Journal of Southern History* 51, no. 3 (August 1985): 357–74.

10. Citizens' Relief Committee report, Keating, 391; Sharon D. Wright, *Race, Power and Political Emergence in Memphis* (New York: Taylor and Frances e-Library, 2003), 10.

11. *Appeal*, August 22. My surmise that Wright was well known and, apparently, trusted, is based on evidence outlined in the text: people in the crowd shouted for him to speak, and they voted as he advised.

12. *Appeal*, August 24.

13. *Appeal*, August 24, 27.

14. *Appeal*, November 3, quoting letter of August 15.

15. Report in Keating, 371.

16. Keating 153, 186; *Appeal*, September 6.

17. Keating, 158.

18. *Appeal*, August 28; Keating, 188, excerpts *Tribune* story.

19. *Appeal*, August 15, September 6; Keating, 193–94.

20. *Appeal*, September 25; Keating, 186; *Transactions of the Grand Commandery, Knights Templar of the State of Michigan* (Grand Rapids: H. H. Colestock, Masonic Printer, 1880), 137, Google Books; Shields McIlwaine, *Memphis Down in Dixie* (Boston: E. P. Dutton, 1948), 171.

21. *Avalanche*, August 30. The official death lists, compiled from reports submitted by physicians, contained only the cases that had come to their attention; Keating considered them a consistent underestimate of the actual death rate. *Avalanche*, September 5, quoted in Keating, 155; *Appeal*, August 28.

22. *Avalanche*, August 30.

23. *The Sisters of St. Mary at Memphis: With the Acts and Sufferings of the Priests and Others Who Were There with Them During the Yellow Fever Season of 1878* (New York: Printed, but not Published, 1879); 66 pp. transcribed by Elizabeth Boggs, AD 2000-2001. Project Canterbury, http://anglicanhistory.org/usa/csm/memphis1.html. Originally, this was a fifty-one-page pamphlet; however, the work appears on Project Canterbury in plain text without pagination.

24. Information about the Sisters of St. Mary is drawn from Sister Mary Hilary, CSM, *Ten Decades of Praise: The Story of the Community of St. Mary During Its First Century* (Racine, Wisc.: The DeKoven Foundation for Church Work, 1965); online at Project Canterbury, http://anglicanhistory.org/usa/csm/mhilary/; DePelchin, September 14.

25. Hilary, *Ten Decades of Praise*, Chapter 8.

26. Ibid.

27. Quotations from Constance's diary, and other material following, *The Sisters of St. Mary at Memphis*.

28. George C. Harris, "Acknowledgements," *The Churchman* 38 (November 23, 1878): 626; Alabama Public Service Commission Report, 1892, 21–22; for an especially good account of Charles Parsons's life and death, see Crosby, *The American Plague*; Project Canterbury, *The Sisters of St. Mary at Memphis*.

29. All of Constance's diary entries are in *The Sisters of St. Mary at Memphis*.

30. Location from Memphis directories and maps, including *Sholes*, 1878, and *Memphis, Tennessee, Insurance Maps*, vol. 1 (Sanborn-Perris Map Company, 1897), which shows location of Mansion House and hotel. Most information here is from Franklin Wright, "Annie Cook: The Mary Magdalene of Memphis," *West Tennessee Historical Society Papers* 43 (1989):

44–55. Probate inventory of Cook's estate, Memphis and Shelby County Archives.

31. Armstrong, August 24.

32. *Appeal*, August 29, 30.

33. Description, *Avalanche*; Citizens' Relief Committee report, including Commissary Report and Report of the Surgeon in Charge of Camp Joe Williams, Keating, 390–95; also Keating, 132; criticism of process, Blum, *Reforging the White Republic*, 169.

34. Keating, Report of the Commissary Department, 392–93.

35. *Appeal*, August 29. Keating, Citizens' Relief Committee report, 391.

36. Brown's occupation, *Sholes* directory, 1878, 181; Keating, 130, 430; *Appeal*, September 14, October 12, November 2; the latter paper explains that the Guards had been on tour throughout the epidemic. See also Young, *Standard History*, 368.

37. Ellis, 47; Bloom, 162–63.

38. Bloom, 178.

39. Bloom, 178–79, report in Keating.

40. Bloom, 162.

41. *Appeal*, September 14, included Camp Henderson in a list of CRC camps; Keating, 191.

42. Keating, appendix, "Report of the Father Mathew Camp," by Father William Walsh, rector of St. Bridget's Church, 395–98.

43. *The Sisters of St. Mary at Memphis*.

44. Ralph Kirshner, *The Class of 1861: Custer, Ames and Their Classmates After West Point* (Carbondale: Southern Illinois University Press, 2008), x, 113.

45. "The Leath Asylum and the Orphan's Refuge," *Appeal*, October 1; *The Sisters of St. Mary at Memphis*.

46. Armstrong, August 28; *Appeal*, August 28.

47. Keating, 185.

48. Keating, 151–52.

49. *Appeal*, September 3.

Chapter 4: The Destroying Angel

1. *Appeal*, September 3.

2. Young, *Standard History*, 180–81.

3. Keating, 131–32; *Appeal*, September 3.

4. Keating, 132.

5. *Appeal*, September 7. The death toll for Monday, September 2, 1878, was listed as fifty-two. According to the September 3 *Appeal*, "few of the physi-

cians made reports yesterday, one undertaker's establishment was closed, and the county undertaker was greatly retarded in his work for want of laborers and burying material."

6. This is almost the entire letter; the only other statement is "Gus home safe." Charles Fisher Papers, Mississippi Valley Collection, Ned R. Mc-Wherter Library, University of Memphis, hereafter cited as Fisher Papers.

7. Parsons letter, September 1. *The Sisters of St. Mary at Memphis.*

8. *Appeal,* September 1. Deaths at two hundred per day, Keating, 141.

9. *Appeal,* September 3; *Avalanche,* September 6.

10. Armstrong, August 24, September 6.

11. Armstrong, August 24, 30, September 1.

12. Choppin quoted in Dromgoole, 16–17; pages 9–59 contain physicians' statements about the fever and its treatment.

13. Mitchell in Dromgoole, 29; on heroic medicine and the move away from it, see John Harley Warner, "From Specificity to Universalism in Medical Therapeutics: Transformation in the 19th Century United States," in Judith Walzer Leavitt and Ronald Numbers, eds., *Sickness and Health in America,* 3rd ed. (Madison: University of Wisconsin Press, 1997).

14. Dromgoole, 17.

15. For the Howards' tally of "foreign" nurses, see Keating, 371–75.

16. Keating, 162; blacks resenting white foreign nurses as unfair labor competition, see DePelchin letters. For insights into class and gender roles as they affected nurses in Memphis, see Randal L. Hall, "Southern Conservatism at Work: Women, Nurses, and the 1878 Yellow Fever Epidemic in Memphis," *Tennessee Historical Quarterly* 56, no. 4 (Winter 1997): 244–61.

17. DePelchin, September 23.

18. Keating, 113.

19. Ibid.

20. DePelchin, November 23.

21. Material on DePelchin background from Harold J. Matthews, *Candle by Night* (Boston: Bruce Humphries, 1942). On Cordelia Buckner, see 30–31; quote from 44. See also "Morris, Joseph Robert," *The Handbook of Texas Online,* http://www.tshaonline.org/handbook/online/articles/fm060.

22. Matthews, *Candle by Night,* 66–69.

23. Matthews, *Candle by Night,* 86; DePelchin, September 3.

24. On Easley, see *Transactions of the American Medical Association,* vol. XXX, 1879, 815.

25. De Pelchin, September 3, 8.

26. Michael Haines, "Fertility and Mortality in the United States," EH-Net Encyclopedia (Economic History Association), accessed August 3, 2011;

http://eh.net/encyclopedia/article/haines.demography. Discussion of prostitution draws from Ruth Rosen, *The Lost Sisterhood: Prostitution in America, 1900–1918* (Baltimore: Johns Hopkins University Press, 1982). For a brief survey of 19th-century Americans attitudes toward sexuality, see Charles Rosenberg, "Sexuality, Class and Role in 19th-century America," *American Quarterly* 25, no. 2 (May 1973): 131–53.

27. Marsha Wedell, *Elite Women and the Reform Impulse in Memphis, 1875–1915* (Knoxville: University of Tennessee Press, 1991), 36.

28. For a discussion of attempts to create red-light districts in American cities, Rosen, *Lost Sisterhood*, 10–11; *Appeal*, July 17.

29. *Appeal*, July 21.

30. DePelchin, September 3, 8.

31. DePelchin, September 17; September 23, letters 1 and 2; October 9.

32. W. L. Coleman, *A History of Yellow Fever: Indisputable Facts Pertaining to Its Origin and Cause* (Chicago: Clinic Publishing Company, 1898), 10–11, 16, 108–9. It is not clear whether Coleman had reached that conclusion by 1878, but he says that after 1879 he believed the South had paid enough for slavery (what with the war and the yellow fever epidemics) and he predicted that no further major epidemics would occur.

33. Quote from Landrum's post-epidemic speech, Keating, 441; fever as punishment for Mardi Gras, Gerald M. Capers, Jr., "Yellow Fever in Memphis in the 1870s," *Mississippi Valley Historical Review* 24, no. 4 (March 1938): 489. Capers quotes Father Quinn, 126.

34. See Robert Ingersoll, "The Gods," in *The Gods and Other Lectures*, Peoria, Illinois, 1875. Many of Ingersoll's works are available online at Google Books, Internet Archive, and Project Gutenberg.

35. See Daniel W. Stowell, *Rebuilding Zion: The Religious Reconstruction of the South, 1863–1877* (New York: Oxford University Press, 1998).

36. See Drew Gilpin Faust, *The Republic of Suffering* (New York: Knopf, 2008), esp. Chapter 6, "Believing and Doubting," and a contemporary source, Elizabeth Stewart Phelps's bestseller, *The Gates Ajar* (1868).

37. Keating, 120.

38. *Sholes* directory, 36; Cornelius James Kirkfleet, *The Life of Patrick Augustine Feehan: Bishop of Nashville, First Archbishop of Chicago, 1829–1902* (Chicago: Matre and Company, 1922), 59–60; Quinn, 53, 142–68.

39. Walsh's death, Keating, 236; Quinn's opening page lists deaths and dates.

40. All from Quinn, 142–68. Quinn knew the "secular," or parish, priests, but did not know the religious priests, i.e., those in orders. He also has very little to say about the non-Irish parishes. St. Mary's was German, St. Joseph's, Italian. See also Keating, 163.

41. Beth Warren, "Staying Power: St. Mary's Catholic Church Keeps on Keepin' On," *Memphis Commercial Appeal*, December 10, 2010. St. Mary's began a soup kitchen in 1870; it is still running. On Wiewer, *The Book of Three States: Notable Men of Mississippi, Arkansas, Tennessee* (Memphis: Commercial Appeal Publishing Company, 1914), 227; Quinn, front page, 170–71; August Reyling, Memphis Letters, 1878–1888. Transcript, translated by Father August Reyling, OFM, 1977 (Quincy College [now Quincy University], Quincy, Illinois). This is a bound volume of typed, transcribed, and translated letters, not published.

42. *Donahoe's Magazine*, vol. 1, 233–34; Sister Mary Jean Ryan, SSM, *On Becoming Exceptional: SSM Health Care's Journey to Baldridge and Beyond* (Milwaukee: American Society for Quality, Quality Press, 2007), 3–6.

43. DePelchin letters, September 30, November 6, 9.

44. Keating, 120, 157; description of curriculum, *Sadlier's Catholic Directory, Almanac and Ordo for the Year of Our Lord 1876*, 39; Nancy de Flon and James A. Wallace, eds., *All Your Waves Swept Over Me*, 100; Quinn, 176; *Donahoe's Magazine*, vol. 1, 233–34; Sister Mary Jean Ryan, *On Becoming Exceptional*, 3–6.

45. *Morning Star*, September 8, 1878; Quinn, 186–89.

46. "Landrum, Sylvanus, D.D.," William Cathcart, Vol. II, *The Baptist Encyclopedia*, 669–70. Reprinted by the Baptist Standard Bearer, Paris, Arkansas, 2001; Google Books; Keating, 443; Sylvanus Landrum, "The Yellow Fever," *The Friend*, November 7, 1878, in Vol. LIL (Philadelphia: William H. Pile, 1879), 117, accessed as Google Book.

47. Keating, 128, 160; *The Friend*, 117; Samuel Boykin, *History of the Baptist Denomination in Georgia*, vol. 2 (Atlanta, Ga.: James P. Harrison and Co., 1881, reprinted by the Baptist Standard Bearer, 2001), 318–19, accessed through Google Books.

48. September 3.

49. *Appeal*, November 3.

50. *Avalanche*, August 20; *Appeal*, August 28, 30; quote from "Nathan Davis Menken Bio Sketch," in Menken Family Papers, Box 1, American Jewish Historical Society; special thanks to Tanya Elder. No author is given for the typed sketch. Internal evidence indicates that it was written by someone who was in Memphis during the summer of 1878; if so, the typed manuscript is a copy. In the quote I have substituted "abroad" for "aboard" on the supposition that the latter is a typo.

51. *Appeal*, September 3; *Avalanche*, September 4, quoted in *Chicago Tribune*, September 7.

52. *Cincinnati, the Queen City*, Vol. III (Chicago: S. J. Clarke Publishing Company, 1912), 326–29; Google Books; *Appeal*, October 4; Keating, 418.

53. *Sisters of St. Mary at Memphis.*
54. Armstrong, September 6.

Chapter 5. The Arithmetic of Sorrow

1. Keating, 329–76.
2. Keating, 152, 180; J. H. Smith, "Secretary's Report for 1878," 335; *Appeal*, August 28.
3. *Avalanche*, September 5, quoted in Keating, 155.
4. Keating, 128.
5. "The Yellow Fever," *The Friend*; Keating, 154, 441; *Appeal*, September 5.
6. *Avalanche*, September 4, quoted in *Chicago Tribune*, September 7.
7. Keating, 373, gives initials.
8. DePelchin, September 8.
9. *The Sisters of St. Mary at Memphis.*
10. Music History: Organists Past and Present, Christ Church Cathedral website, accessed December 29, 2010, http://www.christchurchcathedral .org/default.aspx?name=wm_history; "W. T. D. Dalzell, Caddo Parish, La.," from Maude Herne O'Pry, *Chronicles of Shreveport and Caddo Parish*, 344; in US GenWeb Archives; http://files.usgwarchives.org/la/caddo/bios /dalzellw.txt. DePelchin describes the meeting in a September 14 letter, but internal evidence indicates that it was September 8 or 9 when she met Dalzell at the Howard offices.
11. DePelchin, September 14.
12. Ibid.
13. See *Frank Leslie's Sunday Magazine* IV (June–December 1878): 751 for a brief sketch of Sister Frances's life before Memphis. Google Books, accessed January 2, 2011.
14. Armstrong, September 7.
15. *Dr. Quintard, Chaplain C.S.A. and Second Bishop of Tennessee: The Memoir and Civil War Diary of Charles Todd Quintard*, ed. Sam Davis Elliot. (Baton Rouge: Louisiana State University Press, 2003), 52–53.
16. *Book of Common Prayer*, 1871 Standard. *The Sisters of St. Mary at Memphis* says that Parsons died at ten-thirty on September 6; Armstrong's letter quoted above, dated September 7, speaks of Parsons as dying but still alive at that date. My guess is that Armstrong wrote on his letter the date it was to be mailed (the following morning).
17. This and material below, *Sisters of St. Mary at Memphis.*
18. Armstrong, September 9.
19. *Avalanche*, September 6; *Appeal*, September 4, 6.
20. *Appeal*, September 24. Directions for the construction of a printer (or pressman) hat can found at myriad online sites; see "How to Fold a

Pressman's Hat," http://www.philly.com/philly/video/BC623511839001
.html?results=y; for a selection of cartoons, see Southern Labor History
Archives, "19th and 20th Labor Prints," http://www.library.gsu.edu/
spcoll/pages/pages.asp?ldID=105&guideID=510&ID=4223. Alan Pinkerton, *Strikers, Communists, Tramps and Detectives* (New York: G. W. Carleton
and Company, 1878), 52–57. The Pinkerton Agency's chief job being the
destruction of labor unions, this book must be taken with a grain of salt.

21. *Appeal*, September 6.

22. *Chicago Tribune*, September 9, describes Keating alone in the office:
"Wednesday night, he did all of the editorial work, most of the reporto-
rial work, set several 'sticks full' of type, read proof, and 'made up the
forms' of yesterday's issue of his paper."

23. *Appeal*, September 10. The editorial concludes with prayers: of blessing
for those who have supplied the city's needs during the disaster, for the
safety of those who have come to help care for the sick, "and we ask that
the names of the women and the men who have laid down their lives for
us shall be handed down forever as among the brightest and the best of
earth."

24. Fedder, *History of Memphis*, vol. 2; quote 201; "The Citizens Relief Committee," in Keating, 390; also 157.

Chapter 6: A Contagion of Kindness

1. The Ramsey episode made the wire and was reprinted, with varying details, in papers around the country. The material here comes from Keating, 113–14; *Appeal*, September 14; *New Hampshire Sentinel*, September
19, 1878; Chicago *Inter-Ocean*, September 14, 1878; *New Orleans Times*,
September 15, 1878; see also *Appeal*, September 15, for accusations against
Ramsey and clarifications by Dr. Mitchell. See also interview with a Washington nurse, quoted in the *National Republican*, September 20. Post-
epidemic, see Keating, 113.

2. Keating, 11; *Appeal*, August 25, September 24.

3. Keating, 430.

4. Statistics from Werner Troesken, *Water, Race and Disease* (Cambridge,
Mass.: Massachusetts Institute of Technology Press, 2004), 65; Ellis, 48.

5. Saloon location, 372 Second Street, in *Sholes*, 524; receipts for payments
made to John Overton Jr., Church Family Papers, Series 1, Carton 1, Folder
3, Mississippi Valley Collection, University of Memphis. In *Colored Woman
in a White World*, Mary Church Terrell explains (often obliquely) the
family situation; see 10, 18, 34–38. See also Cherisse Jones-Branch,
"Mary Church Terrell," *Tennessee Women*. It is very unlikely that Church
depended on anyone's charity during the epidemic. According to his

daughter Mollie, Robert had acquired the habit of buying food in bulk while serving as a steward on his father's boat. She said that her father "never bought a small quantity of any thing. My earliest recollection is of seeing barrels of flour, firkins of butter and large tin or wooden buckets of lard. He would buy crates of turkey and chickens. Bunches of bananas used to hang where we could reach them easily. There were always oranges and nuts." *Terrell, Colored Woman in a White World*, 5.

6. Contribution mentioned in *Appeal*, September 15; Annette E. Church and Roberta Church, *The Robert R. Churches of Memphis: A Father and Son Who Achieved in Spite of Race* (Privately published, 1974), 40–41.

7. "contagion of kindess," Keating 116; The appendixes in Keating contain long lists of donations and tallies of sums raised by various Memphis groups. Southern Express, 127; Howard Association Secretary and Treasurer's Report, 365; Masonic contributions, "Report of Memphis Masonic Relief Board," Keating, Appendix, 405–10. Estimate of money values based on Consumer Price Index calculator on *Measuring Worth*, http://www.measuringworth.com/index.php, accessed November 6, 2010; totals from Ellis, 53. Masonic contributions, "Report of Memphis Masonic Relief Board," Keating, Appendix, 405–10.

8. Edward J. Blum, *Reforging the White Republic*; see entire chapter, "The White Flag Waves."

9. Keating, Mitchell's post-epidemic report, 36.

10. *Appeal*, September 14; DePelchin, September 17.

11. *Appeal*, September 8.

12. *Appeal*, October 16; Bloom, 193–94.

13. Howard canteen: Mrs. Heckle letter March 28, 1879, DePelchin Papers; description of Howards as laughing, joking, and cheering each other comes from a Washington, D.C., nurse sent home early because she was so worn out and interviewed in the *National Republican*, September 20.

14. Keating, 192.

15. Keating, 366.

16. DePelchin, September 23 letter, addendum to September 17 letter.

17. Keating, 369–70.

18. W. L. Coleman, *A History of Yellow Fever*, 98–99; reprinted by U.C. Library, 2002, accessed at archive.org, December 28, 2010.

19. Mitchell wrote, "I urged them invariably to leave the city. Even then some would go into the outskirts to work." Faced with willful, suicidal obstinance, Mitchell gave up, called the doctors in question to Howard headquarters, and assigned them to regular duty. Keating, 367–70.

20. Coleman, *History of Yellow Fever*, 90–93. Coleman refers to the physician as "Dr. K." and dates these events to October 17. In the list of unaccli-

mated doctors printed in Keating, 369, it is noted that Dr. M. L. Keating, a resident of New York, died on October 17.

21. Keating, 167; tombstone, Elmwood Cemetery.

22. DePelchin, September 23, addendum to September 17 letter.

23. Keating, 118–19; Dr. D. D. Saunders, in *Society Proceedings, Tri-State Medical Association of Mississippi, Arkansas and Tennessee, Twentieth Annual Meeting* (1903): 678

24. Keating, 119. See Summers, *Yellow Fever* (Wheeler: Nashville, 1879).

25. DePelchin, September 17.

26. "Burial Customs and Cemeteries in American History," *National Register Bulletin*, U.S. Department of the Interior, National Park Service, accessed January 24, 2011; http://www.cr.nps.gov/nr/publications/bulletins/nrb41/nrb41_5.htm. See also "Mourning the Dead: A Study in Sentimental Ritual," in Karen Halttunen's *Confidence Men and Painted Women: A Study of Middle-Class Culture in America, 1830–1870* (New Haven, Conn.: Yale University Press, 1982), for an insightful look at the role of cemeteries in nineteenth century culture. *Sholes*, 1878, 32–33.

27. Keating, 112.

28. Keating, 194.

29. Keating, 190, 441.

30. *Appeal*, September 22.

31. *Appeal*, September 12.

32. Cook probate papers, Memphis/Shelby Archives; thanks to John Dougan, then with the archives, for giving me a digitalized copy of the document.

33. Keating, 424–25.

34. Keating, 431–32.

35. Father William Walsh, "Report of the Father Mathew Camp," Keating 395–404; on funding, The I.C.B.U. Journal, "A Hero in the Strife," *Donohue's Magazine* III (January to July 1880): 129.

36. Walsh, "Report of the Father Mathew Camp," Keating, 395–98; Quinn, 141.

37. Keating, 135–40; DePelchin, September 17.

38. DePelchin, September 17; retrospective note in papers, dated March 1, 1879.

39. Keating, 165.

40. Landrum, "The Yellow Fever," *The Friend*. In 1897 an *Atlanta Constitution* feature story circulated through the press about Herbert Landrum's death. In it, Herbert wears himself out and dies as a result of trying to save the life of Jefferson Davis's son, Jefferson Davis Jr. No mention of this is made in the *Appeal* or in Keating's history of the epidemic. Given

that Davis died a month after Landrum, it seems unlikely. Keating, 190.

41. Keating, 441.

42. DePelchin refers to the man who solicited her help as "Johnson," but the September 17 *Appeal* describes Annie Morrow Johnston's death, listing her mother as Julia.

43. DePelchin, October 6. "In life they were beautiful, and in death they were not separated" is a paraphrase of Samuel II, 1:23: "Saul and Jonathan were lovely and pleasant in their lives, and in their death they were not divided." *Chicago Tribune*, October 6: Julia and Jennie Morrow died on October 5.

44. DePelchin, October 6, 8, 9; reference to castor oil in letter from Mrs. E. K. Heckle to DePelchin, Houston, March 31, 1879.

45. DePelchin, October 6 and 8.

46. Letters, telegrams, and card in Armstrong papers. Date of death, Keating, 369; in *Sisters of St. Mary at Memphis*, date of fever "attack" is given as September 10, with death on September 14, but his card to Lula is clearly postmarked September 16. On the other hand, the list of physicians' illnesses and deaths in Keating says that Armstrong was attacked by fever on September 16, whereas his own note indicates that he had at least passed stage one by that date.

47. Florence to Lula Armstrong, September 22.

48. Benjamin Fithian to Lula Armstrong, September 22.

Chapter 7: Lost Graves

1. Keating, 170; *Sholes*, 35.

2. Official end of epidemic, Keating, 143; DePelchin, October 14.

3. *Appeal*, October 24.

4. Quoted in *Appeal*, October 4, 12; Quinn, *Heroes and Heroines*, 150; Armstrong, September 7 letter; Mitchell, post-epidemic report, Keating, 367; DePelchin, September 23; *Appeal*, September 17.

5. *London Standard* quote October 4; *Herald* quote October 12 editions of *Appeal*.

6. Keating, 141; *Appeal*, September 20.

7. Keating, 165; *Appeal*, September 19, mentions George Harris's dining engagement.

8. *Appeal*, September 28, October 25; Keating, 115, 182, 169.

9. *Appeal*, October 8. Ellis, 54; *Report: Expedition for the Relief of Yellow-Fever Sufferers on the Lower Mississippi* (Washington, D.C.: Government Printing Office, 1878), accessed through Internet Archive, http://www.archive.org/; Keating, 436–37.

10. *Appeal*, October 5, 6, 9.

11. People knew that frost ended yellow fever epidemics, although they did not understand how. Frost, or rather the cold weather that led to frost, brought the *Ae. aegypti* reproductive cycle to an end. The female *Ae. aegypti* stops biting people when she stops laying eggs. At the City Hospital, head physician G. B. Thornton and his staff kept records of daily mean temperatures for the summer. The mean is the average of all temperatures observed during the day. Thornton's data show that in the second week of September the mean temperatures began to decline. From the tenth through the sixteenth, the mean never rose above 69 degrees. After that the mean temperature occasionally dipped into the fifties or rose into the high seventies, but generally fluctuated between the mid-sixties and mid-seventies. See data in Keating, 195–99, and Bloom, 196.

12. Keating, 142.

13. Keating, 153.

14. *Appeal*, September 28; letters from Dr. Mitchell to Governor James D. Porter, Box 6, File Six, Porter Papers, Tennessee State Library and Archives, Nashville; *Avalanche*, quoted in October 17 Anderson County, S.C., *Intelligencer*.

15. President A. D. Langstaff's Report, Keating, 330–34; Keating, 366; *Chicago Tribune*, October 17, 1878.

16. Mrs. E. K. Heckle to DePelchin, March 31, 1879.

17. DePelchin, October 9, 13; in same letter.

18. DePelchin, October 27.

19. Keating, 185, visit of Louisville *Courier-Journal* reporter; DePelchin, October 9.

20. DePelchin, October 8.

21. AP wire story in *Chicago Tribune*, October 22; *Appeal*, October 20.

22. *Appeal*, October 26, 31, November 24.

23. *Appeal*, October 26.

24. *Avalanche*, September 3, quoted in *Chicago Tribune*, September 7; *Avalanche*, September 6.

25. Reference in sermon to inclement weather, weather report *Chicago Tribune*, October 27.

26. *Appeal*, October 23.

27. "Sermon of Rev. Dr. Landrum on the Epidemic," Keating, 439–42.

28. Bloom, 197.

29. Keating, 423, 430; *Appeal*, October 31; date of camp closing, Bloom, 197.

30. Keating, 398.

31. Sedalia, Missouri, *Weekly Bazoo*, September 24, 1878.

32. Keating, 124–25.

33. DePelchin, December 28.

34. DePelchin, letters from Senatobia, October through November.

35. October 31. Although DePelchin liked the people she met in Senatobia, black and white, she detested Sarah Jackson, an African American nurse who had come with her from Memphis. Jackson insisted that as a nurse, she should not be called upon to clean, do laundry, wash dishes, or cook. This made DePelchin angry. It may be that her anger derived from racist ideas about the proper place and duties for black women. However, it should be noted that DePelchin's letters indicate a general willingness to work with black women as colleagues. In her letters, she frequently refers to African Americans by first and last names, a small thing but indicative in a culture that habitually denied black women that dignity. Certainly DePelchin resented that Jackson thought herself above doing the same kind of work DePelchin (and the other nurses) did all the time. "I should very much enjoy seeing someone kick her out of doors," DePelchin wrote, October 27.

36. DePelchin, November 6.

37. *Chicago Tribune*, October 11; *New York Times*, December 13, 1878; *Baltimore Sun*, December 2, 1878.

38. DePelchin, November 16, 23.

39. DePelchin, March 25, 1879. On the Blew family, see Keating, 163.

40. DePelchin, November 23.

41. *Appeal*, December 25.

42. DePelchin, December 8.

43. DePelchin, December 28.

Chapter 8: After the Fever

1. *Appeal*, October 27.

2. The best study of the commission government is Wrenn, *Crisis and Commission Government in Memphis*, see especially "Exit Memphis," 28–40; Keating, *History of Memphis*, 672.

3. Porter quote in Young, *Standard History of Memphis*, 189; Wrenn, *Crisis and Commission Government*; Sigafoos, *Cotton Row to Beale Street*, 59; See also *Digest of the acts repealing the charters of certain municipal corporations: the proclamation of the governor thereon; the acts establishing taxing districts, and the ordinances of the taxing district of Shelby County, Tennessee; together with an appendix, containing the decision of the Supreme Court, settling the constitutionality of these acts; and, also, the by-laws for the government of the legislative council* (Google eBook). This scanned book, originally published in Memphis, was given by D. T. Porter to Dr. J. S. Billings, who presented it to the New York Public Library.

4. Bloom, 199; Ellis, 107–13; Keating, *History of Memphis*, 677.

5. *New York Times*, February 3, October 11, 1879; Bloom, 213–14, 229.

6. Keating, *History of Memphis*, 670–81; "Report on Sanitary Survey of Memphis, Tenn.," Report of the National Board of Health, Appendix L, House of Representatives, Executive Document No. 8, 46th Congress, 3rd Session," 416–41, accessed through Google Books.

7. Ellis, 117–19; Young, *Standard History*, 219.

8. Ellis, 120–21.

9. Ellis, 115–17.

10. *New York Times*, April 27, 1890. The aquifer shows no signs of giving out, and the water today is, in this author's opinion, the best "out of the tap" city water I have ever tasted.

11. The mortality rate for blacks remained higher than for whites, but the gap between black and white mortality rates was reduced by about 70 percent. Werner Troesken, "The Limits of Jim Crow: Race and the Provision of Water and Sewerage Services in American Cities, 1880–1925," *The Journal of Economic History* 62, no. 3 (September 2002): 734–72. I concur with Troesken's suggestion that Memphis did not yet have racially segregated residential patterns: blacks and whites lived in the same neighborhoods, so it would have been difficult to provide water and sewer connections to whites without making them available to blacks as well. He points out that Chelsea, a predominantly black community, still was more than 40 percent white.

12. For insight into the politics behind the visit, see Lester C. Lamon, *Black Tennesseans, 1900–1930* (Knoxville: University of Tennessee Press, 1976). *Scimitar* quote in *National Tribune* (Washington, D.C.), November 20, 1902; *New York Times*, November 18, 1902.

13. In addition to the articles cited above, the *Chicago Tribune*, November 19, 1902; *Washington Post*, November 19, 1902; *New York Sun*, November 20, 1902.

14. *Chicago Tribune*, November 20, 1902.

15. Annette E. Church and Roberta Church, *The Robert R. Churches of Memphis* (Privately published, 1974), 16–18. An article in the New York *Sun*, November 20, 1902, described the scene. The national press (including the AP) wrote about the black reception in a most cursory and humorous manner, and as a rule did not even give the name of the park. The *Sun* did.

16. Ibid.; "Robert Reed Church, Sr.," *Encyclopedia of African-American Business, A–J*, ed. Jessie Carney Smith, Millicent Lownes Jackson, and Linda T. Wynn (Westport, Conn.: Greenwood Press, 2006), 164–67.

17. *Humboldt Argus*, as reported in *Memphis Avalanche*, in Bloom, *The Mississippi Valley's Great Yellow Fever Epidemic*, 231. The statistics are from Campbell Gibson, "POPULATION OF THE 100 LARGEST CITIES AND

OTHER URBAN PLACES IN THE UNITED STATES: 1790 TO 1990,"
U.S. Census Bureau Population Division Working Paper No. 27, 1998.
http://www.census.gov/population/www/documentation/twps0027/twps
0027.html#citypop. Accessed July 14, 2011. These figures are based on the
population in the city limits. An estimate based on the 1892 city directory
put the population at 85,000. Young, *Standard History*, 216, 223; Sigafoos,
Cotton Row to Beale Street, 70–75.

18. Campbell Gibson and Kay Jung, "Historical Census Statistics on the
Foreign-Born Population of the United States: 1850–2000," Table 23. "Nativity of the Population for the 50 Largest Urban Places: 1870 to 2000." U.S.
Census Bureau, Working Paper No. 81, 2006. http://www.census.gov/
population/www/documentation/twps0081/twps0081.html, accessed
July 14, 2011. Memphis historians debate the extent to which the yellow
fever changed the city's course of development. Gerald M. Capers's *The
Biography of a River Town—Memphis, Its Heroic Age*, was published in 1939
and is still the best-known history of the city. Capers argued that the epidemics scared away European immigrants, particularly Germans. In the
post-epidemic years, he says, Memphis drew new population, black and
white, from the rural South. Lynette Boney Wrenn disagrees, arguing that
although the yellow fever epidemics were important, "economic stagna-
tion," municipal debt, bad politics, bad government, changing transportation patterns, and (in the case of the white working class) black
competition for low-wage jobs should be considered significant factors
in shaping Memphis. Wrenn, "The Impact of Yellow Fever on Memphis:
A Reappraisal," 4–18.

19. Young, *Standard History*, 553; Goodspeed's *History of Tennessee* (1887),
891, http://www.wdbj.net/shelby/goodspeed/history/history8.htm#Farm
ers%20and%20Merchants%20Bank.

20. Cookie Lommel, *Robert Church*, 81; picture of saloon in Box 38, Church
Family Papers, University of Memphis; hotel advertisement quoted in
Annette E. Church and Roberta Church, *The Robert R. Churches of Mem-
phis*, 13. Beale Street fight story, John N. Ingham and Lynne B. Feldman,
African-American Business Leaders: A Biographical Dictionary (Westport,
Conn.: Greenwood Press, 1994), 138.

21. See *Measuring Worth*, http://www.measuringworth.com/uscompare/, accessed July 15, 2011. Wrenn, *Crisis and Commission Government*, 12.

22. Earnestine Lovelle Jenkins, *African Americans in Memphis* (Charleston,
S.C.: Arcadia Publishing, 2009), 11–13; Paula J. Giddings, *Ida: A Sword
Among Lions* (New York: HarperCollins, 2009), 126; *The Robert Churches
of Memphis*, 55.

23. Terrell, *Colored Woman in a White World*, 104; *Washington Bee*, November 7, 1891.

24. Wanda Rushing, *Memphis and the Paradox of Place: Globalization in the American South* (Chapel Hill: University of North Carolina Press, 2009), 45.

25. See Bulletin 129, *Negroes in the United States*, Bureau of the Census, 1913.

26. Jenkins, *African Americans in Memphis*, 32; "Robert Reed Church," Ingham and Feldman, *African-American Business Leaders*, 137; see also *The Robert Churches of Memphis*.

27. "Beale Street," *Tennessee Encyclopedia*, http://tennesseeencyclopedia.net/entry.php?rec=67; Carroll Van West, *Tennessee's Historic Landscapes: A Traveler's Guide* (Knoxville: University of Tennessee Press, 1995), 123–24; *The Robert Churches of Memphis*, 21–25; quote from Sigafoos, *Cotton Row to Beale Street*, 116–17.

28. Clipping, not dated, no paper given, in Folder 2, General Correspondence 1863–1911, the Robert R. Church Family of Memphis Papers, Series 1, Carton 1, University of Memphis.

29. Bond and Sherman, *Memphis in Black and White*, 79; see also Lommell, *Robert Church*, 28; *The Robert Churches of Memphis*, 13; Ingham and Feldman, *African-American Business Leaders*.

30. W. C. Handy to Annette Church, December 19, 1956, Box VII, Folder 1, "Annette E. Church," in Roberta Church Collection, Memphis Room, Benjamin Hooks Library; Sigafoos, *Cotton Row to Beale Street*, 117; *The Robert Churches of Memphis*, 22; "Statement by Roberta Church," Robert Church Collection, Box. VI, Folder—Robert R. Church Sr. and Jr.—Business Profiles. Letter from Annette Church to Fred, no last name given, June 29, 1956, in Roberta Church Collection, Box VIII, Church Park, Folder 1. William Christopher Handy, *Father of the Blues: An Autobiography* (New York: Da Capo Press, 1991).

31. Margaret McKee and Fred Chisenhall, *Beale Black and Blue: Life on Black America's Main Street* (Baton Rouge: Louisiana State University Press, 1993), 93–96

Epilogue: Memory

1. Speer, *Prominent Tennesseans*, 45; Young, *Standard History*, 546; advertisements for the sanitarium ran regularly in the *Memphis Medical Monthly* during the 1890s. On the medical community in general, see Patricia LaPointe McFarland and Mary Ellen Pitts., *Memphis Medicine: A History of Science and Service* (Birmingham, Ala.: Legacy, 2011); and Mary P. Moran, "The Life and Times of Lena A. Warner, the Volunteer

Nightingale," in *West Tennessee Historical Society Papers* 49 (1995): 229–37.

2. Clipping from *Memphis Commercial Appeal*. The date, September 21, 1924, has been written on it; evidence of contributions, letters, and deposit slips in Armstrong papers.

3. Finding Guide for the George Carroll Harris Papers, Tennessee State Library and Archives, gives date of death; http://www.tn.gov/tsla/history /manuscripts/findingaids/206.pdf; *Mississippi*, Vol. III: *Contemporary Biography* (Reprint editions, Spartanburg, S.C.: The Reprint Company, 1976; original, Atlanta: Southern Historical Publishing Association, 1907), 378–81; Elmo Howell, *Mississippi Scenes: Notes on Literature and History*, 257–59; both books accessed through Google Books.

4. *Baptist Encyclopedia*, previously cited; Macon *Telegraph*, November 18, 1886.

5. A search for "Mrs. S. Stanwood Menken" will produce multiple hits from the *New York Times*, the *New Yorker*, and *Time* magazine; apparently she was quite the dresser and a social force well into the 1950s. See "Solomon Stanwood Menken," Wikipedia; and Robert D. Ward, "The Origins and Activities of the National Security League, 1914–1919," *Mississippi Valley Historical Review* 47, no. 1 (June 1960). Arthur Menken's obituary, *Time*, October 22, 1973.

6. Simplifying a complex story here; info from *Robert Churches of Memphis*, Church papers; Lamon, *Black Tennesseans*; G. Wayne Dowdy, *Mayor Crump Don't Like It: Machine Politics in Memphis* (2006) and *Crusades for Freedom: Memphis and the Political Transformation of the American South* (2010), both from the University Press of Mississippi.

7. Baker, *Commercial Appeal*, 127. Keating, "The Value of Sanitation from an Economic Standpoint," *Public Health Papers and Reports* VI (American Public Health Association, 1881), 266–78; "The Ultimate of Sanitation by Fire," Vol. 10 (1885): 116–39; *Appeal*, June 23, 1889.

8. J. M. Keating, "Twenty Years of Negro Education," *Popular Science Monthly* (November 1885): 24–37.

9. Curtis W. Garrison, "Slater Fund Beginnings: Letters from Agent Atticus G. Haygood to Rutherford B. Hayes," *Journal of Southern History* 5, no. 2 (May 1939): 232; *The American Missionary* XL, no. 4 (April 1886): 109.

10. Baker, *Commercial Appeal*, 150–54.

11. *New York Times*, November 1, 1889; *Chicago Tribune*, November 1, 1889; Isabel C. Barrows, ed., *First Mohonk Conference on the Negro Question* (Boston: George H. Ellis, Printer), 90; *American Missionary* 43, no. 12 (December 1889), http://www.gutenberg.org/files/16172/16172.txt.

12. *Chicago Tribune*, January 4, February 6, 1890; New York *Sun*, February 10,

1892, contains a wire story from Memphis headlined "Editor Keating Stands by the Union Printers"; Speer, *Prominent Tennesseans*, 382; *Commercial Appeal*, August 18, 1906. Keating's death certificate obtained from Gloucester, Massachusetts Archives lists his age as seventy-six, his residence as Washington, D.C., and his cause of death as nephritis.

13. *Commercial Appeal*, August 18, 1906.

14. See Matthews, *Candle by Night*, for information about DePelchin's life after Memphis.

15. Information from DePelchin Children's Center, http://www.depelchin .org/.

16. DePelchin, December 28, 1878.

17. Virginia Foster Durr, *Outside the Magic Circle* (Tuscaloosa: University of Alabama Press, 1990), 159–60; see Atlanta *Constitution*, February 3, 1901; on the topic of denial and the psychic cost paid, see Nell Irvin Painter, "Soul Murder and Slavery: Toward a Fully Loaded Cost Accounting," in *Southern History Across the Color Line* (Chapel Hill: University of North Carolina Press, 2002).

18. Mother Harriet to Dr. George Harris, November 7, 1878, Box 1, Folder 7, Papers of the Reverend George Harris, Memphis and Shelby County Room, Benjamin Hooks Library; "Constance and Her Companion," St. Mary's Episcopal Cathedral, www.stmarymemphis.org.

19. Wright, "Annie Cook: Mary Magdalene of Memphis."

20. *Avalanche*, September 6, 1878.

21. Kenneth E. Foote, *Shadowed Ground, America's Landscapes of Violence and Tragedy* (Austin: University of Texas Press, 2003), 104.

Index

Originally trained as a journalist, Jeanette Keith obtained her Ph.D. in history from Vanderbilt University in 1990 and is currently professor of history at Bloomsburg University in Bloomsburg, Pennsylvania. She is the author of several books, including *Country People in the New South* and the award-winning *Rich Man's War, Poor Man's Fight*.

MISSISSIPPI RIVER